THE MAN WHO
OUTSHONE THE
SUN KING

THE MAN WHO OUTSHONE THE SUN KING

A Life of Gleaming Opulence and Wretched Reversal in the Reign of Louis XIV

Charles Drazin

DA CAPO PRESS
A Member of the Perseus Books Group

Cataloging-in-Publication data for this book
is available from the Library of Congress.

First Da Capo Press edition 2008
Reprinted by arrangement with William Heinemann
ISBN:978-0-306-81757-1
Library of Congress Control Number: 2008933100

Published by Da Capo Press
A Member of the Perseus Books Group
www.dacapopress.com

Da Capo Press books are available at special discounts
for bulk purchases in the U.S. by corporations, institutions, and
other organizations. For more information, please contact the Special
Markets Department at the Perseus Books Group, 2300 Chestnut
Street, Suite 200, Philadelphia, PA 19103, or call (800) 810-4145,
ext. 5000, or e-mail special.markets@perseusbooks.com.

10 9 8 7 6 5 4 3 2 1

For Dinah, who had the idea

Contents

PART THREE: Quo Non Descendet?

Acknowledgements

I would like to thank the following: my partner Elena von Kassel-Siambani, for staying the course on the long journey from Vaux to Belle-lle and back; Judith Flanders, who with her common sense and practical advice helped to get the project on the road; my agent Clare Alexander, who tempered my enthusiasm with her level-headed, always constructive criticism; my extremely patient and supportive editors – Ravi Mirchandani, Caroline Knight and Alban Miles at Heinemann, and Bob Pigeon at Da Capo; Sarah Fowles, who was an encouraging supporter of the project ever since she whisked me off five years ago to see Nicolas Foucquet make his début on the London stage; Donna Poppy, for her perceptive guidance on both the art and business of writing; Xavier de France, who introduced me to Pascal, Jesuits and Jansenism; Monique and the inspirationally *bavard* Bernard Brosse; James Legg and Simon Heighes, the perfect hosts who were responsible for the tranquil atmosphere in which this book began.

I would also like to acknowledge the assistance of the following libraries; the Bibliothèque nationale de France; the London Library; the Institute of Historical Research; the Senate House Library, University of London; Queen Mary, University of London; and the British Library.

Preface

One evening, during a holiday in France, my friends and I were discussing what to see next. In a guidebook we read the story of a party that Louis XIV's Finance Minister Nicolas Foucquet had held to show off his newly built chateau of Vaux-le-Vicomte – an incomparable masterpiece of seventeenth-century architecture that would inspire Versailles. We read how 6,000 guests had dined off gold plates; how Molière had written a play especially for the occasion; and how the young King was so maddened with envy to see so many splendours in one night, that rather than thank his host, he vowed to destroy him. I hadn't heard of Nicolas Foucquet before and I imagined that these were just a few juicy snippets that had been greatly exaggerated, but I was fascinated enough to want to explore further; and once I did, I found that – in the way of the best stories – Nicolas's became only more spell-binding.

In France there are no public statues of Nicolas Foucquet for reasons that will become apparent, but he is an important, well-known figure who regularly attracts the attention of professional historians. In the English-speaking world, however, he is someone of whom few people have heard. This book, therefore, takes advantage of the outsider's gift of being able to tell a story as if for the first time, cherishing the myths as much as the reality. Whatever it may lack in authoritative historical analysis or an insider's knowledge of his own people, it hopes to compensate for by capturing a very human figure that we can all recognise.

One of the great attractions of seventeenth-century French history is its universal appeal. Voltaire considered the reign of Louis XIV – after Pericles's Greece, the Caesars' Rome and the Italian Renaissance – to be the fourth great age of civilisation, which, in the sheer scale of human achievement, provided an example for all ages. If it was as remarkable for the scale of human folly, this only aided its success as a great stage for drama, full of stirring events and memorable personages, but also of perceptive eyewitnesses to describe them. To mention but a very few names, it was the time of Madame de Sévigné, de Retz and Saint-Simon, of Molière, Corneille and La Fontaine . . .

The wealth of personal testimony, matching the period's colour and incident, made it possible for that great nineteenth-century writer Alexandre Dumas to plunder the time for his stories, and then for Hollywood in turn to plunder him for theirs. The characters may have been drawn from life, yet they were extravagant enough to be larger than life: Richelieu, d'Artagnan and even the Man in the Iron Mask, who were once individual, breathing people, have long since taken on a separate existence as archetypes in fable. This is the appeal of Nicolas Foucquet too: a real person, complex and multifaceted, yet in what he did and suffered as proverbial as Icarus.

A Note on the Name

Since in most published works the name of the hero of this book is usually spelt 'Fouquet', it may seem rather odd that I have chosen to call him 'Foucquet' with a 'c'. I have done so because this is how Nicolas himself used to sign his name:

PROLOGUE: 1644

It is 1644. The King of France is a five-year-old child. Ruling in his name is his mother, Queen Anne of Austria. The deaths in quick succession of Cardinal Richelieu and Louis XIII have rocked the kingdom. The great victory over the Spanish at Rocroi that in May of the previous year blessed the first days of the new reign has failed to end a war that has dragged on now for nearly a decade. It is slowly bleeding the life out of the nation. Few entertain much hope of an early deliverance: Queen Anne's appointment of the Italian Giulio Mazarini to be her first minister is for many only one further step down into the abyss. The death of her little mourned – and even less loved – husband gave her the chance to break the hold of her hated adversary Richelieu, the Red Eminence, who had ruled the late King from beyond the grave. But here she is turning to the very man whom Richelieu had anointed his successor – the very man whom Richelieu, as one of his last acts on earth, had even persuaded the Pope to make a cardinal.

Bowing under the weight of heavy taxes and in many places struggling to cope with famine as well, the people of France face unremitting hardship. Desperate and fractious, many of the country's provinces have already descended into a state of near anarchy. But this new administration – still finding its way and determined to show its authority – is in no mood to make

·concessions. Indeed, rather than rely on local forces to quell the tax strikes and food riots, it is sending into the rebellious provinces the royal intendants, who have instructions from the Chancellor, Pierre Séguier, to act with the utmost ruthlessness.

The Dauphiné is one of the more intractable provinces. Belonging to a remote, mountainous region that was once a separate principality, its inhabitants still retain a tradition of independence, which the magistrates of its own Parlement at Grenoble only encourage. Some of the country's fiercest disputes have taken place in this province.

The intendant who has been assigned to the Dauphiné is a young Master of Requests* called Nicolas Foucquet. He is the son of the late François Foucquet, a distinguished government official who had been a close aide to Cardinal Richelieu.

This is the new intendant's first important mission. He is inexperienced. But the Chancellor makes very clear the policy that must be pursued. In a detailed letter of instruction, he stipulates that Monsieur Foucquet must 'impose the collection of all taxes, tolls and duties outstanding in the province of the Dauphiné forthwith, in accordance with the assessments of the said province, and to bring prosecutions against those who spread the rumour of excessive taxes, sentencing them as insurrectionaries'.[1]

In case there is still any doubt, the intendant has only to think back to the Chancellor's own notorious conduct in the field, when five years previously he was sent to Lower Normandy by the late Cardinal. His mission there was to deal with those who had rebelled against the imposition of the *gabelle* salt tax on the Nu-Pieds – the 'bare-footed' labourers who made salt by evaporating sea water. Calling in 4,000 troops, the Chancellor swiftly crushed the uprising with mass executions. Ever since

*See Glossary.

then, France's royal intendants have known that the surest path to a successful career is unmitigated brutality.

But *this* intendant seems to forget the orthodox methods. Disregarding the harsh measures that were drummed into him in Paris before he set out on his mission, he makes his own independent judgements on the basis of what he finds in Grenoble.

There, the winter stores of grain have rotted in heavy snows, causing the price of bread to rocket. Yet although they are now barely able to feed themselves, the local inhabitants are still being harassed by tax collectors, who – oblivious to their suffering – press as hard as ever for their commission.* Their cruelty and greed provoke angry protests; and the populace in some villages begin to pelt the soldiers with stones.

It is the kind of conduct that is sufficient pretext for an intendant to order heavy reprisals, but Nicolas Foucquet allows simple compassion to determine his response. He sends a despatch back to Paris describing the misery he has seen and queries the policy of the government. The taxes 'have reduced most people to despair', he writes. 'If the King could offer some hope of future relief, it would encourage people to make an extra effort.'[2]

Risking his career here so recklessly, the young intendant will survive this early show of decency to achieve a position of huge importance in his later life. He will a few years later help to win a civil war. He will rise to become the indispensable figure behind some of the most splendid achievements of a time that posterity will label 'le Grand Siècle'. An unusually eventful life – with its

---

* The royal revenues depended on a system of 'tax-farming' that was contracted out to middlemen, known as *traitants*, or 'tax-farmers', who were allowed to keep a percentage of the taxes they collected. This incentive caused the levies to be imposed with a zealous efficiency matched only by the flagrant corruption that occurred among the tax-farmers and the government officials who awarded the contracts.

often dramatic reversals of fortune – furnishes no shortage of conventional reasons to write about him. But it is perhaps this instinct for humanity, at a time when inhumanity was much the more dominant key, that is the root of his appeal.

The Governor of the Dauphiné was the First President of the Parlement, Marshal François de Lesdiguières. Encouraged by the unprecedented support the province had received from a representative of central government, he travelled to Paris to canvass a reduction of the taxes in person. Meanwhile, Nicolas Foucquet continued to rely on persuasion rather than force to restore order. A week after his letter to the Chancellor, he wrote to the bishop of the important Dauphiné town Valence, imploring him to use his influence to calm passions in the surrounding districts, where the uproar over the taxes had been particularly fierce. But while everyone waited to hear back from Paris, there was now nothing else that could usefully be done. So he made the most of the lull to attend the investiture ceremony of his older brother François, who had just been appointed the new Bishop of Agde, in Languedoc.

If the oddly enlightened conduct of the new intendant seemed to offer some brief hope of relief, subsequent events soon exposed his dangerous naïveté. The tax collectors, who feared the drop in commission that would follow any compromise, became only more pressing in their demands. Their heavy-handed methods provoked a series of riots across the province, with protesters in several areas burning the tax lists.

The collectors began to send their own angry letters to Paris, complaining about the conduct of the intendant. He should have brought in troops to quell the riots, but he wasn't even there. He had let the Dauphiné go up in flames while he attended Mass 150 miles away!

The Chancellor was already furious that the intendant had

disobeyed his orders. The only question in his mind was what punishment could possibly do justice to the sheer scale of the misconduct. In this time of slow communications when it took a message many days to get from one corner of France to the other, he had already had considerable time to mull over the matter when he received the new reports. Even more enraged, he ordered the intendant to be relieved of his command and to return to Paris. A new intendant, de Lauzières, was appointed to replace him.

The Parlement of the Dauphiné appealed to the Chancellor on behalf of the dismissed intendant, praising the efforts he had made to establish order in the province and begging that he be reinstated, but to no avail. Nicolas Foucquet had scarcely got back to Grenoble before he had to set off again, this time on a humiliating journey back to the capital. Three members of the Dauphiné Parlement, counsellors Ducros, Coste and Chaulnes, accompanied him part of the way to show their appreciation for his efforts to help the people.

Heading westwards along the Isère river towards where it joined the Rhône, their carriage took a slow, winding path through mountains that loomed precipitously on either side. As Nicolas brooded over the cruel end to a career that had hardly begun, he can't have been very cheerful company. He certainly had plenty of reasons to worry about his future, but at the same time, as he strove to tell his travelling companions a little about himself, at least he could draw some strength and comfort from a prosperous and reassuring past.

Foucquet. It was an old Breton word that meant 'squirrel'. The family of the young intendant had adopted the creature as its emblem. For his travelling companions from the Dauphiné – who had been so eager to express their gratitude but would soon have to turn back and leave him to continue his ignominious journey alone – it was easy to see how the intendant lived up to the traditional qualities of the animal: swift, agile, brave, resourceful, but also, in that instinct for risk, vulnerable. The general direction of a Foucquet might be up, but every now and then a disastrous slip was bound to occur.

In the wider family history, Nicolas's recent misadventure had been the first slip for some time. Over the last hundred years or so the Foucquets had established themselves successfully in Brittany as respected merchants and magistrates. Several of Nicolas's relatives had held high office in the Breton Parlement. It was a detail that Nicolas's travelling companions, seeking to understand him, might well have found significant. Like their own province, Brittany had a long, proud history of independence. The duchy may formally have become part of France over a hundred years previously, but it continued to assert a considerable degree of autonomy, which its own Parlement jealousy guarded.*

Yet the more Nicolas talked about his family, as the tiny carriage rattled along the banks of the Isère, the more it must also have become apparent how hard that family had worked to identify with the prevailing power. Nicolas's father, François, who had been born in 1587, was orphaned as a small child and brought up by his uncle Christophe, who was President à Mortier in the Parlement at Rennes. It was one of the most important

---

*The Breton Parlement sat at Rennes. Originally France possessed only one Parlement, which had its seat on the Île de la Cité in Paris. It had exercised jurisdiction over the entire kingdom, but from the fifteenth century onwards, as the country extended its authority over previously disputed territories, provincial Parlements were established in the regions with the strongest traditions of independence. By the time of the French Revolution, in addition to the Parlements of Paris, the Dauphiné and Brittany, there were also Parlements sitting at Toulouse, Aix-en-Provence, Arras, Besançon, Bordeaux, Colmar, Dijon, Douai, Metz, Nancy, Pau and Rouen.

judicial offices in the province, but the Foucquets were already setting their sights on the capital. Christophe supported his nephew through his law studies and in 1609 used his influence to secure for him an office as a counsellor to the Parlement of Paris. Already in the capital was François's other uncle, Isaac, who was a chaplain to Henry IV. A year later François contracted an extremely advantageous marriage to the twenty-year-old Marie de Maupeou, whose father, Gilles de Maupeou, was Controller-General of Finances in Henry IV's government. The Foucquet family had taken its place in the very highest echelons of the French establishment.

François and Marie Foucquet were a favoured couple, cushioned by privilege, yet at the same time winning universal respect through conduct so clearly inspired by their devotion to Christ, even in this extremely religious age, when a sense of the divine was powerfully present in most people's lives. Their faith could be traced in their practical charity. One of the more striking of the several seventeenth-century churches that line the rue Saint-Antoine in Paris is Sainte-Marie-des-Anges, with its massive but elegant dome that provided a model for the dome of the Invalides. Built by the architect François Mansart for the nuns of the order of the Visitation of Saint Mary, the church received much of its funding from François and Marie Foucquet, who engaged actively with the order.

The nuns of the Visitation called themselves the Visitandines, because their mission was to visit the poor and sick. Their patron was one of the great figures of the Counter-Reformation, Saint Vincent de Paul. Through an irresistible mixture of charm, energy and practical common sense this priest, who had started out as a shepherd in the Landes in south-west France, had established a network of confraternities and missions that brought aid to the destitute throughout France. Madame Foucquet became in 1634 one of his 'Ladies of Charity', a group of high-born women whom the priest organised to aid the sick in Paris's most notorious hospital, the Hôtel-Dieu.

Situated on the Île de la Cité, near Notre-Dame, the Hôtel-Dieu made Bedlam seem like a place of quiet repose. Diderot gives a description of it in the *Encyclopédie*: 'Imagine a long series of interconnected wards filled with every kind of patient, sometimes packed three, four, five, or six into a bed, the living alongside the dead and dying, the air polluted by this mass of sick bodies, passing the pestilential germs of their afflictions from one to the other, and the spectacle of suffering and agony on every hand. That is the Hôtel-Dieu.'[3] Often those patients who were lucky enough to leave the place alive returned home with even worse diseases than when they had entered.

Working here demanded real commitment. In spite of the dangers to her own health – two Ladies of Charity died in the course of their duties – Marie made regular visits to the hospital, comforting the sick but also working hard to be of real practical assistance. She watched the patients carefully, noting the medicines that seemed to bring some genuine relief and those – by far the majority – which did not. She then went away and, on the basis of her observation, concocted her own remedies. Soon she had developed a therapeutic skill that made her far more effective than the Augustinian nuns who were the official nurses in the hospital.

Many years later, after her death, Marie's health potions and cures would be collected together into a book, *Selected Remedies, Tried and Tested against Common Ills, Both Internal and External*. Reprinted many times, it was one of the bestsellers of the age. The preface to one of the later editions (1682) observed: 'If public acclaim and the number of previous editions provide a reliable index of merit, then we can say that no modern work on medicine is better than this one.'

Marie's endeavours seem all the more extraordinary when one

learns that over a period of three decades she gave birth to fifteen children, twelve of whom survived into adulthood.

The first child – who as the eldest son was named François after his father – was born in 1611, and the last, Gilles, in 1637. Nicolas, the second son, was born in 1615. All her six daughters became nuns, most of them joining the ranks of the Visitation. Founded by Saint Vincent de Paul's close friend and supporter the bishop and future saint François de Sales in 1610, the order shared Marie's view that Christians should show a commitment to God not through contemplation and prayer alone but through the performance of good deeds that made a difference in the world. De Sales had wanted – in a departure from the then conventional notion that nuns should be totally cloistered – to encourage spirituality among women who remained a part of everyday society.

The path to Christian perfection was to make the world better, not to run away from it. One of the positive developments of the Catholic revival was a more benign concept of the relationship between man and God. Not everyone could endure hard beds or lengthy fasts, but their reluctance to undergo such mortification did not mean they were less capable of honouring God or less deserving of his love. Such enlightened thinking made it possible for the spirit of God to permeate through secular life. Indeed, sincerely devoted to alleviating the suffering of the poor as the convent of the Visitation was, it operated at the same time as a kind of finishing school, which the daughters of some of the most wealthy families in France attended.

As practical Christians, the Foucquets were also keen supporters of the Jesuit order, which strove to make religious faith an integral part of temporal life. Part of the appeal of the Jesuits lay in the way they seemed to know how to resolve the inherent tensions between earthly and divine obligations; they encouraged the same practical engagement with life that Marie taught her children at home.

Seventeenth-century commentators are unanimous in suggesting that Marie was one of the most admired women of her time. The great chronicler of the reign of Louis XIV, the duc de Saint-Simon, praised 'the virtue, courage and extraordinary piety of this lady, mother of the poor'.[4] And Saint Vincent de Paul himself observed: 'If by some misfortune the Gospel had been lost, one would find its spirit and principles in the conduct and beliefs of Madame Foucquet.'[5]

It is perhaps scarcely surprising that Nicolas should have carried some of his mother's principles with him into the Dauphiné. He was only thirty years old. An upbringing, in which his mother had taught her children that the struggle for Good was the chief purpose of our time on earth, remained a key formative experience. His adult self had yet to be tempered by all those compromises and deceits that are euphemistically called 'lessons of life'. In future years Nicolas's engagement with the world might cause him to neglect many of Marie Foucquet's principles, but the roots of what she had imparted remained there as strong as ever, ready when needed to grow anew.

If the turbulent weeks he passed in the Dauphiné revealed a bedrock humanity, perhaps even more noteworthy was the astonishing courage and vitality with which he battled to redeem himself after his disgrace. An experience that would have demoralised most people seemed on the contrary to galvanise him, so that he was able to turn a major personal setback into a victory.

Nicolas's travelling companions were still with him when his carriage reached Romans two days later, a town close to the end of the Isère valley. They could not possibly have known it then, but they would pay dearly for their decision to escort him.

It would have been wiser if they had marked their gratitude with a warm handshake and farewell embrace back in Grenoble.

In Romans, Nicolas received a message from the Bishop of Valence, to whom he had written before setting off on his ill-fated trip to the Languedoc. The Bishop didn't yet know that the intendant had been dismissed. He was writing to request urgent assistance. All his efforts to reason with the people, as Nicolas had suggested, had proved fruitless. Valence itself was now sliding into chaos. A group of angry women were inciting a rebellion against the taxes. Armed with pitchforks and pikes, they had forced some tax collectors to take refuge in the citadel and they were now rampaging through the city.

Valence was just ten miles to the south-west of Romans, at the point where the Isère joined the River Rhône. As the Governor of the province, François de Lesdiguières, was still in Paris and the new intendant had yet to arrive, Nicolas decided to act as though he were still the intendant. Sending his carriage on ahead to Tournon, a town further north on the Rhône – from where he could eventually resume his journey to Paris – he headed in the opposite direction towards Valence, riding with his companions as fast as possible on horseback.

To reach the town safely they had to skirt a group of over a hundred women, who had received warning of their arrival and had gathered on the main road into the town. Entering Valence as quietly as possible by another gate, Nicolas left his horse at a hostelry and went directly to the Bishop's palace.

There he despatched a magistrate's clerk to invite the protesters to come to the palace to explain their grievances. The women duly gathered outside and, receiving assurances from Nicolas that they would not be harmed, chose eight of their number to form a deputation to enter the building. After he had heard their complaints about the oppressive demands of the tax collectors and their pleas for justice, he promised to do what he could to offer redress, but first, he insisted, they must agree to restore order. The women replied that they doubted they could convince their companions outside without the direct assurances of Nicolas himself. Very well then, replied Nicolas, he would speak to them too.

Asking for the doors to be opened, he suddenly found himself surrounded by a mob of enraged women, brandishing picks, beating drums and screaming. But he remained calm, refusing to speak to them until they had put down their weapons. Knowing that he had sought to reduce the burden of the taxes – although unaware of the price he had paid for his intervention – they acquiesced. Nicolas then repeated what he had said earlier in a firm but conciliatory tone and, reassured, the women left the palace. They persuaded all the armed groups within the city to disband and, finally, went back to their homes. Valence was at peace again.

Returning to the hostelry, Nicolas asked to see city officials and any witnesses who could help him to get a better understanding of the women's grievances. While he listened to the various accounts of what had happened, a woman with two small children arrived. In tears, she begged for the release of her husband, a shoemaker who had been arrested and locked up in the citadel the night before. Nicolas listened to her patiently and agreed to look into the matter. He was told later that the man had taken part in one of the riots, but still he had him released on a caution, insisting only that he and his wife should stay away from the crowds and encourage others to do likewise.

Although it was now eight in the evening, Nicolas decided to resume his journey northwards. The Abbess of Tournon, with whom he had planned to spend the next day, had sent his carriage back to fetch him. Two of the Dauphiné counsellors – Ducros and Coste – continued to keep him company for a while longer. It was a point of honour for them that they should escort him all the way out of the province; they were joined by another man called Saint-Gilles.

As the carriage set off, Nicolas asked the driver to pass by the citadel of Valence so that he could see for himself whether order really had been restored. But when his carriage was spotted heading towards the citadel, a rumour went around that the intendant had decided to release the tax collectors still sheltering there.

A mob of men and women materialised out of nowhere and began to chase after the carriage, pelting the occupants with stones. Nicolas ordered the driver to stop so that he could try to clear up the misunderstanding. But this time the mob, which was now about four or five hundred strong, was in no mood to listen.

There were cries of 'Kill! Kill! Get the thieves!'

The panic-stricken driver whipped the horses hard in an attempt to escape, but one of the beasts collapsed in its traces, leaving the coach stranded. The driver, the postillion and the attendants who had been leading along the saddle horses fled. Two of Nicolas's companions, Ducros and Saint-Gilles, followed them, throwing themselves out of the carriage windows and disappearing into the darkness.

Of a delicate constitution, Nicolas probably thought it point-less to attempt to escape himself, even if his sense of dignity had permitted it. Instead, maintaining the pretence that he was still the intendant, he turned to face the hostile crowd, his last remaining companion, Coste, still at his side. Once again he tried to calm them. But his words were greeted by yet more stones. Coste was badly hurt and pulled into the crowd. Still Nicolas persisted, struggling to make himself heard above the din. If they were killed, he warned, there would be a heavy price to pay. It would be better to take them some place where they might have a chance to explain themselves.

While some of the crowd were ready to listen to him, others

demanded his head, shouting that he had betrayed them. But the more people pressed forward to hit him, the less space there was actually to land their blows. In the mêlée Nicolas begged the women closest to him to shelter him from their companions crowding behind. Forming a protective shield with their bodies, a few of them covered Nicolas's head with their arms. Edging forward in this way, they eventually managed to bring him to the safety of one of their houses. He then begged them to go back for Coste, who was later carried into the house covered in blood and so close to death that Nicolas sent for a surgeon and a priest.

Discovering what had happened, the city authorities despatched a detachment of musketeers to the men's assistance. Leaving Coste behind in the care of a guard, Nicolas returned to the Bishop's palace. Here he learned the fate of his two other travelling companions. Saint-Gilles had found a horse and managed to escape, but Ducros had been caught by the mob, killed, and his body dumped in the Rhône.

Several houses were burned down, as the anger of the mob that had pursued Nicolas and his companions sparked off a more general disorder. The disturbances continued over the next few days. Nicolas, who could easily have slipped out of the town to safety, continued to play the part of the intendant, overseeing the efforts to restore calm. Rather than call in troops from outside, which he thought would only inflame the situation further, he organised a local militia of townspeople to quell the riots, and ordered those responsible for the killing of Coste to be rounded up and put on trial. At the same time he issued a decree to forbid the hoarding of grain, which had been one of the chief grievances of the rioters.

Presiding over a gradual return to order, he established a summary court to ensure that the worst excesses of the riots should be subject to legal scrutiny. When de Lauzières, whom the Chancellor had appointed in Nicolas's place, finally arrived in

Valence some days later, accompanied by a large contingent of troops, he found a city that was still tense but under control.

Nicolas left the next day applauded by a large and – for a change – grateful crowd, leaving his replacement with the difficult task of keeping the peace in his absence. A week after his arrival, de Lauzières wrote to the Chancellor to describe the situation in the town. Three rioters had been condemned to death, but no executioner dared to carry out the sentence, and the tax collectors still remained shut up in the citadel, too afraid to come out. De Lauzières did not want to give any credit to his disgraced predecessor, but had to concede that much of the continuing unrest was due to the widespread belief that Nicolas 'had been relieved of his command for having written to the Council in favour of the people'.[6]

While Nicolas's mother instilled a sense of Christian charity in her son, his father François provided the template for the loyal if often conflicted servant to the Crown – which in the Dauphiné, after all, Nicolas remained even after he had been relieved of his duties. But Nicolas also inherited his father's notable industry, versatility and application, as well as a sharp and enquiring mind. When François began to work for Richelieu soon after the Cardinal became Prime Minister in 1624, he must have regarded his new job as an excellent opportunity – Jesuit-style – to further the works of God on earth, but the association would subject his sense of Christian purpose to some severe tests. For any faith Richelieu himself may have had came second to his determination to build France into the most powerful nation in Europe and to bolster his own authority whatever the cost. In the service of these twin goals, he put religious principle at the expense of cold-hearted, often merciless calculation. It was Richelieu who personally directed the fourteen-month siege of the Protestant Huguenots in La Rochelle, starving to death most of the city's inhabitants; yet it was Richelieu who would build an alliance between France and the Protestant powers against Catholic Spain. 'If God exists, Cardinal Richelieu will have a lot to answer for,' commented Pope Urban VIII on learning of Richelieu's death. 'If God doesn't, then he's had a very successful life.'

Establishing himself as one of the Cardinal's most loyal aides, François undertook many different assignments on Richelieu's behalf, but his chief activity, as Counsellor of State for Maritime and Colonial Affairs, was to fashion and implement a practical strategy that would realise Richelieu's ambition of turning France into a leading maritime power. The country's lack of a proper navy had long been a manifest weakness. Barbary pirates raided its Mediterranean coast,* while the Spanish navy patrolled the Channel seizing French cargos with impunity. In the mid 1620s, France did not possess any warships that could take on the Spanish, nor even the shipyards capable of building such vessels. During the campaign against La Rochelle the Cardinal had to borrow ships from abroad to transport troops and supplies.

Richelieu, who had give himself the impressive-sounding title of 'Grandmaster, Chief and Superintendent General of Navigation and Commerce', looked on jealously at the Spanish, the English and the Dutch, who had used their fleets to build vast trading empires overseas. He was determined that France should at last begin to live up to the length of its coastline and join them. Warships were bought from the Dutch, naval dockyards built at Le Havre, Brest and Brouage, and expeditions sent out to establish settlements in the West Indies.

*Saint Vincent de Paul had been one of their victims. Travelling from Marseilles to Toulouse by sea, his ship was captured and he was sold into slavery in North Africa in 1605. After two years he escaped with the last of his three masters, a renegade whom he converted.

François was responsible for the practical policy that would turn the Cardinal's dreams into reality. In 1630 he oversaw a lengthy review that would result in a complete overhaul of the navy, and four years later joined a panel of scholars and mathematicians, who recommended that the prime meridian should run through the Île de Fer, in the Canaries – a line that drew a natural division between the Old World and the new one that awaited tantalisingly across the ocean. Although the British Royal Navy's subsequent dominance of the seas meant that the designation would fail to catch on, François made a more lasting contribution to posterity when he set up the Compagnie des Îles de l'Amérique to oversee the exploitation of the new colonies. It would be the seed from which France's future empire grew.

The articles of association of this new company suggest an enlightened enterprise, into which François was able to pour a considerable degree of his religious faith and idealism. Not only the colonists and their descendants would enjoy the full privileges of French nationality, but also the native 'savages' who accepted Christianity. François worked to ensure that Catholic missionaries would be an integral part of the colonisation process – especially his favoured order, the Jesuits. The Society's own record of its missionary activity makes clear the active part he played in focusing their evangelistic endeavours. 'Monsieur Foucquet . . . brought the directors of the "Compagnie d'Amérique" to ask our Fathers to help the French settlers and to bring instruction to the savages. As he has a great passion for converting infidels, he wanted to be able himself to put the case to our superiors.'[7]

In the process of overseeing the various overseas trading companies, François often took a personal stake in the enterprise. At a time when, in the seamless web of connections between faith, kin and King, no firm ethical divide existed between the public and private spheres – indeed, when the offices of state themselves were bought and sold – it was deemed only natural to use one's position in this way to advance the standing of one's family. But whatever wealth François Foucquet might have accumulated, it was not in his nature to flaunt it – a restraint lacking in his son. Rather than move to one of the fashionable new *hôtels* being built on the Île Saint-Louis, François was content to remain in the rue de Jouy, a road that ran down towards the river from the rue Saint-Antoine. It may have been rather unfashionable and notorious – as a 1636 municipal report pointed out – for its 'filth, refuse and mud',* but it was just a short walk in one direction up the rue Saint-Antoine to the convent of the Visitation, where François could see his daughters and follow the progress of the order's new church, which was only finally completed in 1632; and in the other, to the Cardinal's new palace opposite the Louvre.

Any taste for luxury or extravagance that François may have possessed was poured into building his collection of maps, ancient coins and medals. He devoted his leisure hours not to outward ostentation, but to study, in the calm of an impressively well-stocked library, perusing books that were each engraved with two enlaced Phis – ΦΦ – the initials of his name. It was a pursuit that he took delight in encouraging visiting scholars to share. To his inquisitive, practical mind, learning was not a fusty or remote thing, but as much an adventure as the ocean voyages he sponsored.

In the library entrance stood a long dugout canoe that had once belonged to the Huron tribe in Canada. Flanking it on either side were two large globes, one of the earth, the other a celestial sphere that mapped out the heavens. All demonstrated the eclecticism and breadth of learning that was such an engaging feature

---

*According to the *Procès-verbal de visite de 1636*, quoted in Alfred Franklin, *Rues de Paris* (Léon Willem, 1873).

of this time still in the shadow of the Renaissance. Whether it was a question of cosmology, literature, medicine, or commerce – François was used to tackling all with equal confidence. His powerful patron Cardinal Richelieu valued him not just for his maritime expertise, but as a man who could give an informed opinion on all things. When pondering on one occasion whether to establish a tapestry factory at the Savonnerie, it was François Foucquet to whom he turned for advice.

In his letters to the Cardinal, François usually took care to sign off with an assurance of profound gratitude that made him ready to serve in any way. This note, for example, on an occasion when Richelieu was away from Paris: 'If you should during your absence honour me with another task, I shall take pains to acquit myself with the care and loyalty you can expect of one who recognises that he owes his fortune to you and remains indebted to you for the rest of his life . . .'[8] This was not just an empty formula, but a true measure of the strength of their ties. François had committed himself completely to His Eminence, who in return would see to it that the Foucquet family prospered.

But in the service of Richelieu it was impossible for such a devout man not to experience some qualms. François had to grapple with the painful lesson that the greater good often involves an apparent evil. Indeed, the very foundation of his career had been built on an act of cruelty that haunted the entire Foucquet family – a crime of such horror that in later years it became natural for any setback or reversal of fortune to be regarded as continuing atonement for what had happened.

A cornerstone of Richelieu's notion of the greater good was that his own personal authority should be unchallenged. Louis XIII, who recognised Richelieu's extraordinary practical command and intellectual brilliance, gave the Cardinal his complete trust, but although he deferred to him in every matter of state, he never warmed to him. Knowing that he had won his power through respect rather than affection, Richelieu was able to banish sentiment from his decisions all the more completely. The only creatures he seemed to show any genuine affection for were his fourteen cats, but only because they lacked the means to plot against him. Otherwise, he maintained a strict observance of his precept that 'reason must be the universal rule and guide; all things must be done according to reason without allowing oneself to be swayed by emotion'. It meant that he countered threats with extreme ruthlessness, yet at the same time took care to reward genuine merit, as François Foucquet discovered when the first major political conspiracy took place against the Cardinal's rule in 1626.

Twenty-eight years old, Henri de Talleyrand, the comte de Chalais, had been a friend of the King since they were both small children. His widowed mother had drawn on her meagre resources to buy him the office of Grand Master of the King's Wardrobe, which would bring him 'close to the royal person'.[9] Soon afterwards he was able to add to this distinction an extremely advantageous marriage to Charlotte de Castille, the daughter of a prosperous financier. Handsome and affable, as well as a brave soldier who had been wounded in battle, Chalais was a much-liked member of Louis's court, but his very openness led him to keep the dangerous company of some disgruntled nobles who had gathered around the King's younger brother Gaston. Spurred on by a combination of Gaston's complaints and promises of advancement, they planned to kill the Cardinal, depose the King and marry the Queen to Gaston, who would be proclaimed Gaston the First of France. Chalais's most significant involvement had been to ensure that such dangerous scheming remained idle talk, but he paid the price for the association. The Cardinal discovered the plot and, rather than risk taking on the principal schemers, who could summon powerful factions in their support, chose to make an example of the hapless Chalais.

In the summer of 1626 the young noble was arrested in Nantes, where the King had gone to attend an assembly of the Estates General of Brittany, and imprisoned in Nantes castle. Disregarding the authority of the sovereign court of Parlement, the Cardinal then created a special tribunal, a Chambre de Justice, to put Chalais on trial for lese-majesty. He chose the judges himself, nominating among them François Foucquet.

At the time of Chalais's arrest, François was already in Brittany, where he had been directing the establishment of an ocean trading company to be based at Morbihan on the Brittany coast near Vannes. When he arrived in Nantes, he found that the chief judge of the trial was none other than his own uncle Christophe, while another judge was a cousin. Richelieu assumed without question that he could rely not only on his aide François Foucquet, but also on his family.

Such kinship turned out to be of very little use to Chalais. When he was first arrested, some of his relatives had offered their support, but now they melted away, fearing the Cardinal's anger. Only his mother made any effort to fight for him, challenging the impartiality of the judges. But her objection was dismissed, and her request that her son be allowed to have a lawyer not even answered. Realising that her son's life was beyond rescue, she strove instead to save his soul, sending a chaplain to help him make the necessary repentance.

The appetite for salacious sensation being as strong then as it is today, unusually detailed contemporary accounts exist of the sad drama that followed. They're worth dwelling on because they capture so well the atmosphere of savagery, loyalty and religious faith that was so typical of the time.[10]

After Christophe Foucquet had given an extremely hostile summing-up, the judges – including François – returned the due verdict of guilty. The accused was sentenced to have his head cut off and his body cut into four pieces, with a chunk being displayed on each of the four gates of Nantes. But his old childhood friend the King eventually intervened to mitigate the harshness of this sentence: out of consideration for his mother, Chalais would only have his head cut off.

Chalais resigned himself to his fate with conspicuous courage. He asked one of his guards to tell his mother that the Lord had granted him a great favour. If he had died in his bed, then he would have been damned, but now he could hope that God would have mercy.

Finding the mother at prayer in a nearby church, the guard passed on the message. 'Tell my son that I am pleased that he will die with God in his heart,' she replied. 'If I didn't think my presence would weaken him and risk undermining some of the spirit he has shown I would stay by his side and not leave until his head had been parted from his body. But as I cannot help him, I am going to pray to God for him.'[11]

It was as well she stayed where she was, for the execution would have challenged her fortitude. Some of Chalais's friends, in a misguided attempt to save him, bribed the official executioner not to turn up. Rather than wait for another experienced executioner to arrive from Rennes, the authorities released a prisoner who had been condemned to the gibbet and ordered him to carry out the execution instead.

Setting about the task with a Swiss sword – the first available blade that came to hand – this amateur executioner was at first able to inflict no more than a light gash. So he asked for the kind of axe he was accustomed to using in his trade as a cooper. But this proved no more effective.

After the twentieth blow, Chalais's head was still fixed stubbornly to his neck. 'Jesus Mary! Jesus Mary!' he cried out again and again. And on it might have continued had not the chaplain – presumably a veteran of such occasions – stepped in to explain to the cooper how the condemned's head had to be pressed more firmly against the block. At last, after the thirty-fourth blow, the mangled head tumbled into the basket.*

Safely above the law as the heir presumptive, Gaston lived to plot another day, while François Foucquet's reward for implementing the Cardinal's will was to be appointed the French ambassador to Switzerland. Chalais's fall cleared the path for his own swift rise. Serving only a year in Switzerland, he was on his return appointed a counsellor of state, an office that gave him admission to the ranks of the nobility. François marked an occasion that was important for all the Foucquets by adding to the family device of the squirrel the motto, *Quo non ascendet?* (To where will he not climb?). Perched confidently on its hind legs, this particular squirrel seemed to suggest that no treetop would be too high.

François's part in the Chalais affair brought him into the Cardinal's inner circle. The Cardinal looked to him not simply to organise fleets and ocean expeditions, but also to undertake assignments of the utmost secrecy. When, for example, the Cardinal's agent captured the English envoy Walter Montagu in Lorraine at the time of the siege of La Rochelle, it was François who was despatched to the Bastille to interrogate him. The information the Cardinal hoped he would extract concerned possible English intrigues with the duchies of Lorraine and Savoy against France, but also the Duke of Buckingham's secret liaisons with France's Queen. Only someone in whom the Cardinal had placed his total trust could be party to such a secret.

*The magazine *le Mercure français* took care to provide its readers with all the gory details, even composing a special *huitain* – an eight-line verse – to mark the occasion. It ended: '*L'arrest dit qu'on te décapite / Et Dieu veut que tu soit haché.*' (The sentence was to decapitate you, / But God wanted to turn you into mincemeat.)

François's work for Richelieu must have involved many crises of conscience. But ultimately he believed that the end justified the often terrible means. After years of internal strife, it was Richelieu who was now establishing France as the most powerful kingdom in Europe, and surely it was Richelieu who would do more than anyone else to restore the true faith.

Whatever sins François may have had to commit in the Cardinal's name, certainly he did the best he could not only to atone for them in private, but also to compensate with practical acts of humanity. Occasionally he risked real danger. The King's continuously meddlesome brother Gaston provides an example. In 1631, two of his supporters fled with him to the Duchy of Lorraine after yet another of his failed conspiracies. Forcibly sent back to France, the two men – La Rivière and Goulas – were arrested and might have expected to suffer a similar fate to Chalais. But Goulas wrote to François Foucquet, who was a family friend, appealing to him for his help. François replied that the two men should pretend to be ill and do whatever they could to put off their transfer to the Bastille. He then took the trouble to travel to their prison and, interrogating them in his capacity as a counsellor of state, pronounced that they had no case to answer. The two men were released and managed once again to escape to Lorraine before they were condemned to death *in absentia* as Gaston's accomplices. 'A good Christian, Monsieur Foucquet remembered the alliance that our family used to have with him,' wrote Goulas in his memoirs. 'As someone who professed to follow the Gospel, it was not to his liking that innocent people should be imprisoned.'[12]

Nicolas was an impressionable child of eleven when Chalais was executed. Richelieu was happy that the awful retribution that the young noble had suffered should be widely publicised as a warning to anyone else who might dare such disobedience. But François was too well known for his sense of honour and decency ever to be regarded simply as one of the Cardinal's pitiless functionaries. For his young son, the most enduring lesson of the Chalais affair was the cruel necessity that could trap a humane but loyal servant of the King, who after all was 'God's Lieutenant on earth'. But what the boy could not possibly have known as he dwelt upon Chalais's terrible fate was that one day he too, having followed his King to Brittany, would be arrested and accused of the same crime.

PART ONE

Quo Non Ascendet?

(To where will he not climb?)

I

The Second Son

De te, Fucqueti, quid non timuere parentes?
Quae non pro puero vota precesque suo?*

As the busy parents of an ever-growing family, François and Marie can have had very little time to devote to any single child, but from early on they knew that their second son was special. He was like some exquisitely worked jewel whose very delicacy suggested its own destruction.

In 1626, when Nicholas was eleven, they entrusted him to the care of the Jesuits, whose school, the Collège de Clermont, across the river on the rue Saint-Jacques, François had success- fully campaigned to have reopened in 1618. The Fathers had been living in exile since Christmas 1594, when an old boy of the school, Jean Châtel, had attempted to kill the King.[1] The gut reaction of the authorities was that his teachers must somehow have been implicated, the Jesuits having long been resented in France for their tendency to place respect for papal authority before patriotism. But twenty years later, after the death of the once Protestant Henry IV,[†] whose switch to Catholicism had

---

* (What fears did your parents not have over you, Foucquet? What prayers and vows did they not offer on behalf of their child?) The quotation comes from a portrait of Nicolas written by his teacher at the Collège de Clermont, Father Vavasseur. It is quoted in Urbain-Victor Chatelain, *Le Surintendant Nicolas Foucquet, protecteur des lettres, des arts et des sciences* (Perrin, Paris, 1905), p. 18.

[†] Assassinated in 1610 by the religious fanatic François Ravaillac, whom the Jesuits had five years before wisely refused to allow into their order.

been more pragmatic than religious, the renewed fervour of the Counter-Reformation made it a propitious time for the Jesuits' return.

One of Nicolas's teachers at the school provides us with our earliest portrait. In a memoir of his time at the college, Father François Vavasseur, who taught humanities and rhetoric, recalled an extraordinarily gifted child whose febrile intelligence required constant challenge.[2] The boy's lightning-quick mind and insatiable curiosity bred a frustration with the limits to discovery that human frailty imposed. Of a nervous, restless disposition, he seemed always to be pushing beyond himself with a force that risked harming an extremely delicate constitution.

Fortunately, the Fathers were able to provide a solid programme of activities to keep his feet on the ground. Classes, which were conducted in Latin, took place six days a week. In accordance with the *ratio studiorum* of 1599, which set out the programme of study in all Jesuit schools, they provided an exhaustive grounding in rhetoric and the humanities, as well as mathematics, astronomy and the other natural sciences. Secular study was encouraged because the Jesuits believed that honing the intellect would aid the apprehension of religious truth.

Nicolas passed his schooldays in an atmosphere of simultaneous erudition and devotion. Aesthetic appreciation and philosophical enquiry shared the curriculum with the practice of Christian faith, a coexistence that often required considerable flexibility of mind. Virgil's *Aeneid*, for example, was a recommended text, but not book 4, in which Dido's tortured, self-destructive love for Aeneas was so clearly morbid and sinful. The great Roman love poets – Ovid, Catullus, Tibullus, Propertius – were on the syllabus, but only in heavily expurgated versions.

The life of a Jesuit scholar involved a continual nibbling of the forbidden fruit only to throw it away. Nicolas's schooling had been intended to equip him with the means to achieve a profound understanding of God, yet at the same time offered the promise of some delightful distractions should he choose to reject Him. Who better than a child of the Jesuits to understand those words of Saint Augustine, 'Lord, make me good, but not yet'? Perhaps this was why the school placed heavy emphasis on Christian doctrine and practice. It was the necessary counterbalance to the possible corruption that might result from such intense study of pagan literature. The pupils said prayers at the beginning of every lesson. They attended Mass every day and confession monthly, when each child was expected to hand over a slip of paper with his name and class so that the confessor could keep a tally of due observance.

The pupils were certainly safe from temptation to the extent that their minds were never idle. Every single moment of their day was provided for, both during their lessons and afterwards. Contests and games were regularly held, the Jesuits believing 'honourable rivalry' to be a powerful incentive to study.[3] Pupils composed their own Greek and Latin verses, the best of which were posted on the classroom walls. Every month, they gathered in the assembly hall to perform public declamations and disputations before the whole school.

The Jesuits favoured such cultural engagement 'as a means of stimulating intellectual interest and relaxing the mind'.[4] In the resulting atmosphere of mental clarity and calm – so the theory went – it would be all the easier to open oneself up to the divine.

But the sense of intellectual freedom was equally congenial to those who were more sceptical in their thinking. The Holy Spirit or free spirits? The Collège de Clermont seemed to encourage both. Among Nicolas's contemporaries were Molière and the libertine Cyrano de Bergerac. Some decades later, after the college had been renamed Louis-le-Grand, Voltaire would follow. It was entirely natural, if ironic, that this great scourge of the Church – who would be refused a Christian burial – should have been the product of such a pious yet enlightened school, where corporal punishment, for example, was discouraged in the belief that the hope of honour and respect was a more reliable incentive to virtue. Those who studied at the Collège de Clermont were inculcated with an essentially humane and liberal outlook – whether or not they chose to build on it in later life.

As a boarder, Nicolas spent much of his five years with the Jesuits cloistered in the rue Saint-Jacques, but holidays at home only strengthened the conviction imparted by his schooling that any darkness in the world could be dispelled through a combination of faith, energy and reason. He closely followed his father's work organising the expeditions that took the fruits of civilisation across the ocean to the newly discovered territories. Often the captains of these voyages, on their safe return to France with cargoes of exotic treasures, would gather in François Foucquet's library to narrate their adventures, tracing the routes they had taken on the great globe of the world.

But if their tales tended to fire up Nicolas's already overly excitable imagination, his father made sure also to acquaint him with the huge labour required behind the scenes, introducing him to his partners in the Compagnie des Îles de l'Amérique, briefing him on the onerous responsibilities involved in running this vast commercial and maritime empire that stretched literally round the world – from Canada, Guyana and the Indies in the west to Madagascar in the east.

If his father's library, with its maps and coins and books on all subjects, was a favourite place to while away the hours, Nicolas's mother took care to save him from excessive daydreaming, prescribing an endless list of charitable and religious duties to soak up spare energy, enlisting him as a willing assistant in her medicinal experiments. Often they would go off together across the river to the market in the place Maubert, where they bought the ingredients for her increasingly ambitious cures.

Back home in the still room, Nicolas would then help her to hang up and prepare the herbs. Amid copper basins, bubbling pipes and cauldrons, he learned how to grind up and mix the ingredients to cure such common seventeenth-century maladies as scrofula, wolf bites and blunderbuss wounds. As Marie infused horse droppings into herbs picked during the month of May or fried in pig's fat a carefully chosen kind of fly that frequented only the backsides of dogs, she inculcated into her son patience, method and a romantic faith in the unlikely.

Her pride and joy was the *Manus dei*, an ointment-impregnated plaster that would keep for fifty years without spoiling. Containing white vinegar, verdigris, opoponax, myrrh, bdellium, olive oil and mastic from trees that could only be found on the island of Chios, it could heal wounds without leaving any visible trace of a scar. It was just one more instance of how you really could work miracles, and for the impressionable Nicolas concocting such remedies would remain a lifetime interest.

It had been expected that the eldest son, François, would follow in his father's footsteps and embark upon a career in the magistracy, but given the religious faith of the Foucquets, no one can have been that surprised when he announced his desire instead to become a priest. Relinquishing the office his father had bought for him as a counsellor in the Paris Parlement, the younger François became a cleric in the diocese of Chartres. It was the first step in a rapid ascent, which would see him become – in spectacular fulfilment of the family device of the climbing squirrel – Bishop of Bayonne at the age of only twenty-six.

What made the eldest son's sudden discovery of a vocation particularly fortuitous were the increasing doubts that François and Marie had been having about their plan that Nicolas should go into the Church. A few perfunctory steps had already been taken to put the boy on this path. Aged sixteen, Nicolas left the Collège de Clermont, in January 1631, because his great-uncle Isaac Foucquet – the former chaplain to Henry IV – had given up his living as treasurer at the Abbey of Saint Martin de Tours, passing on the benefit of this office to his nephew. The following month Nicolas received the monastic tonsure, but the negative response of an otherwise enthusiastic child caused a general disquiet. According to one account,[5] it was Cardinal Richelieu himself who, after meeting Nicolas, advised that such a sharp mind could be put to much better use in service of the King. Perhaps the precocious Nicolas reminded the Cardinal a little of himself in youth. The third son of a noble family, Armand-Jean du Plessis de Richelieu had trained to be a soldier, but was pushed into the Church by his family after an older brother refused to accept the see of Luçon, a benefice that had been granted to the Richelieu family by Henry III.

So Nicolas grew back his hair and, abandoning the monastery in late 1631, returned from Tours to enrol as a law student at the Sorbonne, just across the road from his old school, the Collège de Clermont. Two years later, at the age of only eighteen, he passed his exams with such distinction that his achievement was cited in a report to the King. He was now well placed to embark upon a fast-track career.

As he began to make his way in the adult world, Nicolas was able to rely on not only a fierce intelligence but also considerable personal charm. He may have possessed a frail constitution that made him more than usually susceptible to headaches and fevers, but he was tall, with handsome, engaging features that inspired goodwill. His dark brown eyes were sharp and penetrating, but a habitual smile softened their regard, giving him an aspect of benevolence – if also a hint of mischief. He wore his hair at shoulder length, but even in later life resisted the fashion for elaborate wigs that was such a feature of the seventeenth century.

With his older brother François withdrawing into ecclesiastical seclusion, Nicolas began to play a more prominent role at home, acting as the next presumed head of the Foucquet family. It was Nicolas, for example, who, on 4 February 1633, carried Marie's youngest child, Louis – born that very day – into the parish church of Saint-Jean-en-Grève, near the Hôtel de Ville, and vowed as a godfather to provide the child with moral guidance – guidance that in practice would take on a more worldly character. After all, with six sisters in Holy Orders and an older brother well on the way to becoming a bishop, this latest addition to the family was never going to want for spiritual advice.

As for Nicolas's spiritual guidance, François and Marie had, on his leaving school, turned to his former director of studies at the Collège de Clermont, Father Pierre Deschampsneufs, who was an old friend of the family. With the approval of his Jesuit superiors, Deschampsneufs became Nicolas's personal chaplain, who would over the years come to take up permanent residence in his various households. A Hebrew scholar of considerable repute, he spent much of his time working on translations of the Scriptures, but theoretically he was on call for Nicolas to consult on spiritual matters whenever he felt the need.

Looking to give his son the best possible start in life, Nicolas's father was careful to consult with the Cardinal, who suggested that he buy Nicolas an office in the new Parlement of Metz. Richelieu had created the Parlement as part of his campaign to extend France's domination over the Duchy of Lorraine. As the obviously capable son of one of his most trusted *créatures*,

Nicolas, he believed, would be able to provide useful assistance in his efforts to impose France's jurisdiction over the disputed bishoprics of Metz, Toul and Verdun.

Upon his arrival in Metz in September 1633, Nicolas's first assignment was to visit the bishopric archives, which were kept in the palace of the bishops in the nearby town of Vic-sur-Seille. Here the eighteen-year-old conducted a painstaking investigation of documents, often hard to decipher, that went back four centuries and, in a long, closely argued memorandum, catalogued all the infringements that the ducs de Lorraine had made on French sovereignty. Months later, presumably pleased with a report that made the desired case, Richelieu ordered the complete annexation of the duchy.

Nicolas was appointed a member of the occupation authority established in Lorraine's capital, Nancy, where he arrived in September 1634. But his most important task had really already been accomplished in the dusty cellars of the bishops' palace in Vic and, far from home, he was now free to cultivate for perhaps the first time in his life an appetite for diversion that would prove to equal his capacity for hard work.

After a series of sightseeing tours that took him as far as Frankfurt, he took up residence in one of the larger houses of Nancy. Father Deschampsneufs arrived from Paris to take up his place in the household, but his sober presence did not deter Nicolas from hosting a series of lavish balls and feasts.

Holding pride of place at these occasions were the Mademoiselles de Pré – nieces of the King's Lieutenant in the town, the marquis de Fouquières, who was in charge of the occupation. They returned Nicolas's hospitality by inviting him to join their salon, which, offering a pale imitation of the famous Hôtel de Rambouillet in Paris, became a refuge for frivolity among young officials posted to a city that otherwise struggled to shake off the gloom of an occupation. The salon members whiled away the hours fashioning riddles, penning verses and creating mock chivalrous orders. The eldest of the de Pré sisters, for example, presided over an 'order of the Egyptians' under the assumed name of Queen Epicharmis. Her followers, who won admission to the order through some conspicuous act of gallantry, wore on their chests the device of a golden claw with the words 'Nothing Escapes Me'.[6] To the seasoned courtiers of Fontainebleau or Saint-Germain, these amusements of a provincial town would probably have seemed rather juvenile, but they offered a perfect opportunity for a young aspirant to their world to cut his teeth.

The twenty-year-old Nicolas remained in Nancy through most of 1635. It can perhaps best be regarded as a kind of 'gap year' in which, having no serious duties to discharge, he was free to broaden his horizons. His parents, trusting in Father Deschampsneufs to deter the more harmful excesses of youth, were content to see him make the most of this opportunity to enjoy himself, aware that in the years ahead, as he began to take an increasing responsibility for the family fortunes, he would never be so carefree again.

Back in Paris, Cardinal Richelieu was brooding over a decision that would help to keep Nicolas's hands full for the next twenty-five years. In May 1635, declaring war on Spain and Austria, he finally committed France to the long conflict – which we know today as the Thirty Years War – that had been ravaging central Europe since 1618.* Under pressure to find extra revenue to pay for France's armies, in December the Cardinal resorted to a policy of creating new offices in the Parlements to be sold to the highest bidder.

---

* Although the Peace of Westphalia in 1648 ended the Thirty Years War itself, France continued to be at war with Spain until 1659.

As Richelieu had centralised power in the hands of the monarchy, relying on the intendants to implement royal authority throughout France, it was impossible not to regard the measure with some cynicism. Since in practice the intendants, as instruments of Richelieu's will, overrode the traditional authority of the Parlements, there seemed very little practical call for the new offices, which would only dilute the authority of these institutions even further. But they were, nonetheless, an excellent stepping stone in a political career if you had the Cardinal's backing.

Among the offices created were eight new Masters of Requests in the Parlement of Paris. Once again, in consultation with Richelieu, Nicolas's father François bought one of these posts for Nicolas, the Cardinal signing a special dispensation to allow the twenty-year-old to take up an office that usually required its holders to have reached a minimum age of thirty-two.

On 18 January 1636, a few days before his twenty-first birthday, Nicolas swore his oath of office before the Chancellor of France, Pierre Séguier, and took up his position two weeks later. After the months of leisure he had enjoyed in Lorraine, Nicolas threw himself into his new job with enthusiasm and, familiarising himself with the way the Parlement worked, steadily began to build up his influence. The goal – effortlessly assumed, since it was a natural part of belonging to the Foucquet family – was to become a man of consequence, who would follow in his father's footsteps as one of the Crown's most faithful servants.

These were years of unremarkable but steady achievement in which Nicolas built for himself a reputation as one of the more able and popular of the Masters of Requests. Having established a foundation for what was clearly going to be a high-flying career, in 1640 he improved his prospects even further with a judicious marriage. Louise Fourché was the daughter of a rich Breton landowner who had been a counsellor in the Rennes Parlement. As part of her dowry, she brought 160,000 livres, as well as the estate of Quéhillac, north-west of Nantes. Nicolas's parents, for their part, bestowed on the couple a near equal amount.

Twenty years old, Louise was a niece of Father Deschampsneufs, who had recommended the betrothal. If the marriage clearly made sense from the point of view of her fortune, a surviving portrait, which shows a heavy-featured young woman of exceeding plainness, suggests that it was probably not much of a love match. But Nicolas's father François, who was now ill and anxious about the fortunes of the family after he was no longer around to protect it, urged an alliance that brought such obvious material benefit.

Too sick to attend the wedding, which took place in the cathedral of Nantes on 24 January 1640, François wrote his last will nearly a month later.[7] 'I, François Foucquet, miserable sinner . . .' he began, specifying in detail the religious orders – from the Benedictines to his favourite Jesuits – that he wished to pray for his soul. Then, after requesting that his body be buried without ceremony in the church of Saint Mary of the Visitation, he set out a clear division of responsibility between his first and second son. 'I entreat my eldest son, the Bishop of Bayonne, to take care that his brothers and sisters live in fear of God and at peace with one another, and that he say a prayer to God for me every time he celebrates Holy Mass.'

Turning to his second son, he reverted, for the only time in the entire document, to secular concerns. 'Having conferred considerable benefit on my son Nicolas, Master of Requests, through his contract of marriage, I hope that he will take special care to help his mother in the conduct of her business, and that he will act as a father to his brothers and sisters in their daily lives. I bequeath to him my books and antiques, which do not amount to a considerable enough collection to divide . . .'

Two months later François Foucquet was dead. Henceforward, the second son would have to find his own way in the world.

2

The Road to the Top

Since the Foucquet family had provided a substantial part of the funds that had enabled the Saint Mary of the Visitation church to be built, it was perhaps only fitting that the head of the family should be one of the first to find a resting place within its walls. In spite of François's wish that he should receive only a simple burial – he expressly stipulated that his corpse wasn't even to be swathed in a winding-sheet – no expense was spared in providing him with one of the most extravagant funerals that Paris had witnessed in years.

On his funeral bier, displayed like trophies, stood not only the heraldic squirrels of the Foucquets but also the coats of arms of other allied families, while the major achievements of his life were chronicled like the *res gestae* of an emperor. It is not hard to imagine which of the two eldest sons was responsible for organising such a send-off. While the austere Bishop of Bayonne would surely have frowned on such display, the young Master of Requests, Nicolas, had already shown his taste for extravagance during his year away in Lorraine.

If we must surely attribute this piece of theatre to Nicolas, such a radical departure from the terms of the will was less an act of disobedience than the gesture of a munificent host overcoming the polite 'No, thank yous' of a well-bred diner. If François had preferred thrift and simplicity, his son Nicolas showed a tendency always to pile the plate high. He wanted to make the most of this opportunity to remember his father, but also to show his pride in the family that he now headed.

'*Quo non ascendet?*' read the family motto. 'To where will he not climb?' While François had in practice been content to consolidate the family fortunes, his son Nicolas – led on by his ever restless imagination – treated present-day achievements as challenges for even more splendid feats in the future. As the young Master of Requests stood beneath the Visitation's great dome, surveying the august coats of arms that lined his father's bier, with their decorative devices of castles and portcullises, what could he have been thinking? Probably that he would get a castle of his own, complete with manorial forest where the Foucquet squirrel might be free to scurry across the treetops.

Less than a year later, in February 1641, Nicolas bought from François Lotin de Charny, a fellow counsellor in the Paris Parlement, the estate of Vaux, situated near the town of Melun, about thirty miles south-east of Paris. With this purchase came the title of Lord and Viscount of Vaux, providing Nicolas with formal admission to the ranks of the nobility.

The estate consisted of a crumbling fourteenth-century castle with a moat and drawbridge, a number of dependencies that included farm, stables, watermills and dovecote, as well as a park and forest. The impoverished Lotin de Charny had allowed the buildings to fall into a considerable state of disrepair – there was really no solution for the old castle but to pull it down, but if Nicolas had just become the lord of a ruin, there was nonetheless plenty of potential for improvement.

The increasing reliance the Cardinal was placing in him after his father's death encouraged the hope that he would soon be able to announce some grand schemes for refurbishment. But then an extraordinary run of bereavements turned all his plans to dust.

Within days of the purchase of Vaux, Nicolas's grandfather,

Gilles de Maupeou, died. Gone were the wisdom and steadying hand of a man who had, in the time of Henry IV and Sully, held one of the highest offices of state. Then, a few months later, in August 1641, Nicolas's wife, Louise, died, leaving Nicolas to care for a baby daughter, Marie. There's no record of Nicolas's reaction, but so soon after the loss of his father and grandfather, the death of a young wife and mother of just twenty-one must have shaken him badly. There but for the grace of God . . .

Then, on 4 December 1642 occurred the most grievous loss of all. Cardinal Richelieu died, the man who had been the Foucquet family's greatest protector and benefactor, from whom Nicolas had confidently expected to receive swift preferment. The death of Louis XIII five months later, on 14 May 1643, confirmed the passing of an era. Nicolas, who had been the beneficiary of unusual wealth and rare privilege, was suddenly on his own, responsible for making his own destiny.

The new King, Louis XIV, was only four years old. By long custom his mother, Queen Anne of Austria, would have been expected to become, for the duration of his minority, the regent ruler of France, as Marie de' Medici had in 1610 when the nine-year-old Louis XIII acceded to the throne of Henry IV. But Anne had been involved in far too many plots to be trusted. Fearing what might happen if she were allowed to rule unchecked, her late husband had in his last days stipulated that the affairs of the kingdom be determined by the majority vote of a Regency Council. Anne would be a member of this council, but safely protected against herself by the presence of the great notables of state – the King's brother and Lieutenant-General of the Kingdom Gaston d'Orléans;* the first prince of the blood

*Gaston had been involved in at least as many plots as Anne, but he was too important to be disregarded, and the King hoped that, in the harness of the Council, he would be an effective counterbalance to her.

Henri II de Bourbon, prince de Condé;* the Chancellor, Pierre Séguier; the Superintendent of Finances, Claude Bouthillier; and two former advisers to Richelieu, the comte de Chavigny and Cardinal Giulio Mazarini – or Jules Mazarin as the Italian was now calling himself.

In the event, Anne enlisted the support of the Parlement to dissolve the Regency Council. After years of being marginalised, its members hoped that the Queen, who had cause to hate Richelieu even more than they did, would use her unfettered power to restore their former importance.

The first public act of Louis XIV was to revoke the decree of his father. On 18 May 1643, the Grand Chamberlain carried the little child – like the puppet he in practice was – into the great hall of the Palais de Justice. Here he sat quietly before the assembled gathering of counsellors to the Parlement, while the Chancellor, Pierre Séguier, playing the ventriloquist's part, declared on the child-king's behalf that his mother the Queen should have 'free, complete and absolute control of the kingdom's affairs during His Majesty's minority'.[1] Nicolas was one of the counsellors present to witness the Parlement confirm the decree.

But if the gathered assembly really expected the occasion to usher in a new era of partnership between the royal government and the Parlement, they were to be deceived only a few hours later. That evening the Queen announced that Jules Mazarin would be her Prime Minister.

It was an extraordinary return to the agenda of her adversaries, who had gone out of their way to express their high esteem for the Italian. Not only had Cardinal Richelieu persuaded the Vatican to make him a cardinal, but the dying Louis XIII had chosen him to be godfather to the Dauphin. The inference was

* Father of France's young military hero the duc d'Enghien, who won the decisive victory over the Spanish at Rocroi in 1643, and would become known as 'the Great Condé' after Henri's death in 1646.

clear. Mazarin was the favoured candidate of the previous dispensation to guide the affairs of the realm. The fact that Anne had accepted this inference meant that although she was now able to rule with the full powers of a regent, the real force to reckon with was this mysterious stranger from Italy who had won the trust of the late Cardinal and King but was little known among the wider establishment.

With his favoured place in Richelieu's circle, and the long association of his father before him, Nicolas had felt confident of his position, but what was he to expect now? It was true that Mazarin had been one of Richelieu's closest confidants, but he showed no sign of placing the same trust in the Foucquet family that his master had done. Nicolas's posting the next year to the distant province of the Dauphiné – far from Paris and his new estate at Vaux – only confirmed his sense of having been knocked back a peg. The one crumb of comfort he was able to draw was that at least this engagement in the service of the Crown would give him a chance to prove himself, but in the event it had turned out be a disaster.

Had Nicolas been a little less well connected, maybe his career would have ended under a Dauphinoise cloud, but the Queen Regent, who admired and encouraged the good works of Nicolas's mother, Marie, chose to take an indulgent view of an esteemed friend's child. The boy had made a mistake through his youth and inexperience, but both she and Cardinal Mazarin had been impressed with the way he had managed to redeem himself – the initiative and considerable heroism he had shown in staying behind to quell the riots in Valence. While the Chancellor would have been happy to see the young Master of Requests thrown into the Bastille, they decided that he deserved to be given a second chance.

So after a few months sitting as a Master of Requests again on the benches of the Palais de Justice, Nicolas was appointed to serve as an intendant first with the French army besieging the town of Lerida in Spain, then, in 1646, with the army Gaston d'Orléans was commanding in Flanders.

Nicolas acquitted himself well in both missions, but since he was profoundly unmilitary, he can hardly have found these years of running after generals particularly rewarding. They were a period of sterling but unspectacular achievement. The slow, static nature of the war in Flanders, which involved one lengthy siege after another, afforded plenty of time for relaxation. Nicolas arrived to find that Gaston wasn't even there, but taking the waters in Bourbon. The real campaign for Nicolas wasn't on the ramparts at all, but rather in the salons of Amiens, where the Court had gathered to follow the progress of the war. Here, he launched a charm offensive.

In this small town far from Paris it was possible to get to know – and impress – the Queen Regent and the new Prime Minister Jules Mazarin in an atmosphere of comparative informality. Here, Nicolas first began to sense their closeness. The Spanish-born queen and the former Italian diplomat were both outsiders who, facing the same challenge of a grafted existence in the French Court, instinctively turned towards each other. Informed by his family's familiarity with the dynamics of power, Nicolas realised that their bond would become every bit as strong as the one that had existed between Louis XIII and Richelieu. Fresh from the lesson of the Dauphiné, he also realised that any future advance he was to make in his career depended upon the backing of such powerful protectors. From this moment on, therefore, he was single-minded in his efforts to win their approval, aspiring to serve the new power in the land as his father had served the old.

Cardinal Jules Mazarin is such an important character in Nicolas's story that we must pause at this point to take a closer look at him. While François Foucquet had shown total deference to Richelieu, his more ambitious son ultimately looked at Mazarin less as a master than as a model to emulate – an object lesson in what you could achieve if you exploited the principles of patronage with sufficient intelligence and imagination.

The rigid society of the time may have expected you to know your place and to stay in your place, but if you were resourceful enough, if you played the game of connections well enough, there was no limit to how far you could climb. The man the Queen Regent made Prime Minister of France was said to be the grandson of a Sicilian fisherman. During the reign of Louis XIII he traded on his lowliness with genius. As Richelieu's favourite, he had achieved the considerable feat of making the forbiddingly austere Cardinal laugh, his self-effacing manner drawing forth such fond nicknames as Rinzama (an anagram of Mazarin), Colmardo or its French equivalent *Frère Coupechou* (Brother Cabbage-Cutter) – the friar who took on all the most humble tasks in the monastery. Previously only the Cardinal's fourteen cats – the beneficiaries of a considerable settlement under his will – had been able to command such affection. But while Lucifer, Félimare, Soumise and the rest would be murdered after their master's death by the Swiss Guard (who grew sick of having to feed them), Mazarin lived to receive the due reward for a winning combination of extreme intelligence and absolute fidelity.

Born Giulio Mazarini in the Abruzzi village of Pescina in 1602, he was the son of Pietro Mazarini, steward to Don Filippo Colonna, the Constable of Naples. Educated at the Jesuit college in Rome, he emerged from his studies with the worldly and sceptical cast of mind that such an education so often seemed to encourage, but with a passion for gambling that no appeal to the *ratio studiorum* seemed able to curb.

Alarmed by his son's reckless dedication to cards, Pietro Mazarini arranged for him to become tutor and companion to the Constable's second son, Don Girolamo, who was going to Spain to study law at the University of Alcala. The two-year sojourn (1620–2) gave the young Giulio a fluency in Castilian that would much later stand him in good stead with the Spanish Queen of France, but when he returned to Italy he still seemed more concerned to taste *la dolce vita* of Rome – then approaching the height of its baroque decadence – than to settle down to a serious profession. He eventually tumbled into a career more than chose one, when a cousin of Don Filippo Colonna, the Prince of Palestrina, offered him a captain's commission in a regiment he was raising for the papal army.

With his sharp mind and natural charm, Giulio made rapid progress. In 1628 he became secretary to Gian-Francesco Sacchetti, apostolic commissioner to the papal army, who had been appointed Papal Nuncio to Milan. Possessing the perfect cast of character for an age that prized the social as much as the intellectual, he had ability, but also – crucially – affability. Soon he had made himself a firm favourite not only of Gian-Francesco but also of the prominent Florentine family to which Gian-Francesco belonged.

Embarking on an apprenticeship in diplomacy under the nominal tutelage of Gian-Francesco, he received copious advice and encouragement from all four Sacchetti brothers. In one of many notes addressed to '*mio Giulio*', the youngest brother, Marcello, wrote, 'Live in the hope of being supported by your merit: that is the true way.' But of course both he and Giulio knew that it was just a part of the way. Referring to his brothers, Marcello went on, 'As for us, we shall serve you any time we can, with all our heart.'[2]

Of his actual work with Gian-Francesco Sacchetti, Giulio would later comment, 'I made myself important at that time more through my handling of affairs than by my actual post, which consisted only of informing my patrons of what was happening in Lombardy.'[3] Here was his vocation – the 'handling of affairs', finessing, wheeling and dealing – managing people, oiling the wheels of communication. The rise of Mazarin – for anyone such as Nicolas who took the trouble to examine his career closely – was a perfect example of the art of friendship and influence, of establishing an effective network for personal progress.

Sacchetti thought so highly of his secretary that when he returned to Rome in 1629, he left the legation in his control. In the new year Giulio helped Cardinal Antonio Barberini – the nephew of Pope Urban VIII – to mediate between France and Spain, who were fighting in northern Italy over the Mantuan succession.

This dispute was caused by the death in 1627 of Vincenzo Gonzaga, Duke of Mantua and Prince of Monferrato in Piedmont. Having no children of his own, Vincenzo bequeathed his territories to the Duke of Gonzaga-Nevers. Refusing to accept the heir, Spain besieged Casale, the principal fortress in Monferrato. Supporting Gonzaga-Nevers's claim, France sent an army to relieve Casale in 1629. After a brief occupation the French had to abandon the fortress, but threatened to attack again soon with an even greater force.

With full power to speak on behalf of the Pope, Mazarin travelled to Lyons to attempt to negotiate a peace. Here, on 29 January 1630, he met Cardinal Richelieu for the first time.

Mazarin's own recollection of the occasion suggests a *coup de foudre* in which the two arch intriguers found themselves instantly drawn to each other as surely as any pair of star-crossed lovers. Recalling an astrologer's prophecy that he would make his fortune in France, he later wrote, 'I confess that the first time I saw the Most Eminent Cardinal-duke, at Lyons, I remembered it and resolved to devote myself entirely to him.'[4] While Richelieu enjoyed the reputation as the most powerful man in Europe, Mazarin was an obscure twenty-seven-year-old functionary of little importance. Yet at the end of his hour-long audience he had persuaded Richelieu to allow him to conduct direct negotiations with the military commanders.

As the months passed, Richelieu grew tired of the endless talks. In an attempt to force a victory, he sent an enlarged army, of over 20,000 men, back to Casale to lift the Spanish siege once and for all. It turned out to be Mazarin's finest hour.

The order to attack was given at teatime on the afternoon of 26 October 1630.[5] As the French soldiers advanced to engage the forces surrounding the fortress, they were bewildered to see the papal legate – who had earlier secured a promise from the Spanish that they would give up their siege – galloping towards them on a horse, crying, 'Peace! Peace!'

The Pope then sent Mazarin to Paris in order to negotiate a formal treaty. Here he made friends with France's Secretary of State, the comte de Chavigny, and also quickly won the confidence of the chief French negotiator, the Minister of War Abel Servien. An agreement – known as the Treaty of Cherasco – was finally concluded on 19 June 1631.

Richelieu was hugely impressed by Mazarin's skill in the talks. The papal legate had hinted his private support of the French position, yet assumed the role of the Pope's neutral representative with total credibility, deftly ensuring that the negotiations would permit France to hold on to the strategically important frontier town of Pignerol in the Alps. Delighted with the outcome, Richelieu instructed Servien to 'assure M. Mazarin that everything he has been told about me is false and that I love and esteem him as much as he could possibly desire'.[6]

Mazarin returned to Rome, but kept in constant touch with his new friends in France, accepting no employment without sounding out Chavigny or Servien first. His true allegiance henceforward was clear. Still in name a representative of the Holy See, he made an all too brief trip to Paris in the spring of 1632, but longed to return there permanently to work for

Richelieu. In the meantime he spared no effort to communicate his devotion, sending the Cardinal endless gifts – antique statues, old paintings, a gilded vase inlaid with coral.[7]

The Pope demonstrated his own satisfaction with Mazarin by offering him the benefice of two churches. With the official status of Canon, Mazarin was allowed to wear ecclesiastical garments, even though he had not been ordained. In December 1634 the Pope sent him back to France as a Nuncio Extraordinary (the title of Nuncio was already taken) with the mission to persuade France to avoid further conflict with Spain and also to give up its recent annexation of Lorraine.

Mazarin arrived in Paris with four Titians and a Pietro de Cortona for the Cardinal's gallery. Richelieu seemed to treasure the envoy's company as much as the gifts, inviting him to attend not only his soirées but also those of the King. The two men would even match their wits over the card table, confirming Mazarin's view that gaming was less a vice than a necessary career skill. 'A good diplomat,' he would observe many years later, 'must avail himself of all means to get to know those on whom the favourable outcome of his negotiations depends.'[8]

In the event, the outcome of the negotiations was not so favourable, but Mazarin himself emerged from the trip a considerable personal success. Although this time an implacable Richelieu refused to budge an inch, he was as charmed as ever by the manner in which Mazarin continued to plead for peace.

'His Eminence,' wrote Mazarin, 'rose and retorted that I courted peace as if it were the lady of my dreams, and pressing my hand, he concluded, "You have not yet abandoned France."'[9]

France's declaration of war on Spain of 26 May 1635 did nothing to affect the warmth of the relationship. Indeed, it was now quite impossible for Mazarin to act any longer as an honest broker. Embarrassed by his obvious preference for France over Spain, the Pope asked him not to take any further part in mediation efforts between the two countries and appointed him instead as a vice-legate to the papal possession of Avignon.

Here, as he really had no practical duties to undertake, Mazarin only worked harder to make himself indispensable to his chosen patron. When the Spanish army pushed deep into France in the autumn of 1636, reaching the royal town of Compiègne in Picardy, less than fifty miles from the capital, Mazarin gathered together as much weaponry and gunpowder as he could find and sent it to the French forces. 'It must be admitted that only the Italians, and particularly Jules, know how to do things properly,' Richelieu wrote in thanks. 'In times of peace they distribute powders that smell sweet, and in times of war those that thunder.'[10]

But still the Cardinal kept Mazarin dangling on a string, considering him to be more useful in the Pope's employ than his own. It was a perception that Mazarin took care as gently as possible to challenge. His life in the Pope's palace in Avignon, he wrote to Chavigny, was 'the most melancholy in the world. I have converted one of the ancient drawing rooms into a gambling den, but after playing for an hour I am more bored than ever . . . I would gladly exchange my lot with that of the gardener at Rueil' – Rueil was Richelieu's chateau, near Paris – 'and would work all day long at the fountains . . . if my consolation could be to hear myself called Colmarduccio or Nunzinicardo by that personage whom one must adore even if one has spoken to him but once.'[11]

But Richelieu had far grander plans for him. After the death of his close adviser Father Joseph at the end of 1638, he put Mazarin forward in Father Joseph's place as the French Crown's candidate to be appointed a cardinal. He wrote to him, 'Monsieur Colmardo is well aware how useful it is to attach oneself to the service of great princes and good masters, such as the one we both serve. He will know in due course that it is useful to have good friends and that I am not the least of them that he has in the world.'[12]

In January 1640 Mazarin at last took up permanent residence in Paris. In the three years that followed he proved himself so invaluable an aide that the ailing Richelieu would comment shortly before his death, 'I know only one man who could succeed me, though he is a foreigner.'[13] On his deathbed he advised Louis XIII that he should rely on Mazarin for guidance in state affairs, and the King duly appointed the Italian a minister, instructing officials to report henceforth to Mazarin as they had previously reported to the Cardinal. And when the King himself died, Mazarin seemed able effortlessly to win over the Queen.

Indeed, his relationship with Anne was so close it was rumoured that they had married in secret. One of the wilder conspiracy theories even maintained that it was Richelieu who had deliberately encouraged a romance to develop between his admired Rinzama and a woman who had lived in a state of virtual separation from her husband ever since their marriage in 1615. Louis XIII, who much preferred the company of the young gentlemen of the court, then turned a blind eye while the Italian lover gave Anne the kind of satisfaction that Louis had been so loath to provide himself. When, to everyone's surprise, in 1638 Anne gave birth to a baby boy after more than twenty years of marriage – Louis Dieu-Donné, Louis the God-Given – the King, who knew that the child was in reality more Jules-Donné than Dieu-Donné, was happy to go along with the fiction of a sudden rapprochement.*

---

* The inexhaustible passion for this kind of historical gossip means that there are plenty of rivals for the honour of being the Sun King's father. Perhaps the leading candidate was François de Vendôme, duc de Beaufort, the illegitimate grandson of Henry IV. According to the legend, he was locked up as the Man in the Iron Mask – that convenient solution for so many of France's seventeenth-century mysteries.

But whatever the truth, one thing was undeniable. Tall and handsome, with a generous moustache and goatee beard, Mazarin was a bright, genial presence who inspired affection as well as confidence, and brought to the Queen the warmth that had been so notably lacking in her relationship with her late husband. The strong affinity that existed between them cemented his position as the key political figure during Louis's minority, regardless of the mostly hostile sentiment he inspired in the kingdom at large. With careful diplomacy and statecraft, he would bring to fruition Richelieu's long-term plan to establish France's ascendancy over Spain, even if in the minds of ordinary people these elusive skills came second to a fabled extravagance and thinly veiled larceny.

Nicolas's efforts to win Mazarin's confidence were soon repaid when he was appointed to be intendant for Paris in May 1648. With responsibility for internal order within the capital, this was a strategic position that would have been entrusted only to the most dependable of loyalists. But it was a dangerous time to be identified too closely with the Cardinal.

The Paris Parlement, of which Nicolas was a prominent and popular member, resented Mazarin's influence. Cheated of the consultative role they had expected to have after the death of the previous king, its members had never forgiven Anne her treachery, and regarded her chosen adviser as quite as damaging to their authority as Richelieu had been. Over the years that followed, the Parlement's sense of grievance grew in proportion to the degree it was ignored. Cardinal Mazarin may have had the grandest of visions for France's place in Europe, but he knew little – and cared even less – about the Parlement de Paris's place in France. To the extreme anger of its counsellors, he treated the institution as little more than a rubber stamp.

Matters came to a head at the beginning of 1648, only a few months before Nicolas's new appointment. Not content with introducing a whole roster of additional taxes to finance the interminable war against Spain, the Superintendent of Finances, Particelli d'Emery, sought to bring in extra revenue by selling off several newly created posts in the Parlement. As the effect of such a policy was to diminish the importance of the offices already held by existing members, it was greeted with open hostility.

A group of nearly sixty counsellors to the Parlement gathered together and swore on the Bible not to agree to the new offices. Meanwhile, disturbances were taking place among the city populace, who were just as angry about the new taxes. A mob seized and barricaded three churches on the rue Saint-Denis.[14] When the Queen attended Mass in Notre-Dame, a group of about 200 women followed her into the cathedral, begging her to give them justice. They wanted to kneel down before her, but the guards wouldn't allow them to.[15]

For a brief moment the indignation of the people and the privileged magistrates who sat in the Parlement seemed to be joining together. But the protests only hardened the royal government's resolve. Rather than seek a compromise, it held a formal *lit de justice* to force the Parlement to ratify all the financial measures. On 15 January the nine-year-old King made a second visit to the Palais de Justice. This time he was able to walk into the chamber, but his face – bearing the ravages of smallpox, from which he had just recovered* – made his vulnerability plain. With all the authority he could muster, the child began in a frail and piping voice to recite the edicts that the Parlement was expected to pass, but after just a few sentences he faltered, forgetting what he had been schooled to say. The Chancellor, Pierre Séguier, quickly stepped in to complete the

---

*A Mass to thank God for the young King's survival had been held in Notre-Dame Cathedral just the day before.

litany of demands on the child-king's behalf, leaving Louis to run back sobbing to his mother. If this mishap revealed the clear contrivance of the occasion, the active part the despised Chancellor played in pulling the strings only further provoked the counsellors' anger. No one could have provided a better symbol of oppression.

The final straw occurred when the Queen Regent let slip a vindictive little guffaw of laughter as the Chancellor read out the edict concerning the creation of the new offices in the Parlement. Incensed, the Advocate-General, Omer Talon, took the floor. Famed among his fellow counsellors for his fearlessness and oratorical eloquence, he gave a speech that seemed as heartfelt as the previous presentation of the King's edicts had been contrived. His words captured the mood of the assembly perfectly.

Addressing himself to Louis, who was still clinging to his mother's lap, Talon declared that once the people had welcomed the King's meetings with the Parlement because they knew that a genuine debate would take place:

> The Parlement was allowed to disagree and to say freely: 'Sire, that is not right.' But today, through lack of courage and political trickery, edicts are brought here preordained, with the assumption that they will be inevitably passed. Once this court vetoed a tax that François I, aged thirty years old, wanted to levy on his people. But now it fears to challenge Your Majesty, even although you are still a child.[16]

Talon went on to enumerate the human suffering that the long war with Spain had caused. Whatever victories France might boast, they did nothing to diminish the tribulations of the people. Whole provinces had to subsist on scanty rations of bread, oats and bran. Once Frenchmen had prided themselves on their freedom. 'But now they see themselves treated like slaves and convicts.'[17]

Reaching his conclusion, the Advocate-General now addressed the Queen, amid loud applause from the assembly: 'It is up to you, Your Majesty, in the privacy of your office, to consider all these matters and to reflect on the miseries of the age. Don't forget that when you make war, it is countless poor people in the provinces who pay the penalty.'

Stepping back from the brink, the Parlement still went on to confirm the King's edicts, but this gesture of protest was an unmistakable threat of worse to come. Visibly shaken, the Queen took Louis's hand and turned angrily to leave, without saying a word. As her retinue passed out of the chamber, no one gave out the customary cry of 'Long live the King!'

The next day, a group of Masters of Requests gathered to discuss the edict concerning the new offices, which was specifically aimed at them. Concluding that the King had no right to introduce such a measure during his minority, they resolved to challenge it.

Enraged to learn of this meeting, the Queen summoned them to her apartments in the Palais-Royal. Wearing their long robes and hats, they entered to find her waiting for them with the King, the Cardinal and the Chancellor. As the fifty Masters of Requests crowded around, the Queen turned sharply as someone stepped on her dress, but, recognising an embarrassed-looking Mazarin, quickly replaced her look of fury with a nervous smile.

She then invited the Chancellor to speak. Addressing them like miscreant schoolchildren, Séguier took them to task for holding debates that were needlessly long for the resolutions they passed, but too short properly to consider the issues. Itching to intervene and unable to observe for very long the silence of royal decorum, the Queen cut in herself: 'Really, you are fine people to doubt my authority!'[18] She would soon show them, she added, that she could create as many new offices as she liked!

At the end of the audience the Masters of Requests filed out if anything even more disgruntled and fractious. The meeting served only to make change seem all the more vital. In the weeks that followed, the counsellors to the Parlement met at every opportunity to discuss what form its relationship with the government ought in future to take. In May 1648 the Parlement and the other sovereign courts – the Grand Conseil, the Chambre des Comptes and the Cour des Aides – formed a new assembly to discuss measures for reform. The deliberations of the Chambre Saint-Louis, as this assembly was known, resulted in an avalanche of proposals to limit royal power.

Enraged by their impudence, Anne dismissed this chamber as an absurdity –'a republic within the monarchy'[19] – and ordered it to disband. But when it became clear that the counsellors would not back down so easily, Mazarin suggested that it could do no harm at least to negotiate a little.

Nicolas had witnessed all the turbulence of these momentous months. He had been among the counsellors who cheered the speech of Omer Talon. He was one of the Masters of Requests whom the Queen had scolded in the Palais-Royal. Indeed, many of the counsellors to the Parlement expected the people's hero of the Dauphiné to play a leading part in demanding the new reforms. But whatever his liberal sympathies, ultimately Nicolas belonged too much to the prevailing system of patronage to depart from his family's tradition of service to the Crown. Instead, the newly appointed intendant turned his intimate knowledge of the Parlement to Mazarin's benefit, becoming as close an adviser to the new Cardinal as his father had been to the previous one.

As a conciliatory gesture, it had been agreed that the First President of the Parlement, Mathieu Molé, would head a deputation to the Queen to assure her that, finally, the Parlement wanted only the best for France and did not intend to obstruct the royal government. On the eve of the meeting Nicolas wrote a long memorandum to the Cardinal with advice on how the Queen might best receive this deputation.[20]

> They should be told that while the Queen has never doubted the Parlement's loyalty and affection, the behaviour of some individuals has caused her to suspect their motives. But she would be very happy for any constructive criticism and advice that the Parlement might have to give. If its members want to meet with the members of other sovereign courts, then she has no objection, as long as it is understood that such a gathering should set no precedent for the future.

The correct tactic, Nicolas argued, was to isolate the extremists, but to win over those who held moderate views. For 'in the present heated atmosphere, a huge effort has been required to get them to adopt such an attitude'.

By 'huge effort' he meant his own effort. As the Cardinal's chief means of persuasion in the Parlement, Nicolas took care to underline how indispensable he was at every opportunity. So long as he had the backing of Rinzama the Godfather, the road to the top was clear.

3

Slings

France did not have a ruling team that could command much respect – a Spanish-born queen, an Italian gambler and diplomat who was possibly her lover, and a ten-year-old boy. It was hardly surprising that the 'fine people' of the Parlement doubted the Queen's authority. Nor did a near-total inconsistency in decision-making help the situation. While the Queen – who tended to regard all talk of political reform as a personal slight – defended impossible positions, refusing to yield an inch, the Cardinal – always pushing for accommodation and usually with some hidden motive in mind – was prone to make spectacular concessions that his wiser self knew he could not keep even as he was making them.

The visit of the Parlement's First President, Mathieu Molé, to the Queen, concerning which Nicolas had given such considered advice, was an example of how wildly government policy veered between the two poles. On 26 June 1648 the Queen received him with frosty contempt, but four days later her Prime Minister agreed to the formal union of the sovereign courts. Where Nicolas had advocated a policy of measured conciliation, Cardinal Mazarin chose total surrender. The newly sanctioned reform body proceeded to draft its wildest dreams: habeas corpus, the abolition of the arbitrary exercise of royal authority through *lettres de cachet*, the right of the Parlement to veto taxes, the establishment of a special court to investigate the abuses of tax collectors . . .

Mazarin's capitulation was so complete that few people doubted that there must be some trick. And indeed, two weeks later it began to become clear what that trick was. On 9 July, sacking the Superintendent of Finances, Particelli d'Emery, the Cardinal announced that the government could no longer honour its debts. Such an extreme measure, he implied, had been forced upon him by the Parlement's demands for reform, which were undermining the government's ability to raise revenue. Intoxicated by their new-found power, the counsellors seized upon the bankruptcy as a pretext to launch prosecutions against the financiers who lent money to the government or organised the collection of taxes, both areas rife with corruption. But the government's insolvency hit just as many distinguished families of irreproachable reputation. With its increased militancy and patently unsustainable demands, Mazarin calculated, the Parlement would quickly lose support and discredit itself.

The following month the Parlement arraigned some of the largest tax-farmers in the country. Its reformist zeal – blind to the needs of practical government – was so radical that any investor not already deterred by the government bankruptcy made himself scarce. The royal coffers were empty with no immediate prospect of replenishment, yet there was still an army to keep supplied and a war to be won.

Towards the end of the month a great victory over the Spaniards in Flanders seemed to provide a timely opportunity for the royal government to pull the noose. With the Battle of Lens, France's flamboyant young general, the Great Condé – now First Prince of the Blood and third in line to the throne after the recent death of his father, Henri II de Bourbon – had not only turned the war decisively in France's favour, but also delivered a splendid practical feat of royal power to set against the fairy-tale dreaming of the Parlement.

Determined to take advantage, the Queen ordered a Te Deum, a Mass of thanksgiving.* On the morning of Wednesday, 26 August, the young King led a procession of the Court from the Palais-Royal to Notre-Dame. Soldiers of the Royal Guard lined the route all the way to the entrance of the cathedral, where cheering crowds crammed the vast square. The mood of jubilant reconciliation assured total surprise when the very same day the Queen's guard arrested two of the most outspoken counsellors in the Parlement, Pierre Broussel and René Potier de Blancmesnil, but the subsequent turn of events afforded very little time for the Queen to savour her revenge.

The celebrations in the streets quickly turned into enraged protest, as the news of the arrests spread. The crowds began to chant the names of the two counsellors, whose opposition to taxes had made them popular heroes, and demanded their release. Soon an angry mob, which had gathered outside the Palais-Royal, was threatening to storm the building and, in a humiliating climbdown, the Queen was forced to authorise the release of the two men.

But the day of reckoning had merely been postponed. In the early hours of 6 January 1649 the royal family stole away from the Palais-Royal to the Château de Saint-Germain outside the city. Here it would not be so easy to take them hostage. On the same day the Queen sent the Parlement an ultimatum. Its members were to leave Paris and to reassemble in Montargis, over sixty miles to the south. Ignoring the injunction, the Parlement instead ordered the citizens of the capital to prepare themselves for a siege.

---

* So named after the opening lines of the hymn that was sung on the occasion: *Te deum laudamus . . .* (We praise you, God . . .).

The latest of France's many civil wars had begun. Just about the only thing the warring sides seemed able to agree on was its name, the Fronde. A 'fronde' was a kind of sling. During a particularly heated session of the Parlement, a counsellor known as Bachaumont observed, in a moment of levity, that the assembly was behaving like the schoolchildren who fought against each other with slings outside the city walls. The name stuck, capturing some of the senseless, juvenile nature of the four-year conflict, if not the scale of the bloodshed and destruction.

A military legend at the age of just twenty-seven, the Great Condé – otherwise known as the prince de Condé or Monsieur le Prince – was a fearless soldier who had, with his victory at Rocroi, established himself as the nation's saviour in the very opening days of the King's reign. As a twenty-one-year-old, with no previous experience of battle, he had inflicted upon the Spanish their first great defeat in a century. Now his latest triumph at Lens added to this aura of invincibility. Hailed as the Alexander of his age, this veteran of countless sieges in Flanders, Spain and Germany was the obvious choice to command operations against the rebel Parlement, his reputation enough to ensure the speedy surrender of most cities.

Swiftly cutting off all roads out of the city with an army of 8,000 men – mostly German, Swiss or Polish mercenaries, who were immune to the pleadings of the populace – he imposed a near total blockade of the city, which was made only more cruelly effective by the worst winter floodings Paris had seen in years.

This time Nicolas allowed no ambiguity to exist in where his loyalties lay. He aligned himself squarely behind the sovereign authority. He became the Cardinal's chief confidant in the development of a strategy against the recalcitrant Parlement. Mazarin may often have disregarded his advice, but nonetheless he knew that Nicolas's intimate knowledge of what the counsellors were thinking made him indispensable. Furthermore, as intendant for Paris, Nicolas was at the heart of the attempts to subdue the city. His chief responsibility was to deny supplies to the populace and, marshalling all available resources in the countryside, to feed the besieging army. This role must often have involved harsh measures – the compulsory levies that he imposed can hardly have been popular – but he behaved with a civilised correctness that stood in stark contrast to the savage maraudings of Condé's mercenaries, which many of the less fortunate villages had to endure. An index of his essentially humane nature was his concern to make amends once the city finally succumbed in early April. As soon as peace terms were agreed, he hastened to make contact with the mayor and the other authorities, offering to do whatever was in his power to facilitate the swift resupply of the city.

Naturally open and sympathetic, Nicolas expected to be liked, but the return of peace did not make up for the fact that, as Mazarin's aide, he worked for the most unpopular man in France. A striking aspect of the Parlement's rebellion against the government was that it continued all through the siege to profess its loyalty to the King, attributing the failures of the Queen's regency instead to her heavy reliance on Cardinal Mazarin, who was regarded as having bewitched her. By this reasoning, the goal of Parlement had been not to overthrow royal authority but to rescue it. The sentiment was near universal. Even after a treaty had been agreed to end the siege – a treaty from which the Parlement was lucky to emerge with an amnesty as well as many of the concessions that the government had made before the rebellion – there were violent protests because one of the signatures belonged to the Cardinal. The streets echoed to the refrain: 'Long live the King! Down with Mazarin!' Through the length of the siege printing presses in the city had poured out a never-ending supply of mocking pamphlets, public letters and songs, known as 'Mazarinades', that helped to turn him into the great hate figure of the age. By the end of the Fronde, over 5,000 had been published.

Two of the milder examples suffice to suggest the common tone of hostility in a genre that could often take the form of virulent, obscene abuse. *Letter of a Priest to Monsieur le Prince de Condé*: 'The whole of Paris (and no doubt the whole of France and the whole of Europe too) can hardly believe that you wish to protect, contrary to the well-being of King and country, such a troublemaker – the Enemy, the Destroyer, the Scourge and Ruin of France . . .'[1] An apocryphal *Confession by Jules Mazarin of the Crimes He Has Committed against God, the King and Himself*: 'I threw into prison 25,000 people for not paying enough tax. Six thousand of them died from hunger during the six years of my rule . . . It is also true that I only took charge of the King's upbringing so that I could dominate him and have him act as I saw fit. At Court, I conquered virtue with vice, invented all kinds of decadent games, used magic charms to loosen women's inhibitions . . .'[2]

But Mazarin's qualities more than made up for such loathing. With his privileged access to the inner circle, Nicolas was able to appreciate that the Queen-Regent's reliance on the Italian was not just a case of blind passion, but a genuine recognition of his political genius. As Richelieu had realised before her, in times of crisis, when new threats seemed to arrive daily, there was no one who could better anticipate the moves of the enemy or match his gambler's instinct for finding a sure path through the confusion of unpredictable events. The way Mazarin went on in the months to come to handle the now dangerously powerful Condé was an example that served as an important masterclass for Nicolas.

It had been gratifying for Anne to see the Great Condé put the Parlement in its place, but yesterday's friend was beginning to become today's rival. Condé would never have thought to challenge the right of the King to his throne, but nor did he consider the King to be his superior; he was merely a *primus inter pares*, to whom, as the First Prince of the Blood, he need show no deference. Indeed, on the contrary, he felt that the onus now was on the monarchy to discharge its very heavy debt to him.

In the months following the siege, Condé made one demand after another for himself, his family and his supporters. He wanted back the estate of Montmorency, which had many years ago been confiscated from an uncle who had rebelled against Richelieu. He wanted to be appointed commander-in-chief of the navy; he wanted his brother-in-law, the duc de Longueville, to be awarded the stronghold of Pont de l'Arche . . . The list was endless, but what made these demands especially difficult was the aggressive manner in which he asked for them. He treated the Queen-Regent's chief minister like a lowly servant, making no effort to hide his contempt for this low-born Italian who had somehow mananged to wangle his way into the highest office in the land. Routinely hurling abuse at him, on one occasion he even pulled the Cardinal's carefully groomed beard. Condé expected to play a part in the affairs of state, yet at the same time undermined rational government with his often arrogant, capricious demands.

In public Mazarin abased himself, meekly enduring Condé's insults, as if he were as wretched a creature as the Mazarinades were suggesting, but privately he began to consider how best to tackle this dangerous new challenge to his authority. He took steps to build up his social standing so that he would seem less an outsider. His lineage could barely compete with a country squire, let alone the First Prince of the Blood, but his two sisters, Margarita and Girolama, had married into the Roman nobility and had five pretty daughters. Some time earlier the Italian had brought these girls to live at the French Court, where they became the childhood companions of Louis and his brother Philippe. Now, he decided, it was time to seek a return on the investment. If he could marry off his nieces – the Mazarinettes, as they were popularly known – to leading figures in the French aristocracy, he would establish roots in high society that not even the Great Condé could hope to pull up.

Just weeks after peace had been restored in Paris, he began negotiations to marry his niece Laura Mancini to the duc de Mercoeur, a member of the prestigious Vendôme family. The negotiations, which continued through the summer, went well. Mazarin agreed to make the bridegroom Viceroy of Catalonia, which France had conquered from Spain, and granted equally valuable state offices to other members of the Vendôme family. But just as the contract was finally about to be signed, he discovered that this marriage involving such an important family required the approval of the First Prince of the Blood. Condé refused to give it. Instead, hurling more insults, he browbeat the Cardinal into signing a humiliating document in which he undertook to consult Condé on not only his nieces' marriages but also all important decisions of state.

A lesser man might have despaired of ever loosening Condé's grip, but Mazarin simply began to look for another way round. He feigned complete submission to Condé's wishes, but undertook a series of top-secret meetings in which – smuggling some of France's most influential figures, including several former rebels, into the Palais-Royal at the dead of night – he built a powerful alliance against Condé, bartering every privilege he had at his disposal. He promised to give the duc de Vendôme the post that Condé had so prized of commander-in-chief of the Navy; he promised Vendôme's son, the duc de Beaufort, that he would be the successor to this office; he promised the marquis de Châteauneuf that he would be made Keeper of the Seals . . . Through into the winter, as the nightly negotiations continued, a long line of cloaked figures passed each other awkwardly in the dark cloisters of the Palais-Royal, on their way to add their names to the Cardinal's ever-growing catalogue of promises.

Early in the new year of 1650 Paul de Gondi, the Co-adjutator – or assistant – to the Archbishop of Paris, who had been a leading rebel during the siege, joined the queue of petitioners hoping to trade their loyalty. Turning up at midnight in the cloisters, he recalled in his memoirs being escorted up a hidden staircase by the Queen's train-bearer to a private chapel, where he found Anne waiting for him. 'She pledged to me all the goodwill that her hatred of Condé and her devotion for the Cardinal could inspire, the last seeming much greater than the first. She must have repeated at least twenty times, "Oh, the poor, poor Cardinal!"'[3]

About half an hour later, the 'poor Cardinal' himself entered, full of greetings and compliments and, not least, promises for a man who had not long ago been one of his most implacable enemies. Knowing that de Gondi wanted to be nominated in Rome as a candidate to be made a cardinal, he expressed himself heartbroken that he could not give him his own cardinal's hat then and there, but no doubt in due course something could be arranged . . .

With his elaborate network of alliances in place, the Cardinal saved one last promise for Condé himself. On 16 January 1650 he wrote to him, 'I promise Monsieur le Prince, according to the good pleasure of the King and the Queen-Regent, his mother, that I shall never swerve from his interests and that I shall always be devoted to him come what may, and beg His Highness to think of me as his very humble servant and to favour me with his protection, which I shall earn with all the obedience he can desire of me.'[4] But days later he had Condé, as well as his brother the Prince de Conti and brother-in-law the duc de Longueville, arrested and locked up in the Château de Vincennes. All those who might once have come to their defence had systematically been bought off.

If Nicolas had ever wavered in his support of Mazarin, then Condé's sudden downfall confirmed the wisdom of standing firm. The Cardinal had once again demonstrated his extraordinary ability to slip free of the most formidable fetters and to out-manoeuvre his opponents to deadly effect. In the years to come he would test Nicolas's patience many times, but Nicolas continued to back him through all the twists and turns of fortune, no doubt partly from that powerful sense of loyalty that emerges as a persistent feature of his character, but perhaps also remembering Condé's fate, which, in other circumstances – he had no doubt from his knowledge of the Cardinal – could so easily have been his own.

In the days that followed Condé's arrest, Nicolas joined the government's efforts to neutralise the resistance of the remains of Condé's allies and sympathisers, travelling with the Court around the country to tackle the hot points of sedition. When Condé's sister, the duchesse de Longueville, arrived in Dieppe, seeking to encourage an uprising in Normandy, Nicolas slipped into the town and persuaded the governor to open up its walls to the royal army. During March and April 1650, he was with the Court in Burgundy, where armed forces loyal to Condé had occupied the town of Bellegarde (today known as Seurre). No sooner had this rebellion been put down than he was on the move again, travelling down to Libourne, which became the Court's base while the royal government struggled to counter the factions that supported Condé in Bordeaux.

During this lengthy odyssey through France, Mazarin was able to observe Nicolas closely. He appreciated his commitment, determination and intelligence, but what impressed him most of all was the combination of charm and authority with which he seemed able to win over even the most inveterate opponents. The

Cardinal's own knack for pleasing had long since evaporated. With the arrest of Condé, Mazarin had shown his mastery over the sort of influence that bribery or blackmail could achieve; but, always suspected as an outsider, he struggled to win people's simple goodwill. It was here perhaps that Nicolas could contribute his most precious asset: people liked him.

4

Fighting for the Cardinal

Perhaps nowhere were friends more badly needed than in the Parlement of Paris. It had been forced by Condé's blockade into reaching a settlement, but as the chief forum of debate it still played a critical role in marshalling opinion for or against the government.

A key means of influence was the office of attorney-general. The most important law officer after the chancellor, the attorney-general was supposed to communicate to the Parlement the decisions of the royal government, but also to let the government know of the mood and concerns of the Parlement. He was in practice a mediator who needed to enjoy the confidence of both parties to be effective.

But the trouble with the present attorney-general was that he enjoyed the confidence of neither. A docile functionary who had been appointed years ago by Richelieu to manage a then equally docile assembly, Blaise Méliand had been left floundering by the Parlement's new militancy. He was booed virtually every time he entered the chamber, as were those members of the Parlement who were foolish enough to come to his defence.

When Méliand at last bowed to the inevitable and put the office up for sale, Cardinal Mazarin was only too happy to encourage Nicolas to bid for it. Here was an opportunity at last to exert some effective influence over this deeply troublesome body. In an elaborate deal, Nicolas agreed to give 300,000 livres to Méliand, but also his office of Master of Requests. The only obstacle that remained was to win the approval of the King's uncle, Gaston d'Orléans, the Lieutenant-General of the Kingdom, who – jealous of his own importance and authority – had to be made to feel that he was granting a serious favour.

Mazarin already had an idea of who could undertake the necessary lobbying. Since Condé's arrest at the beginning of the year, his principal activity had been racing around France with the Court to put down this or that uprising. The near daily meetings with the Minister for War, Michel Le Tellier, which were one of Mazarin's more tiresome duties in 1650, became only more tedious with the arrival of the Court in Libourne at the beginning of the summer. The strategy for confronting the rebel factions within Bordeaux and the province of Guyenne was unusually tortuous, requiring a grasp of local affiliations that eluded a prime minister who had lived most of his life in Italy. The endless briefings on the shifting state of the alliances taxed even the Cardinal's formidable intellect, but he found a godsend in the form of Le Tellier's secretary, Jean-Baptiste Colbert.

A rather dour young man, Colbert came from a prosperous merchant family in Rheims. Before entering Le Tellier's service, he had worked for a bank and in a notary's office. He possessed the soul of an accountant, but also complete discretion, which made him ideal to be the Cardinal's agent. Usually dressed in a black doublet and a plain jabot of starched white cotton, he reminded one of those Roundheads who had recently gained the ascendancy on the other side of the Channel, but he was able to explain the situation on the ground with analytical precision and a total command of detail. His extreme reserve and unflappable calm were a reassurance to a man of the Mazarin's contrasting excitability. Eventually, the Cardinal had decided, he would like to add this talented young man to his own staff. But meanwhile, here was the perfect person to lobby on Nicolas's behalf. For Colbert had the ear of Le Tellier, who in turn had the ear of Gaston d'Orléans. He had also got to know Nicolas a little in the course of the year as they had both travelled with the Court from one trouble spot to another. He had come to admire Nicolas's intelligence and his application, which so mirrored his own. To put it in modern terms, they were the sort of people who now might well find each other working late at the office long after everyone else has gone home. Nicolas was someone the conscientious Colbert knew he could safely recommend.

In a note to Le Tellier, Colbert wrote:

Monsieur Foucquet, whom His Eminence sent here, has already told me on three separate occasions that he is very keen to be counted among your servants and friends, both because of the great esteem in which he holds you, and because he has no particular attachment to any other person that might prevent him from receiving this honour . . . Since he is a man of good birth and rare merit who is in a position to enter high office some day, I felt that it was appropriate to tell him that you have the same regard for him. If you agree, I beg you to let me know as soon as you can. I assure you that I don't think it would be possible to repay some part of all I owe to you in a better way than by winning for you a hundred friends of this kind . . .[1]

The note suggests the delicate network of reciprocal patronage that governed a political career in the seventeenth century. Implicit was the assumption that Le Tellier would profit as much from the contact as Nicolas. After receiving the due recommendation from Le Tellier, Nicolas was in October 1650 granted an audience with the Lieutenant-General. Gaston demurred at first, but finally, with some pleading from the Queen, gave his blessing to the appointment.

The inauguration took place in the Palais de Justice on 28 November 1650. By tradition, the attorney-general and the two advocates-general, with whom he worked in the Parlement closely, were known as the *gens du roi* – the King's Men. The members of the Parlement knew that Nicolas's first loyalty would be to the royal government, but even the more radical among them welcomed his appointment. They remembered the independence of spirit he had shown in the Dauphiné, but also valued the deep understanding he had gained of their work in nearly ten years' service as a Master of Requests. As one of Nicolas's contemporaries wrote, 'So many important and delicate subjects were debated every day in the Parlement that it was badly in need of minds as discerning and subtle as his.'[2]

For the first time in his life, Nicolas had a sense of having become an important personage. He commissioned a portrait of himself wearing the black satin robes of the attorney-general. In the background, an angel high in the sky bore a banner with the squirrel and the familiar motto: '*Quo non ascendet?*' There was something almost brazen about the way he flaunted his ambition, as if the chief satisfaction of any single accomplishment lay in the promise it offered of an even greater one to come. He had managed to secure one of the great offices of state, but already he was looking forward. It was time to marry again. Death had toppled his first attempt to build a dynasty, but now, with his important new office, he suddenly found himself one of France's most eligible suitors.

On 29 January 1651, at the church of Saint-Germain l'Auxerrois, next to the Louvre, the banns were published for Nicolas's forthcoming marriage to Marie-Madeleine de Castille. Fifteen years old, Marie-Madeleine belonged to a rich merchant family that had many important connections in government and finance. Although her dowry of 100,000 livres was less than that of Nicolas's first wife, Louise Fourché (160,000), she was an only daughter who would in due course inherit a fortune of 1,500,000 livres.

But the turn of events did not bode well for future domestic happiness. Early on the day that the marriage contract was due to be signed, Saturday, 4 February 1651, Nicolas was summoned to an emergency all-day session of the Parlement in the Palais de Justice. Gaston d'Orléans had demanded the release of the Princes and was refusing to take part in meetings of the Royal Council so long as the Queen continued to support her Prime Minister, Cardinal Mazarin. The Parlement, who had taken Gaston's side, were meeting to discuss a resolution to expel the Cardinal from France. Nicolas not only had to be present during the all-day debate, but also in the evening, as Attorney-General, had to head the deputation that would present the decision of the Parlement to the Queen.

He fared little better the next day. The wedding took place in the church of Saint-Nicolas-des-Champs, but Nicolas had to leave the festivities early to discuss the latest dire turn of events with the Queen-Regent and Mazarin at the Palais-Royal: Gaston had ordered the country's two most senior generals, the duc d'Epernon and Marshal Schomberg, to refuse to obey the Prime Minister. Nicolas found himself spending most of his wedding night with the Cardinal as he sought to calm the growing panic.

The next day he had to attend the Palais de Justice at dawn. In a speech that set the tone for the occasion, the Co-adjutator to the Archbishop of Paris, Paul de Gondi – who had swapped sides again – made the most of the opportunity to crow over the Cardinal's reverses. 'At last the day has come where God has distinguished between the good and the evil!'[3] The Parlement went on to confirm Gaston's order of the previous day.

Across the city, effigies of Mazarin were being strung up to cries of 'Kill the Cardinal!' Fearful of what might happen if he continued to remain in Paris, Mazarin slipped out of the Palais-

Royal that Monday evening. Burying his face in a red cloak and pulling a large felt hat with feathers over his head, he made his way through the streets on foot, exiting the city by the Porte de Richelieu, where an escort of 200 mounted guards were waiting to take him to the royal palace at Saint-Germain.[4] He hoped to be able to sit out the storm at this discreet distance from the capital, but the angry speeches of the counsellors in the Parlement the next day made it clear that even the most remote spot in the country would not be far enough.

On the evening of Wednesday, 8 February, Nicolas returned with the advocates-general to the Palais-Royal to explain the Parlement's mood. There was every danger of a violent uprising, he warned the Queen. She had no choice but to order the release of the Princes and the Cardinal's exile from the kingdom, 'without hope of return'.[5]

The next day, Thursday, the rumour went round that the Queen intended to leave the city with the young King as she had done two years previously. Fearing another siege, angry crowds gathered in the rue Saint-Honoré and outside the palace itself. By midnight they had become so loud and unruly there were fears that their protests would turn to violence.

An envoy arrived from the Luxembourg Palace, where Gaston had been following events closely. Warning the Queen not to think of escape, if that had been on her mind, the envoy told her that, instead, she should make it absolutely clear to the crowds that she intended to stay with the King in Paris. Inviting him to see the King fast asleep in his bedchamber, the Queen suggested that the envoy tell the crowds himself.[6] But when they refused to believe him, the Queen agreed to allow them into the palace so that they might see their sovereign with their own eyes.

'For a long time they just watched him sleeping,' recalled the Queen's lady-in-waiting Madame de Motteville. 'The sight of their King filled them with respect. They wanted all the more that he should remain among them, but now they felt this desire through a sense of devotion. They no longer felt impatient. The mob that had entered the chamber full of anger left it as subjects full of goodwill, with all their heart praying to God to protect their young King, whose presence had so charmed them.'[7]

With the Queen-Regent and the King effectively hostages in Paris, Mazarin realised that he had no choice but to make the best of a totally new situation, which he did with alacrity. Aware that an official deputation was about to set off for Le Havre castle, to where the Princes had been moved, he travelled to Le Havre himself.

Arriving there on the morning of 13 February 1651, well ahead of the deputation, he released the Princes without condition, entertained them to lunch and, making endless professions of friendship, even kissed Condé's boot, as if all that had happened before had just been a terrible misunderstanding. After a long interview with Condé, in which he begged him to be faithful to the Queen-Regent and the King, he escorted him and the other two Princes to a carriage waiting at the entrance. As the vehicle set off, the Cardinal could hear guffaws of laughter from the occupants inside.[8]

It was an obsequious but oddly impressive performance, Mazarin's self-willed humiliation revealing the same flair for the dramatic imaginative gesture that had once sent him galloping between the opposing armies at Casale – even if this latest peace overture was far less likely to have a successful outcome.

Three days later, on Thursday, 16 February, virtually the entire Court set off to welcome the arrival of the Princes' carriage. In the streets, fireworks were let off and barrels of wine opened to celebrate their liberation. The Queen-Regent chose to stay with the King at the Palais-Royal, but Gaston, who brought the Princes into Paris in his own coach, thoughtfully dropped them by in the evening. Glumly, the Queen got up from her daybed to welcome them back and the King reluctantly greeted them too. They then went off to Gaston's palace, where they had dinner and danced until two in the morning.

Meanwhile, Mazarin was wandering aimlessly through Flanders, not sure whether he would ever see Paris again. Eventually he settled in Brühl, where the Elector of Cologne had offered him sanctuary. The King of Spain, who had allowed him safe passage through Spanish-held territory, sent an emissary inviting him to serve Spain as he had once served France. But he turned down the invitation. 'I shall end my days serving France in my thoughts and in my wishes if I cannot do it otherwise.'[9]

Mazarin spent the first days of his exile in a state of profound melancholy, self-pity and paranoia. It was only natural for him to suspect that some of his ministers had turned against him when the rest of the country had done so long ago. What sustained him was the belief that he had the support of the two people who most counted in France – the Queen-Regent and his godson the King – and that they would be working for his return. For he had been much more than just a royal servant. A genuine regard and love underpinned the relationship. Unlikely as it might have seemed, they were in some sense a family. But it was still difficult to accept that it was the Queen herself who had signed the order for his expulsion. His reason might tell him that this public act was contrary to her private will, but always preying on his mind was the fear that sooner or later she would conclude that protecting him was more trouble than he was worth. 'Whether or not I have her good opinion means everything to me,' he wrote soon after his departure. 'When it is put in doubt, I lose myself to despair.'[10]

Because the principal ministers in the royal government – Michel Le Tellier, Abel Servien, Servien's nephew Hugues de Lionne – were compromised by their long association with him, Mazarin began to place increased reliance in Nicolas as a faithful ally who could nonetheless put on a credible act of neutrality. As the Attorney-General of the Parlement, he had a pivotal position in what was effectively the chief crucible of political opinion and influence. As long as he maintained the appropriate attitude of official disapproval that the present mood dictated, he was perfectly placed to limit the damage to the Cardinal's interests and to prepare the way for an eventual return.

Since the traditional loyalty to the Crown of the Foucquet family was a chief motivating factor in Nicolas's conduct, it was perhaps only natural for him to turn to his family for help. Unable to maintain open contact with the Cardinal, he enlisted the support of his brother, Basile, to keep open the secret lines of communication.

Seven years younger than Nicolas, Basile was the latest of the Foucquets to enjoy the ecclesiastical sinecure of treasurer to the Abbey of Saint-Martin de Tours. Although he styled himself the Abbé Foucquet, he possessed no more of a religious vocation than Nicolas. The two brothers were close, but starkly different in their characters. Physically frail, erudite and charming, Nicolas had won a reputation for his ability to placate and conciliate, but Basile was notorious for a quick, often violent temper, more likely to pick a fight than stop one. Recklessly brave, always wearing a sword at his side, he was a born adventurer. Over the next few months Basile Foucquet went back and forth between Paris and Brühl, often risking capture or worse as he passed through the many miles of enemy territory that lay between the two towns. 'I know the danger you're running,' Mazarin wrote to him on one occasion. 'I'm always delighted to see you, but in the name of God don't put yourself in any further jeopardy.'[11] Basile became the crucial link that sustained the Cardinal's morale, making it possible for him to continue to work his web of influence.

With Nicolas and Basile maintaining an underground network

of political contacts, the Cardinal was able to exert a huge hidden influence, but he also needed someone who could take charge of his personal affairs. His exile had forced him to abandon control of a byzantine jumble of properties, works of art and other investments that he had been quietly amassing ever since he had first come to France over a decade earlier.

The most suitable candidate to manage this fortune was obvious. Even while he was still on the road not even sure of his place of exile, the Cardinal wrote to Michel Le Tellier to request the services of his grimly efficient secretary. 'As I need someone to look after my financial affairs in Paris and I have complete faith in Monsieur Colbert, I'd be very pleased if he would like to undertake such a job, for which I would pay him handsomely.'[12]

In agreeing the terms and conditions of his employment, Colbert did everything he could to build the post into one of real consequence. 'A single person,' he wrote to Mazarin,

> must have the management of all your affairs and, besides possessing integrity, experience and devotion to the service of Your Eminence, that person must not be one of those base-hearted men who would run and hide in a well rather than even be suspected of a connection with yourself. This person must go about with his head high, making no secret of his mission. Further, Your Eminence must honour him with his utmost confidence and must not hold him to blame for any vexing contingencies that may delay or ruin, wholly or partially, any of the affairs entrusted to his discretion. The man must speak out and must have judgement enough only to involve the Queen in important matters and only to make her intervene when those matters shall be of grave consequence.[13]

In theory Colbert was just a private servant, but as servant to the Queen's most trusted adviser – albeit an exiled adviser – he had in one leap assumed influence at the very highest level of the state, although he was careful not to take this for granted. Realising the precarious nature of his new master's position, he insisted that he should be accredited to the Queen. That way, if Mazarin failed to be restored to public favour, there would be no risk of accusations of treachery.

In these early days it is likely that Nicolas – who, after all, owed his own high office partly to Colbert's efforts – regarded the Cardinal's capable new secretary as less the dangerous rival he would later become than a welcome addition to the team, whose help would alleviate the considerable pressure on him.

The Cardinal was often begging Nicolas to use his influence over the most trifling matters in a way that made it extremely difficult to maintain a semblance of impartiality. When, for example, the Parlement passed a motion confiscating several of his possessions, the Cardinal asked Nicolas to do what he could to retrieve them. 'I thank the Attorney-General with all my heart for the kindness he has shown me,' wrote Mazarin after Nicolas agreed to do what he could. The trouble was, however, that such kindness only encouraged the Cardinal to expect even more help no matter how compromising it might be. 'I shall never forget my gratitude, and I beg him to continue with his efforts, for there is no one else in the Parlement prepared to defend my innocence.'[14]

The Cardinal waited impatiently in Germany for news, but was soon writing again to single out a few items that might deserve special attention. 'I'm furious about the sale of my beautiful tapestries . . . I have slaved for twenty years to put together such a collection and now I lose them in an instant. I beg you . . . to see if I might at least be able to keep the *Scipio* and the *Paris*.'[15]

Since it was still impossible to speak openly in his favour, every intervention Nicolas made on Mazarin's behalf had to be routinely cloaked in an appeal to some other consideration.

When he intervened to prevent the Parlement from auctioning off the Cardinal's book collection, for example, he secured a royal order in the name of the public interest to forbid the sale. The injunction noted, 'It would be impossible even in the course of an entire century to put together such a library.'[16] But no amount of dissimulation could counter the suspicions that Mazarin was still pulling the strings. So, at the beginning of July 1651, the Parlement passed a measure, by 117 votes to fifty, forbidding anyone to have 'commerce with the Cardinal'.[17]

The Great Condé wanted to go much further. Reclaiming his position at the heart of political life in Paris, he was now pressing the Queen to declare the Cardinal's exile to be 'in perpetuity'. He also demanded that Mazarin's former ministers, Le Tellier, Servien and de Lionne, should not only give up their positions in the government but also leave the capital. Le Tellier and Servien were able to retreat to their spacious country houses in the Île-de-France, but de Lionne had nowhere to go. Once again it was Nicolas who came to the rescue with another act of kindness, inviting de Lionne to stay at the Château de Belle-Assise on the Marne, a house that belonged to Nicolas's young wife Marie-Madeleine.

Displaying all his old arrogance, Condé had wasted no time since his return in making a series of demands that once again made a mockery of responsible government. He wanted the post of commander-in-chief of the navy to be peremptorily removed from the duc de Vendôme and given to him; he wanted the control of Provence to be assigned to his brother the Prince de Conti; he wanted the fortress of Blaye – which, with its strategic position on the Gironde, commanded access to Bordeaux from the sea – to be given to his friend the duc de la Rochefoucauld.

His behaviour was so impossible that the Queen was soon making secret overtures once again to the Co-adjutator of Paris, Paul de Gondi. Still waiting in vain for the cardinal's hat that had been promised to him over a year before, de Gondi had used his influence in the Parlement to undermine royal authority at every turn. But although he was a chief instigator of the Parlement's virulent anti-Mazarin stance, he feared Condé even more and hoped that the Queen might at last help him to win the longed-for hat.

The Cardinal was quick to take advantage of the discord. 'Your Majesty should have no scruple about reaching an accommodation with people who previously harmed you,' he wrote to the Queen. 'Your conduct should not be governed by such sentiments as love or hate but what is best for the country.'[18] Soon afterwards a heavily cloaked de Gondi was attending a second night-time tryst in the Queen's private chapel. Meanwhile Condé, who had no intention of being trapped in the way he had been before, went about Paris with a formidable escort of armed men that made the King's Guard seem small by comparison.

Reflecting on these dangerous, confusing times, the Cardinal commented in one of his letters from exile, 'We live in an age when we must pretend with everyone!'[19] In the summer of 1651 the double game had reached its height. The Queen passed ever more hostile measures against Mazarin in public, but depended on Nicolas and Basile to provide him with the maximum support in private. 'It bothers me how each day I become more and more obliged to you without being able to do anything in return,' the Cardinal wrote to Basile towards the end of August.[20]

But all the members of his clandestine camp expected this situation to change very soon. On 5 September 1651 the King was to celebrate his thirteenth birthday, which would mark the official end of his minority. After that date it would become increasingly difficult for the opponents of Mazarin – all of whom claimed nominal loyalty to their sovereign – to argue that the King was somehow still under his undue influence.

On 7 September the King held a *lit de justice* before the

Parlement to mark the occasion.²¹ Every effort was made to hail the event as the dawning of a new era. The royal procession, which marched slowly from the Palais-Royal to the Palais de Justice, was one of the most superb in living memory. As the royal cavalcade set off at nine in the morning along the rue Saint-Honoré at slower than a walking pace, the city's church bells tolled and the guns of the Bastille thundered a salute. Soldiers of the French and Swiss Guards lined the route to keep back the vast crowds. Yet more people were packed into tall stands that reached almost to the rooftops. All were crying over and over again, 'Long live the King! Long live the King!' Whatever people may have thought of Queen Anne or the Cardinal or the Great Condé or the Co-adjutator of Paris, or any of the other aspiring leaders of the time, this faith in the young King himself seemed universal – a longed-for cure for all the ills of the time.

Sitting astride a magnificent horse caparisoned in gold, Louis, who held a wooden baton in his right hand, acknowledged the greetings with a calm and self-assurance far beyond his years, as though it were a relief at last to assume the role to which he had been born. It was the first time that he had commanded such public attention separate from his mother. Queen Anne followed at a distance that had symbolic force, her carriage, with its substantial escort of royal bodyguards, forming a splendid but clearly lesser jewel in this display of regal munificence. With her sat Gaston d'Orléans and the King's younger brother, Philippe, the duc d'Anjou.

Reaching the Palais de Justice at about eleven, the royal party entered the Sainte-Chapelle, where a celebratory Mass was held. After a greeting from the presidents of the five chambers that made up the Parlement, the King was then escorted through the gallery that connected the chapel to the Great Chamber, the drums, fifes and trumpets of the Swiss Guard providing a fanfare.

During this short passage there occurred an incident not in the protocol. The Prince de Conti stepped forward to hand Louis a letter from his older brother, the Great Condé. Unruffled, the King handed the unopened envelope to an attendant and continued on into the Great Chamber.

The King climbed a dais in the far corner, the 'lit de justice', and settled himself down on a pile of blue velvet cushions embroidered with the fleur-de-lys. As he looked to his right, where the royal family were supposed to stand, he would have noticed for the first time the gaping absence of the First Prince of the Blood.

It was an act of disrespect that must have been on the minds of everyone in the chamber, but Louis, who did not appear at all disconcerted, began his address in a firm, steady tone. 'Gentlemen, I have come before my Parlement to tell you that in accordance with the laws of my realm, I wish to take up the reins of government myself, and I hope, through the goodness of God, to rule with justice and piety.'[22] A little later, he formally thanked the Queen for the care she had taken over the governance of his kingdom and asked her to continue – no longer as Regent, but as the head of his Council – to give him good advice. In practical terms nothing had changed, but the King's expression of his will gave the Queen's rule a renewed legitimacy.

As Attorney-General, Nicolas sat at the very front of the chamber within feet of the King. From here, he would have been able to notice for himself the boy's composure as he went on to ask the Chancellor of France, Pierre Séguier, to speak on his behalf to the Parlement. In a clear, distinct voice the Chancellor summarised the state of France under Louis's nine-year reign. God had blessed the country with a string of great victories from Rocroi to Lens, but internal divisions had prevented these victories from leading to a final peace.

A rigid, inflexible man, Séguier usually observed the dictates of ceremony to the letter, but Condé's extraordinary snub made it impossible to disregard reality entirely. Departing from his carefully rehearsed words, he confided to the gathering that Condé's absence left him speechless, but he was sure that the King would be forgiving, since he knew all that the First Prince of the Blood had done for France.

The snub was even more shocking because an important purpose of the ceremony had been to offer Condé an olive branch. When the court clerk read out the first decrees to be signed by the King in his majority, they included a declaration of Condé's innocence. But his absence made a mockery of the gesture. This day, which had been intended to demonstrate royal authority and unity, instead exposed the continuing division.

After the ceremony was over, the King did not remount his horse, but instead climbed into the Queen's carriage for the return journey to the Palais-Royal. In this comparative privacy, perhaps he would have had a chance at last to read Condé's letter, printed copies of which had already been circulated around Paris by Condé's supporters. Citing the many grievances against the King's government that had caused the Prince not to attend the ceremony, the letter amounted to a quiet laying down of the gauntlet.

The King waved to his cheering subjects, the fountains flowed with wine and from dusk celebratory candles lit up windows throughout the city. The thirteen-year-old boy played his part in this fairy tale to perfection, but he also knew how to give the necessary assurances behind the scenes. Two days later he despatched to Brühl a secret note that was a much needed morale booster for the Cardinal, who had lost count of the number of orders the Queen had under the duress of political circumstances publicly signed against him:

Having given you my word when you left Paris that I would summon you back as soon as I had the power, I do not think I can better start my majority than by letting you know of the intense displeasure I feel at all the sufferings seditious groups in my realm have caused you in respect of your person, your honour and your property. I assure you that I will ask you back as soon as I can safely do so. I long for this moment more than I can possibly convey, being impatient to abolish as completely as possible all the measures that have been so unjustly taken against you during my minority.[23]

The Great Condé had sensed that the net was closing. The fact that his ally Gaston d'Orléans had given up his office of Lieutenant-General upon the King's majority only added to his foreboding. Feeling cornered and suspicious, he finally chose to commit himself to open revolt rather than surrender his demands. Leaving the capital on 6 September, the day before the King's appearance before the Parlement, he set off for Bordeaux, where he began to raise an army.

The government was left with no choice. A month later the Queen issued an edict declaring Condé to be guilty of treason and sent a force to besiege his stronghold of Montrond in Burgundy. A new civil war had begun.

Although France's greatest general had taken up arms against his own nation, Cardinal Mazarin thought that at least there was the recompense that he would be able to return from exile. But as soon as he declared his intention to do so, Nicolas warned him that he would be making a serious mistake. Condé's fall from grace did not mean that the Cardinal was any less hated. His return would only undermine the Parlement's support for the war against Condé. On the contrary, now was just the time to allay their fears of such a return. With that sometimes wayward independence of his, Nicolas even went right on, as Attorney-General of the Parlement, to request the King to issue a decree confirming Mazarin's exile. He argued that it was a necessary deception, the only way he could maintain his influence over an assembly that was so hostile to the Cardinal, but Mazarin was far too fed up with Brühl to listen. On 12 December 1651, he had the King order his return at last. Crossing into France on 24 December with a Christmas present for the King of 7,000 German soldiers, he arrived early in the new year at Poitiers, where the Court had moved to follow the campaign against Condé's forces in Guyenne. Some days later, he wrote to Basile, scarcely troubling to veil his criticism of Nicolas, 'I really don't understand how anyone could have suggested that my return to France would cause rebellion and bring down the state. Without my having made any effort to win support or anyone even being aware of the King's order, I have been applauded everywhere I've been and encountered only delight at my appearance'![24]

But Nicolas still insisted that the return had been too early. When the Royal Council proposed an order to annul the measures against the Cardinal, he wrote to the Queen warning her that the Parlement would not accept it.

A messenger arrived from Poitiers with the answer that the decision was final, but just hours later a second messenger arrived to countermand the first: Nicolas was authorised to act as he thought best. A third messenger arrived some days later with a note from the King to commend Nicolas for his frankness. No doubt it was the Cardinal who had prompted it. He realised that Nicolas's readiness, when necessary, to tell his superiors what they did not want to hear was a valuable quality that deserved to be encouraged.

Yet nonetheless the situation led to inevitable strains between the two men. Practically every day in the Parlement Nicolas was presiding over debates that vilified the Cardinal. Mazarin's reason may have told him that it was a necessary sham, but he must have wondered whether to some extent Nicolas shared the hostile sentiment. It was galling to have to express his gratitude to him when a much stronger feeling was resentment. Nicolas's secret support may have been vital to his political survival, but it was also an unpleasant reminder of his weakness.

Nicolas would have been wise to make more effort than he did to play down the sense of a debt. But behind all the skilled dissimulation he had practised on the Cardinal's behalf lay a basic integrity that made him only too aware of what he was owed. The Cardinal's wordy assurances of rich rewards fired his indignation. Sick of all the promises that never seemed to be kept, he was too proud not eventually to hold the Cardinal to account.

Indeed, his patience snapped just weeks before the Cardinal's return from exile at the end of 1651. Complaining to Colbert that Mazarin had still to honour an undertaking to provide a church benefice to his brother Basile, Nicolas wrote, 'After having his hopes encouraged, my brother put himself up for the Abbey of Noailles. But since then he has been kept dangling with the usual fine words . . . I am astonished that His Eminence has made no effort to change his attitude after having got so little out of his customary dictums: the one about doing nothing for those he considers to be attached to him by honour and loyalty; and the other of thinking that if he keeps people waiting, they will always be prepared to perform yet some new service the better to merit their reward. It seems to me that if he fails to appreciate what has been done for him up until now, then he should consider what I still can do – both for and against his interest here.'[25]

It was an extraordinarily dangerous threat that betrayed arrogance and a reckless disrespect in a society that depended so heavily on hierarchy and patronage. Behind all Nicolas's cleverness and sophistication lay a strange, potentially fatal naïveté – a touching faith in some irreducible principle of loyalty that made him extremely vulnerable to those who had long ago sacrificed such a notion to expedience. A more sensible man would have worried about the effect that such a letter would have on not only the Cardinal but also his quietly ambitious secretary.

Going on to express further anger on his brother's behalf, Nicolas concluded, 'I hope you will be so gracious as to let [the Cardinal] know that I am shocked by such behaviour and that nothing can offend me so much as to treat my brother like someone ordinary, when his service has been far from ordinary.'

Colbert, who kept the exiled Cardinal updated with regular bulletins, not only reported Nicolas's anger but even included a copy of the original letter. Wishing to bolster his own standing as the most loyal of all the Cardinal's loyal servants, Colbert – who never allowed his mask to slip – took advantage of an extraordinary gift, worth any number of abbeys. Commenting on Nicolas's outburst, he wrote to the Cardinal, 'The sad state of your affairs has reduced you to the point where you need such people, and the more you need them, the more they seek to demand of you things you are not in a proper position to give to them. [Foucquet] is one of my friends, and I am obliged to tell you that he has served you well since I became responsible for your affairs. However, I cannot prevent myself from finding fault with the way he has behaved here.'[26]

5

The Scoundrel's Return

Whatever fears Nicolas's angry letter may have raised, he and Basile gave the Cardinal, in the months that followed his return to France, more cause than ever to be grateful to them.

Condé's plan of turning Guyenne into an impregnable fortress, from which he would be able to force the Court into submission, soon crumbled into a series of defeats across the giant province that must have made the great general wonder whether he had lost his touch. But then, at the point when his situation seemed most hopeless, with his army cornered in the hostile town of Agen, he engineered one of those unexpected lightning moves – probably a surprise even to himself – that made him such a brilliant soldier but poor statesman. Slipping out of Agen on 24 March 1652 with a handful of his closest companions, he journeyed northwards, in a series of rapid marches, to take command of an army that his ally the duc de Nemours had raised in the Low Countries. The royal army, hurrying back northwards in pursuit, tried but failed to stop him on 7 April at Bléneau, about sixty miles to the south of Paris.

Only the timely arrival of General Turenne with fresh forces prevented Condé from taking the royal family and Cardinal Mazarin prisoner. For once considering discretion to be the better part of valour, he broke off the action, deciding to make for Paris instead. On the eve of his departure he invited the commander of

Turenne's rearguard to supper. As they said goodbye afterwards, Condé observed, 'What a pity brave people like us should cut each other's throats for the sake of such a scoundrel!'[1] The remark captured the personal nature of a conflict that always seemed to return to one name. Thousands of men had committed their lives to a struggle that Condé would have been happy to settle with a duel at dawn – if only Mazarin were likewise ready to choose his weapon.

Instead, the destiny of France depended upon that familiar scenario in its history, where the final triumph belonged to whichever side could win over the capital. Here, increasingly adrift, seemingly unaware of the two hostile armies approaching ever closer, the Parlement continued in its favourite activity of issuing decrees against the Cardinal even though he was now openly serving as the King's Prime Minister. Protesting itself as loyal as ever to the King, it justified such measures on the grounds that the King had become Mazarin's prisoner. Given the over-whelming hatred that the counsellors continued to feel towards the Cardinal, Nicolas's delicate task remained to manage the mood, to steer sentiment gradually in Mazarin's favour, without voicing any overt support that would undermine his influence.

But from the outside, Parlement appeared to share a unanimous loathing of the Cardinal. Hoping that it would be possible to make common cause against 'the scoundrel' after all, Condé rushed to put his case, appearing before the Parlement on 11 April. But the speed that had worked so well on the battlefield seemed like indecent haste in the Palais de Justice. Only five days previously he had been spilling the blood of the King's loyal subjects at Bléneau. It was too soon to expect anything other than a frosty reception.

The angry rebukes he received made him appreciate the importance of engineering some political support, but the methods he chose were typically violent. He took his campaign of persuasion on to the streets. Thugs were hired to stop carriages crossing the Pont-Neuf. Forcing the occupants to get down, they would then order them to shout 'Long live the King! Down with Mazarin!', threatening to throw anyone who refused into the Seine.

The great scoundrel himself followed events from the safe distance of Saint-Germain, where he had taken up residence with the royal Court, but he was able to rely on the two Foucquet brothers to execute his business in the city for him. An obvious priority was to organise some effective counter-propaganda. 'It would be an excellent idea', he suggested in a note to Basile, 'to make some banners attacking Monsieur le Prince, which show him preventing the King's return to Paris and bringing disaster on the people. If you need to hand out any money, I beg you to do it, and the resources will be quickly provided.'[2]

The thought was as good as the deed. At once Basile recruited an atelier of designers to churn out lurid posters of an ogrish Condé attempting to devour a blameless France, paying his own gang of men to display them around Paris. One of these banners depicted the Prince pitching Guyenne into war and then abandoning the province after the people of Agen turned against him. The caption read: 'So now in his desperation he has come to Paris in an attempt to incite the same revolt, disorder and division being the sole foundation of his power.'[3] In the way of the best propaganda – as the occupants of the carriages commandeered on the Pont-Neuf could have testified – it was based on a kernel of truth.

When Basile wasn't masterminding the Cardinal's propaganda campaign, he continued his courier duties, running messages to the Court at Saint-Germain. This often involved having to elude the patrols of Condé's rebel army. But towards the end of April he was caught by Condé's soldiers at Corbeil to the south of the city, with a coded letter for the Cardinal. Brought before the

Prince at his *hôtel* in Paris, he refused to decipher the message or to give the name of the person who had sent it, although everyone suspected it was his brother Nicolas.

Condé would normally not have hesitated to use terrifying methods of persuasion to make a prisoner talk, but in this case he delivered Basile to his brother's house on the very same evening of his interrogation – he even supplied his own carriage for Basile to travel in. The gesture was a recognition of Nicolas's critical influence over the Parlement. Condé had sought to portray himself as the innocent victim of the royal government, which, under the malign influence of the Cardinal, had heaped humiliation after humiliation on the saviour of France, leaving him no choice but to take up arms to defend his legitimate claims.

Up until now it was Nicolas who had done more than anyone else to undermine his case, arguing in speech after speech that the assembly should not talk to a traitor. Yet Condé still hoped that the Attorney-General – who he was sure detested Mazarin every bit as much as he did – might change his mind. For with his support it would be easy to persuade the Parlement to sanction the union of the Princes, and then the game would be over for the Cardinal once and for all.

To Condé's frustration and anger, Nicolas remained resolutely loyal to the royal government – although that didn't mean he was any more comforting a presence for Mazarin. As the activities of the two opposing armies in the countryside of the Île-de-France made living conditions in Paris increasingly intolerable, he argued in private to the Court that the best way to end the chaos would be for the Cardinal voluntarily to go back into exile. Mazarin refused, fearing that such an exile would become permanent, although as usual he was careful to express 'every possible gratitude to the Attorney-General'.[4]

So the stand-off dragged on into the summer months, the clashes between the factions in the city becoming more and more violent. On 25 June, an enraged mob set upon members of the Parlement as they left the Palais de Justice. Several people were killed. Nicolas, who managed to reach the carriage of his brother Basile, was lucky to escape with his life as the coachman drove a pair of frightened horses on through a hail of stones and musket fire.

'The peril your brother risked in your carriage and the other dangers you've mentioned make me worry constantly about what might happen to you both next,' the Cardinal wrote to Basile the following day. 'In the present situation, your efforts are more vital than ever, but, I beg you, please try to minimise the chances you are taking. Don't place yourself in any unnecessary jeopardy.'[5]

A week later Nicolas played a decisive part in ending the murderous stalemate. Expecting an attack sooner or later from the royal army, on the night of 1 July Condé ordered his forces to leave their camp at Saint-Cloud, a little to the north-west of Paris, and to regroup to the south at Charenton, which was a more easy position to defend. He had hoped that they would be able to pass through the city, but the municipal authorities refused to open the gates. When Nicolas learned of the manoeuvre, he sent a note to the Cardinal: 'They have seven cannons and are marching in such great disorder that a force of 500 cavalry, swiftly despatched, would defeat them easily.'[6]

The information was passed on at once to the royal army's commander Turenne, who duly ordered a detachment of cavalry to mount a surprise attack on the rearguard of Condé's army. The troops fled in disarray. Reaching the Porte Saint-Martin, they tried to take refuge in the city, but once again were refused entry. Caught between the steep ramparts of the city walls and Turenne's cavalry, they were driven on to the next gate. Here they were pressed back into the vast semicircular concourse before the Porte Saint-Antoine. Defeat seemed certain with the arrival of dawn, but Condé ordered them to prepare for one last stand.

Cardinal Mazarin, who had been following the events of the night closely, hurried to the village of Charonne as soon as the sun began to rise. Built on a hill to the south-east of the city, it offered a bird's-eye view of Condé's army hastily improvising what defences it could, but hopelessly exposed, with the great fortress of the Bastille looming behind.

As the two armies engaged, fierce hand-to-hand fighting ensued. After several frustrating weeks of negotiating the endlessly shifting ground of Paris politics, Condé was happy to be back on the battlefield, where his skills unquestionably made a difference. He was everywhere, urging on his men and inspiring a confidence they had no good reason to feel, since the odds against them were overwhelming. Even from the distance of the hill, it was easy to see why he was France's greatest general. Cardinal Mazarin may have been on the point of triumph, but, for a man who was as practical as he was deeply sentimental, it must have been a cause of some regret to witness the waste of such an extraordinary asset.

Condé's cornered army continued all day to offer the fiercest possible resistance, but in the evening Turenne brought up two detachments of artillery. It seemed now just a matter of minutes before the exhausted men would be cut down by cannon fire. But as the first volleys sent them scattering, the giant doors of the Porte Saint-Antoine slowly began to open and they fell back on this unexpected refuge, hurrying to pass beneath the gate's three great arches.

At first disconcerted, Mazarin gave a shout of joy as next the guns of the Bastille opened fire, with great billows of smoke. He was convinced that Condé must have been lured into a trap. Within the walls the fortress's lethal guns, fired from such short range, would quickly pulverise the rebels. But as further blasts from the Bastille's towers followed, it became clear that the guns were trained not on Condé's army, but on the royal army that was pursuing it.

The Cardinal and the King, witnessing the scene from their hilltop vantage point, had enjoyed a kind of Olympian detachment. But now a scorching-hot cannonball, which skimmed across the hill of Charonne, sent the royal party scattering and brought home the disastrous turn of events. A merciless strafing from the Bastille was forcing Turenne's soldiers into a headlong retreat. At the end of a day when even Condé himself expected annihilation, instead he found himself in undisputed control of the city.

The cause of this reverse was just one more example of the kind of princely presumption that so needed curbing. Inside the city, Gaston d'Orléans, who was regretting his alliance with Condé, had been undecided for days. Increasingly sceptical of Condé's ability to command support, he was on the verge of seeking a reluctant rapprochement with the royal government. The latest fighting, in which Condé faced imminent defeat, only served to confirm the necessity. But then his daughter, Anne Marie Louise – who was a fierce partisan of Condé and had at one stage even entertained hopes of marrying the general – marched into his office and, demanding a letter of authority, forced him into yet another about-turn. Through her mother Marie de Bourbon, Anne was the heiress of the duc de Montpensier, which made her the richest woman in France. The effect of this independent wealth was to make the Great Mademoiselle – as she was popularly known – even more contrary and unpredictable than her father.

At once she set off for the town hall and, brandishing Gaston's letter, persuaded the city officials to give her permission to open the gates. She remained at the Porte Saint-Antoine just long enough to see Condé stagger through to safety. 'His hair was tangled and his face covered with dust,' she would later recall in her memoirs. 'Although he had not himself been wounded, his shirt and collar were covered with blood. His armour had been dented by several heavy blows, and, having lost his scabbard, he carried his sword in his hand.'[7] She then rushed off exultantly to the nearby Bastille, from where she gave the order to fire the guns.

The Great Condé proceeded to terrorise Paris into obedience. On 4 July his men set ablaze the Hôtel de Ville after a meeting of the city authorities decided to make peace overtures to the royal government. As the counsellors fled from the burning building, they were set upon by an angry crowd that Condé's men had incited into a frenzy of anti-Mazarin hatred. Many people were killed.

The day amounted to a brutal but very effective demand for support. The population in the city, afraid of more violence from Condé's soldiers, took to wearing stalks of straw in their hats, an emblem that Condé's army had adopted in battle to distinguish itself from that of the King. On 6 July the Parlement, equally cowed, passed an edict appointing Gaston d'Orléans, who had reaffirmed his alliance with Condé, to be once again the Lieutenant-General of the Kingdom. To justify the absence of a royal assent, they fell back on the familiar argument that the King was the Cardinal's prisoner, but the irony of course was that the Parlement was as much a prisoner of the Great Condé.

Many of the most influential figures in the Parlement had begun to leave the city and to take up residence with the Court at Saint-Denis. On 8 July Nicolas joined the exodus. He arrived at Saint-Denis to find the Cardinal lamenting over his mortally wounded nephew Paul Mancini, who had been shot in the thigh during the fighting at the Porte Saint-Antoine. The wound had now turned gangrenous and all that could be done was to wait for his death.

In his grief, the Cardinal seemed incapable of facing the growing chaos within the city. As uncomfortably forthright as usual, Nicolas tried to shake him out of his lethargy. 'Most people, both at the Court and in Paris,' he wrote, 'are hesitating to commit themselves to one side or the other, because matters are so uncertain and they do not know how events will turn out. This would not be the case if definite decisions were made.'[8] Once again he urged Mazarin to go into voluntary exile, since it would remove the chief pretext for the continuing rebellion. But although the Cardinal allowed the possibility to be raised in negotiations with the rebels, he could not hide his distaste for this course and stayed on at Court mulling over the possible alternatives, as exasperatingly indecisive as ever.

Nicolas had better luck with his advice that the King should order the Parlement to reconvene at Pontoise, a small town about fifteen miles to the north of Paris. Intended to separate the loyalists from the rebels and invalidate any decisions made by those who continued to remain in the Paris Parlement, the decree was duly issued on 31 July. Nicolas, in his capacity as Attorney-General, drafted a declaration to urge obedience. The King's edict, he wrote, was intended 'to rescue his Parlement from the oppression it had suffered in Paris for some time'.[9] Those deputies who continued to exercise their offices and to attend debates in the Paris Parlement 'would be declared traitors'[10] and put on trial as such.

He wrote a separate note to his own assistants: 'I hope that none of you will disobey the King or disappoint me by behaving in a manner different from my own. It's why I've considered it appropriate to tell you that I intend to remain steadfast in the loyalty that I owe the King; and to discharge my duty to the Parlement in the place where it has pleased him to re-establish it. And I invite you to come here to perform your duty with me. Those who do, will afford me great pleasure. But I'm not so unreasonable as to make this demand of those who for domestic reasons will have great trouble leaving their families so quickly. Each person must be free to decide this question for himself; although I hope at least that those who stay behind in Paris will not go to the Palais or continue to carry out their offices. Otherwise I will have cause for complaint, and they will be sorry for having given it to me.'[11]

On Wednesday, 7 August 1652, a group of about twenty-five deputies gathered in a barn to inaugurate the Pontoise Parlement. The setting may have been modest and the number of those who attended tiny, but this assembly had the huge advantage over the Paris Parlement of possessing the authority of the King. The next day, in a manoeuvre that had at last received the agreement of Mazarin himself, Nicolas persuaded the deputies to pass a decree requesting the King to exile the Cardinal. In response, the King issued a declaration that praised the qualities of his godfather, but promised to make him leave the Court for the sake of peace. With this compromise the stage was set for a quick return, which Mazarin hoped would be within weeks.

In his absence, Nicolas became the most influential figure not only in the loyalist Parlement but also at the Court. On 19 August 1652 he helped the Cardinal into his carriage at the beginning of a long journey to what Mazarin hoped would be just a temporary exile at the Château de Bouillon in the Ardennes. As Mazarin waved farewell, it would have been only natural for him to entertain some doubts about Nicolas's motives – he must have considered him as much a future rival as an aide. But in the weeks that followed Nicolas wisely went to lengths to prevent the Cardinal from feeding on such possible resentment, keeping him informed of every detail of the developing politics, consulting his opinion on every decision, making him continue to feel indispensable even in his exile.

As Nicolas had predicted, the Cardinal's departure soon had the desired effect: it undercut any support for the Princes that still remained. The bourgeoisie of Paris, who had long tired of the ill-behaved army in their midst and the taxes that the rebel authorities sought to levy, decided to make a direct address to the King, appealing to him to return to Paris.[12] At the same time more and more members of the Paris Parlement were abandoning the city for Pontoise.

Nicolas was full of yet more initiatives to hasten what now seemed like the inevitable restoration of the King's authority. He helped deputies to escape to Pontoise; he urged an amnesty for the rebels that would further weaken their determination to hold out; he recommended a distribution of money to solidify royal support among the citizens of Paris.

Within Paris itself, Basile continued to apply his more nefarious talents to the cause. On 24 September he organised a demonstration outside the Palais-Royal. The crowd replaced the stalks of straw in their hats with bits of paper and cried that soon they would bring the King back to Paris in spite of the Princes. 'The straw has broken,' they cried. 'No more Princes. Long live the King, our one and only sovereign!'[13]

From this point onwards the Princes' only hope was to salvage what honour they could. Both Basile and Nicolas took part in the negotiations designed to accommodate their retreat while the Cardinal followed events with increasing frustration from his isolated castle in the Ardennes Forest. His long letters of policy advice contained as much whingeing self-pity and petulance. 'I was supposed to have been away from the Court for just a month,' he complained to Basile in a letter dated 9 October. 'However, it's nearly two months now since I left, and thirty-six days that I've spent in a tiny room in this castle, which is no better than a hole, and where I am exposed to the vagaries of the weather. I can't even ward off the wind and rain. But as I trust your brother as much as I trust myself, I am sure that he will do everything within his power to vindicate me.'[14]

Condé finally left Paris with the remnants of his army on 13 October. Arrogant to the last, he refused any settlement with the King and joined the Spanish army in Flanders. Gaston d'Orléans, who left a week later, spent the remaining years of his life in exile from the Court at Blois.

On 21 October 1652 Queen Anne of Austria and the King made a triumphant entry into Paris. Accompanying them was the exiled Charles II of England, who still had some years to wait until he could enjoy the same fortune.* They took up residence in the Louvre, with its solid walls and ramparts, 'the King having learned from his terrible adventures at the Palais-Royal that private houses without defensive ditches were not right for him'.[15]

But the Parisians' delight to have their King back did not extend to his godfather. The still deeply unpopular Mazarin would have to endure a few more months in the provinces, finally making his return to Paris at the beginning of February 1653. The King's own maître d'hôtel summed up the unaccountable caprice of the crowd that made this comeback possible. 'As the hatred of the people is often without foundation and its inclinations without good cause and judgement, it is not surprising if its love and hate are both of short duration. So, on the third of February, this outlaw, this disturber of public order and obstacle to the general peace, who had a price on his head of 50,000 écus, came back to this great city, not only without any protest or murmur, but in triumph and covered in glory.'[16]

---

*Charles II made a birthday entrance into London on 29 May 1660 four days after landing at Dover. The day was declared a public holiday to mark 'His Majesty's return to his Parliament' and, as 'Oak Apple Day', celebrated for the next 200 years.

PART TWO

Summi Montes

(The Highest Peaks)

6

A Promotion

Even before his return to Paris, the King – doubtless, receiving close advice from his mother and godfather – had breathed some new life into the 'royal we' with a letter to the Pontoise Parlement: 'All authority belongs to Us. We alone hold it from God alone, without any claim from any other person . . . The officers of the Parlement have no power other than what We have deigned to grant them in order to administer justice . . . Will posterity credit that these officers once presumed to preside over the government of the Kingdom, to formulate policy and to collect taxes, indeed to usurp the plenitude of power that belongs only to Us?'[1] The letter set out pretty accurately the way things were going to be for the next fifty years.

On 22 October 1652, rather than deign to make the traditional journey across the river to the Palais de Justice, Louis summoned the Parlement of Paris instead to the Louvre. The whole purpose of the occasion was humiliation. The deputies gathered in the Grand Gallery as supplicants. The boy-king then strode in like a conquering general, a vanguard of soldiers heralding his entrance with a roll of drums. 'His displeasure,' commented an eyewitness, 'was only too clear in both his eyes and manner: he was grave, serious, with a proud, haughty expression.'[2]

A first declaration set out the terms of a general amnesty, a second re-established the legitimate Parlement in Paris, and a third forbade the Parlement 'to take any part in the affairs of state and its finances'. The deputies sat there meekly, accepting their enslavement without a murmur.

As Attorney-General, Nicolas made a reply on the Parlement's behalf, which, reflecting the new reality, had as much the tone of a courtier as a magistrate. After praising the King's clemency and wisdom, he extolled the far-sighted policy by which the sovereign had transferred his Parlement from Paris to Pontoise. 'When he saw [the Parlement] under oppression and without liberty . . . like a good father, who takes care of his children and faithful servants, he removed them from the place where they were suffering persecution . . .'[3] As Nicolas himself had been chiefly responsible for such a policy, he was able to bask in the reflected glory.

If the Cardinal's small band of supporters had worked tirelessly to restore his authority, they had been sustained not only by their often professed loyalty to the Crown but also by the hope that one day they would get their reward. With the end of the civil war, Nicolas was quick to suggest what would be an appropriate recompense for the huge part he had played in the victory. The Superintendent of Finances, Charles La Vieuville, had died at the beginning of January 1653. The very next day Nicolas wrote to Mazarin asking for the job, this time being careful to employ all the habitual phrases of respect. He pointed out that it called for someone who enjoyed great public esteem and was of known probity, as well as possessing excellent financial connections. He could think of no one better than himself. Not only did he have eighteen years' experience in the royal service, but he also had an impressive range of high-level financial contacts through his wife's family.

Perhaps what is most striking about the letter to a contemporary reader is the effortless mixture of the public and private.

In support of his candidacy, Nicolas stressed not only the service he could provide to his King and country, but also his personal devotion to the Cardinal. 'No one in the world cares more zealously or passionately for the advantage and glory of Your Eminence.'[4] As Nicolas had already allowed his mask to slip, it's likely that Mazarin – whom Cardinal de Retz once described as having 'a lot of spirit but no soul'[5] – regarded such protestations as the 'the usual fine words', but nonetheless such professions of allegiance were a mainstay of seventeenth-century life.

If the Cardinal took a whole month to make up his mind, it was perhaps a reflection of the fact that the office was the most important ministerial position after his own. There were plenty of other candidates he might have chosen, but Nicolas had achieved too much personal prestige of his own to be easily turned down. Finally, he announced that there would be not one but two superintendents. Sharing the office with Nicolas would be Abel Servien, the veteran diplomat who had been close to Mazarin since the days of Richelieu.

The decision amounted to a deliberate check on Nicolas. Sixty years old, Servien had enjoyed a distinguished career. In 1648 he had negotiated the Treaty of Westphalia that ended the Thirty Years War and he was already a minister of state. For him, the office of superintendent was not an instrument for further ambition, but one final prize to crown a career of long and loyal service. Mazarin could rely on him to supervise the conduct of his younger partner. In effect, Nicolas had been placed on a kind of probation. But, not yet forty, at least he knew that time was on his side.

Basile Foucquet was also to be rewarded for his services. Once Cardinal Mazarin was safely back in Paris, he made up for his hesitance over the Abbey of Noailles, by providing him with a small fortune in ecclesiastical livings and benefits.

Unlike his older brother, Basile may have had no grand title that could be openly celebrated, but as the instrument of the Cardinal's arbitrary power he remained as vital a part of the inner circle as ever. Appointed to run a network of spies, his chief task was to monitor all the elements that might provide any renewed threat to royal rule, whether disgruntled factions within the recently subjugated Parlement or sympathisers of de Retz and the Great Condé.

In a note to Basile towards the end of 1653 Cardinal Mazarin wrote, 'We must put an end to the freedom with which people are once again beginning to talk, publish seditious pamphlets and hold meetings in public and private against the King's interests.'[6] In practice speaking out against 'the King's interests' meant speaking out against Mazarin. Basile rounded up the trouble-makers with such efficiency and speed that the Cardinal would regularly turn to him with some new errand. 'If we can find that woman who spoke out so insolently in Saint Elizabeth's Church, it would be a good idea to confine her in Petites-Maisons . . .'[7]

Basile's most important task in the months that followed the end of the Fronde was to foil a plan to assassinate the Cardinal. The alleged plotters were Christophe Bertaut, who possessed the incongruously serene title of 'Grand Master of the Waters and Forests of Burgundy', and an adventurer whom Basile referred to in his reports as Ricous. In a note to Mazarin dated 16 September 1653, the Abbé wrote, 'I have spies in ten places to catch him, and as this matter concerns Your Eminence, I shall work to that end day and night.'[8] Days later both Ricous and Bertaut were arrested, and confessions extracted from them under torture. Basile remained on hand to ensure the smooth fulfilment of the Cardinal's wishes at every stage. A court was established at the Arsenal to try the two accused. When one of the judges expressed some doubts over the verdict, Basile paid him a visit to strengthen his resolve. Once the men had been duly convicted, he then arranged the confiscation of their property. He even supervised the details of their execution. 'It passed off extremely well,' he reported to the Cardinal. 'The hangman burned their letters, then strangled them and broke their bodies on the wheel.'[9]

Such was Basile's dedication to his work that he had to assure the Cardinal that he had not been behind an attempt to assassinate the Great Condé, who, after all, in spite of his treachery, was still a prince of the blood. But he made it clear that he would not hesitate to provide such a service should it be called for. 'When I believe that Your Eminence desires something, I am prepared to risk everything to bring it about.'[10]

But if a degree of recklessness was perhaps necessary to the special services that Basile tended to provide, it had the serious drawback of expressing itself, as well, in a lack of discretion that continually threatened to make him a liability to both the Cardinal and his older brother.

The Bertaut affair was an example. Bertaut's confession had implicated the beautiful young Duchess of Châtillon, whose many admirers had included the Great Condé, the exiled King of England Charles II and even the young Louis XIV himself, when he was barely into his teenage years. A scurrilous verse of the time ran, 'Madame de Châtillon save your charms for some other conquest. You may be ready, but the King is not.'[11] Basile had been infatuated with her ever since they had crossed paths during the Fronde. Turning up at her chateau at Merlou, he quietly offered to forget the matter in return for the usual favours. Only too acquainted with his reputation, the Duchess sacrificed what little was left of her own without a moment's hesitation. But not trusting him to keep his word, she slipped out of the chateau at the first opportunity. With Basile hot on her heels, she fled from one out-of-the-way lodging to another disguised as a monk, surfacing some weeks later in Brussels, where she sought the Great Condé's protection. Eventually, she returned to France, to undertake a scheme on Condé's behalf. During the Fronde, the governor of Péronne had joined the long list of the princes, dukes and generals to fall in love with her. Now she was going to try to persuade him to deliver this important frontier town to the Spanish.

Mazarin had her arrested, but then, no doubt wishing to accommodate his loyal servant as far as he possibly could, released her again into Basile's supervision, which, in the words of Madame de Sévigné, 'amused everybody'.[12] The Duchess, who hoped to profit from Basile's powerful connections, encouraged his hopes, but at the same time continued to keep in close contact with the Great Condé.

On one occasion, according to Mademoiselle de Montpensier,[13] she went to his lodgings when he was away from Paris, talked her way past his servants by taking advantage of what had become her accustomed role as mistress of his household and stole back some letters he had taken from her. Furious, Basile stormed round to her home, where in his rage he smashed several mirrors and threatened to take back all the gifts he had given her. The Duchess fled her home once again, this time seeking refuge with her friend Madame de Saint-Chaumont.

Still helplessly in love, Basile was unable to endure their separation for long, and enlisted his mother's support when he discovered that the Duchess was visiting a convent on the rue du Vieux-Colombier. Appearing before the Duchess with the Mother Superior of the convent, Marie Foucquet made a plea on behalf of her prodigal son: 'Madame, I implore you to allow my son the Abbé to visit you.'

'In the name of Jesus Christ, have pity on him!' added the Mother Superior.[14]

'It was a marvellous farce,' commented Mademoiselle de Montpensier,[15] but only the latest in a succession of scandals that would keep Paris gossiping about the odd couple for years to come.

In spite of such behaviour, the Cardinal continued to indulge

Basile. Genuinely fond of his wayward assistant, he treated him a bit like the fierce dog that shows its master total devotion but terrorises its master's enemies, every now and then tossing him bones in the form of one honour or another. To the disgust of the nobility, the Cardinal conferred on him membership of the order of the Saint-Esprit. To see such a thug wear the blue ribbon and cross of this distinguished order seemed to make a mockery of the privilege. With the Cardinal's blessing, the Abbé was able to pass through any door, whether it belonged to church, dungeon or even council chamber. Acquiring the office of attorney-general in the parlement of Metz, he became entitled to wear the dark robes of the magistracy. 'I am not unhappy to see you take on this new role,' wrote Mazarin in a note of congratulation. 'It is wise to have friends in both heaven and hell.'[16]

It's possible too that, ever wary of Nicolas, the Cardinal valued the one brother as a useful means of embarrassing the other. In the check and balance politics that the Cardinal deployed with such skill it was always wise to have a backup. The way Nicolas would wriggle free from the oppressive partnership he had been forced to enter with his fellow Superintendent of Finances Abel Servien soon provided an example.

Years of war and then civil strife had taken an enormous toll on the state finances. The ability of the Superintendent of Finances to raise funds was critical to the nation's recovery, but in spite of Nicolas's much vaunted banking connections, Mazarin had at first stipulated that it should be Servien who decided financial policy, although he was least qualified to do so. His distinguished service as a diplomat may have brought a certain grandeur and dignity of bearing, but they were a poor preparation for the kind of complex financial juggling a superintendent had to undertake.

Nicolas, on the other hand, had given serious thought to the peculiar difficulties of how to fund a country embroiled in a long war, having discussed the problem at length with the financiers and businessmen he had come to know through his wife's family. Brimming over with ideas, he was eager to put them into practice. But his colleague, who was more than twenty years his senior, made no effort to encourage his thoughts. Haughty and aloof in his manner, Servien was the kind of disconcerting presence to freeze youthful exuberance. He had just one eye – having somehow managed to lose the other as a young man while playing tennis – and thin, upturned lips that gave the unfortunate impression of a supercilious sneer, even on those rare occasions when he was actually in a good mood. Taking refuge in his seniority, he treated Nicolas not as an equal partner but as a little respected assistant. Ignoring his suggestions, he required him only to countersign the orders that he had already settled. Conflict quickly became inevitable. No more capable of blind obedience than he was of blind loyalty, Nicolas fell out with his colleague repeatedly.

While the two Superintendents squabbled and looked to the Cardinal to settle their differences, the state of the finances became worse and worse. The costs of the continuing war against Spain were mounting, but credit dried up as potential lenders lost confidence in the ability of the government to pay them back.

The unpredictable nature of warfare meant that sudden unexpected expenses often occurred. In July 1653, for example, the governor of La Fère refused to open the gates of this strategic frontier town to the royal army. In order to persuade him to change his mind, the Cardinal offered a payment of 150,000 livres. Stationed with the Royal Court close to the front, he wrote back to his secretary Colbert in Paris with various instructions concerning the necessary financial arrangements – anxious and often panic-stricken notes that help to convey the desperate and ad hoc manner in which affairs were conducted. 'I'm sending you the complete particulars of this affair,' he wrote on 19 July, 'so you can inform the Queen and the Superintendents. Please beg them on my behalf to help us as quickly as possible.'[17] Having set out the specific details concerning the hastily arranged bribe, he concluded his note with a disturbing afterthought. 'The truth is that the day after payment there won't be a penny left for the court, not only to give the army what the Superintendents have already sent us but even for its own subsistence. It's why I am begging you, without wasting a moment, to press the Super-intendents to send us right away at least 100,000 francs, and if they need my jewels to help them raise this money on the spot, they can have them.'[18]

It wasn't the first time that Mazarin had given up his jewels as security. Routinely mixing up public and personal sources of finance, he would often complain of the great sacrifices he had to make on behalf of the nation, although those sacrifices tended to work out finally to his own advantage.

Slow, correct and inflexible, Abel Servien would raise count-less obstacles for why the Cardinal's various demands for cash could not be met. Nicolas, on the other hand, was always able to suggest practical solutions. In September 1653 the Cardinal was at first dismayed by the time the Superintendents were taking to find the money to pay for the winter quarters of the troops. If provisions weren't sent soon, he feared the army would have to be recalled and the frontier put at risk. But when Servien left Paris for a few days at the beginning of October, Nicolas emerged from behind the considerable cloud that his colleague had cast over the exchequer and, using his contacts, secured the necessary funds with lightning speed. He made borrowing the money seem effortless.

'You can tell the Attorney-General,' wrote one of the Cardinal's confidants shortly afterwards, 'that he has not wasted his time while he has been alone.'[19] Profuse expressions of grati-tude soon followed from the Cardinal himself.

The incident served to highlight the gulf between the two Superintendents. Their dislike for each other was now common knowledge. A few weeks later one of the Cardinal's aides wrote this note to Nicolas's brother, Basile: '[The Cardinal] has several times asked me how the Superintendents get on together, and told me that it was important that they tried their best not to trip each other up. I can't give you all the details of the conversation, but I said what needed to be said.'[20] The letter was discreetly phrased, but the tenor obvious. It was time that everybody else clubbed together to trip Servien up. In public, the words of respect due to the venerable old diplomat who had negotiated the Treaty of Westphalia continued to pour forth unabated, but in private everyone agreed that he was useless. The Cardinal allowed Servien to continue to present himself as the supremo of the treasury, but henceforward relied on Nicolas to solve the more knotty financial problems.

Probably the Cardinal, ever suspicious of Nicolas's ambition, would have preferred this ad hoc arrangement – Servien projecting the majesty of office, Nicolas providing the practical advice in the background – to continue indefinitely. But the fact that Servien's authority had not been openly challenged was in itself enough to put off the financiers. As he glared at them with his one eye and treated them brusquely like crooks (and by present-day standards they certainly were), they looked around elsewhere for investment opportunities. By the middle of 1654 the state's credit had dried up. The shortage of money was so acute that even the Swiss Guards who patrolled the King's palaces were threatening to go home.

In desperation, the Cardinal spoke several times of defaulting on the government's debts but finally he did not dare, for he remembered the chaos that had been caused when the country last declared itself bankrupt in 1648. With his usual indecision, he allowed this atmosphere of impending disaster to drag on to the end of the year, his ill-concealed panic making potential investors only more reluctant to provide funds.

At the last moment he confronted reality. Summoning Nicolas to a private meeting, he confided that Servien had let him down badly. The situation was hopeless, he declared, he could see no way out. The calculated note of despair amounted to a cue for Nicolas to provide the reassurance that the Cardinal had been seeking. Things weren't so bad, he replied. If he hadn't addressed himself wholeheartedly to the problem before, it was only because the necessary solution was so completely at odds with Abel Servien's style. The way to win over the financiers was to reassure them, not browbeat them. Access to credit required an atmosphere of calm and confidence. The bankruptcy of 1648 should never even be mentioned except to decry it as the cause of all the chaos that followed. An equally awkward subject to be avoided was the idea of taxing financiers and businessmen; after all, this was killing the golden goose. Instead, one should praise them and, rather than wrangle over their assets and legitimate profits, offer them rewards for their good faith whenever they provided timely assistance. 'The key secret, in brief, was to give them something to gain, this being the only reason why anyone would be happy to take on a risk, but above all to establish so powerful a reputation for honouring an agreement that they didn't even feel they were running a risk.'[21]

Nicolas's obvious ability forced the Cardinal to put aside his other reservations. In future, Nicolas alone would be responsible for securing the state finances; Servien would be allowed to keep his title, but henceforward his brief would be restricted to the allocation of state expenditure. Nicolas insisted that Mazarin set out the division of duties in writing, so that there might be no confusion. The resulting decree was issued on Christmas Eve 1654.

Once Servien realised that he would not only be allowed to

keep his robes and chains but also have a lot more leisure to pursue his own interests, he was stoical about his demotion. With the Cardinal's blessing, he devoted his remaining years to building up a show of authority in place of the real authority he had lost. He bought the Château de Meudon, to the south-west of Paris, from the once powerful Guise family, repaired the considerable damage it had suffered from Condé's troops during the civil war and built an orangery, whose vast terrace still dominates Meudon today. Here he achieved the final epiphany of prestige, when he invited the Royal Court to a feast in celebration of the marriage of his daughter Marie-Antoinette to the great-grandson of Henry IV's legendary chancellor, Sully. All the leading members of the royal family, including the King himself, signed the marriage contract. The writer and scholar Gilles Ménage penned an ode to mark the occasion: 'This powerful minister whose vast domain / Occupies the banks of the Sarthe and the Maine / And who watches over our prince's gold, / Offers us a feast for a century of gold.'[22] Nicolas may have had little faith in Servien's ability to raise money, but he couldn't help admire the style with which he spent it.

Previously Nicolas had longed for Servien's freedom of action, but now that his old colleague enjoyed the trappings of the job without the responsibility he could envy him for different reasons. When in the new year an anxious Cardinal confided the true state of France's financial chaos – to which his own penchant for sudden unplanned expenditure had considerably contributed – it challenged even Nicolas's ability to see the bright side. 'The Cardinal told me things so extraordinary that I wouldn't have believed them if I had discovered them for myself,' he recalled. 'He spoke as though I alone could save him, as though the only hope for both his future as a minister and his own livelihood lay in my devotion to the King's service, my fond gratitude towards him the Cardinal and the efforts that I and my friends might make on his behalf.'[23]

If this account suggests an image of the Cardinal practically hugging Nicolas's knees, other descriptions of Mazarin's often obsequious behaviour suggest that it was nonetheless a pretty accurate portrait. As fawning as he was powerful, the Cardinal gave Nicolas the impression of total licence: 'He assured me that he would give me the King's authority to do whatever I wanted to do, and that I would be absolutely free to grant such concessions, privileges or handouts as I thought fit, generally to do whatever I considered appropriate, just so long as I could provide for the necessary costs, a statement of which he would provide every year.'[24]

When some days later the Cardinal sent the first of these statements, it was broken down into wartime expenditure on the one hand and domestic expenditure on the other. The long list of ships and fortifications suggested the grim times that the sailors and soldiers of France had to endure, but also threw into relief the frivolous expenditure of the other list. There were the games and amusements of the King, ballets, plays and so on. In each case the Cardinal expected the expense to be met without going into any specific detail. The impression for a modern reader is of a narrow élite – not quite enlightened yet – blindly on the take, incapable of imagining that there might be anything untoward about the extravagance of the luxuries that the rest of the country had to pay for, regarding them somehow as their due, because it was their station in life to enjoy such privilege. The notion of '*Liberté, Egalité, Fraternité*' was still well over a century away.

In such a hierarchical society, it was natural to reward the support of your servants with generous handouts and to buy influence, wherever possible. In this respect Nicolas, who was still the Attorney-General in the Parlement, was a model of the seventeenth-century political fixer. Dispensing the vast sums and privileges that he acquired as the Superintendent of Finances, he worked hard to secure a docile Parlement for the King, as well as important allies for himself. Maintaining a façade of propriety – for this was also a society in which appearances were important – he relied on a number of agents to organise the deals behind the scenes. Of these, Jean Hérauld, sieur de Gourville, was the one in whom he placed the most reliance.

Ten years younger than Nicolas, Gourville had started out as a servant in the household of the duc de la Rochefoucauld. His intelligence and personable nature quickly drew him to the attention of the author of the *Maximes*, who asked him to become his personal secretary. During the Fronde, when La Rochefoucauld allied himself with the Great Condé, Gourville, displaying the reckless loyalty so characteristic of the time, involved himself in every intrigue and danger, including kidnap and theft, to further his master's interests. When La Rochefoucauld finally sought a reconciliation with the Court, Gourville took charge of the successful negotiations. Cardinal Mazarin was so impressed by his ability that he sent him to Spain with the task of persuading the Great Condé likewise to bury his differences. But when the Great Condé turned down these overtures, the Cardinal, who feared that his erstwhile peace envoy was secretly working in Condé's interests, had him imprisoned in the Bastille. With the help of his brother Basile, Nicolas interceded to have Gourville released, in this way winning a devoted and extremely capable collaborator.

After Nicolas had complained of the difficulties he sometimes had getting the Parlement to confirm decrees, Gourville set about getting to know the counsellors, drawing up detailed lists of those who wielded the most influence among their colleagues. The compliant would then receive a payment from the Superintendent of 500 écus and a promise of further help in the future. In his memoirs Gourville spoke of such activity as though it were the most natural thing in the world – simply the operation of the prevailing system of patronage. With his capacity for friendship and open-minded good nature, he effortlessly oiled the wheels, dispensing the Superintendent's favours in such a way that the notion of such conduct being in any way untoward was usually far from anyone's mind.

The President of the Parlement, Le Coigneux, was an example of Gourville's effectiveness. When Nicolas told Gourville that he needed to secure his co-operation, it turned out that Gourville had already been out hunting with Le Coigneux several times. So it was easy to find the opportunity to suggest an arrangement of mutual benefit. 'One day, when he told me about some improvements he was making to his country house, I told him he ought to try to act in such a way that the Superintendent would help him to finish the terrace he had just started. Two days later I received instructions to give him 2,000 écus and the promise of more to come.'[25] Le Coigneux quickly became one of Nicolas's most consistent supporters.

The state finances depended upon the same manipulation of personal connections. Although over the years a whole host of other taxes had been added, the following were the chief sources of revenue for the state treasury: the *taille*, which was levied directly on land; the *aides*, a tax on goods with the exception of salt, which had its own special tax called the *gabelle*. The responsibility for gathering these taxes did not belong to state officials, but had been granted to independent agents (*fermiers*), who collected the tax in return for a commission. They imposed their levies on the populace with a brutality that often led to riots – as Nicolas himself had discovered in the Dauphiné – but the advantage of the arrangement was that these highly motivated collectors guaranteed a steady flow of revenue to the treasury. To win one of these highly valuable tax-collection contracts inevitably required inside influence. As these taxes were not enough in themselves to meet the continuing costs of the war, Nicolas was also – like other superintendents before him – constantly dreaming up elaborate incentives to coax financiers into lending money.

One scheme involved the redemption of worthless treasury notes that had been issued to lenders in the aftermath of the 1648 bankruptcy. 'In business with the King,' explained Gourville, 'the custom arose that Monsieur Foucquet would renew these notes for a certain sum: one bought them usually for about a tenth of their nominal value; but after the Superintendent had assigned them to certain securities, they were good for the entire amount.'[26] As this practice of 'assignation' guaranteed a tenfold return on an investment, lenders were tripping over themselves to take advantage, but yet again some kind of inside influence was required to reach the head of the queue. As Nicolas's aide, Gourville was in a position both to witness and to take part in the casual graft of the inner circle. On one occasion he secured the Cardinal's backing to take over the tax-collection contract for the province of Guyenne. Concerned about Gourville's ability to make the huge advance payments that such a contract required, Nicolas questioned the arrangement with the Cardinal. 'The Cardinal replied that he was owed 2,700,000 livres in return for advances he had made to the King. As Monsieur Foucquet ought to reimburse him in the form of assignations, he would be more than happy if my tax-collection contract served as security.'[27] Probably the Cardinal's 'advances' had taken the form of treasury notes, which he would have acquired at a fraction of the cost. Steadily gathering the tax due under the contract over the next fifteen months, Gourville paid the 2,700,000 livres to the Cardinal's secretary, Colbert, and took a healthy commission for himself.

His participation provided a convenient intermediary that enabled the Cardinal to keep his name out of the transaction.

Time and time again the Cardinal, who involved himself in every kind of enterprise from arms trading to tax collection, would ask that his involvement be cloaked under the name of a third party. Twice driven into exile, Mazarin did not want to be embarrassed by unseemly details that might make himself even more unpopular, although there is no evidence that he regarded his conduct as in any way improper.

The correspondence with his secretary Jean-Baptiste Colbert, preserved in the official archives, contains numerous examples of what today would be considered gross corruption. It captures not only the Cardinal's readiness to take maximum personal benefit from his office but also the system of patronage that led to such an attitude. As the Cardinal's *créature*, Colbert defended his master's interests zealously, placing them before even the needs of the state.

When the Cardinal agreed to provide supplies to the French army in Spain, Colbert warned him that it was an ill-advised enterprise: 'The contract will be difficult to fulfil and, above all, it will be extremely expensive to Your Eminence.' It wasn't that the Cardinal wouldn't make a handsome profit eventually, but Colbert feared that he would have considerable cash flow problems in the interim, since Nicolas had advised him that the treasury couldn't make a monthly payment as in the case of other war expenses, but would have to give the Cardinal an 'assignation' instead. 'I'm beginning to realise that we will deliver most of these supplies, perhaps all of them, before we have received a penny. A swift return on assignations cannot be made without regrettable consequences, since it would be impossible to prevent the name of Your Eminence appearing. Those who are responsible for paying the assignation will make your name known everywhere since they derive so much prestige from the association.'[28]

Robustly pragmatic, the Cardinal replied, 'You will tell the

Attorney-General that in return for the supplies to Catalonia he has led me to expect not only some good assignations but also ready cash, since I have already maintained the army for some considerable time.'[29] As for the use of his name, the Cardinal merely commented, 'This difficulty can be overcome by using Albert's name or some other name you consider appropriate, it being absolutely vital that my name should not appear.'[30]

Whatever fears the Cardinal had concerning his wider reputation, he did not hesitate to appear importuning among his colleagues in government. The note above was typical of the constant pressure he exerted on Nicolas to provide extravagantly generous returns on his various investments in state enterprises.

When it was impossible to claim any semblance of a commercial transaction, the Cardinal merely took advantage of the royal prerogative to make secret payments, known as *ordonnances de comptant*. In such circumstances the Superintendent, on behalf of the King, would write on a request for payment the words 'I know the reason for this expense' and the sum would be released without any account having to be made.

Since Servien was in charge of expenditure, such a discretion theoretically fell within his ambit, but the Cardinal, who had long grown tired of his annoying rectitude and inflexibility, in practice relied on Nicolas to authorise such payments and then to push them past his colleague under some pretext, concealing the real reasons. 'I'm sending you an *ordonnance de comptant* for 300,000 livres,' the Cardinal wrote to Colbert on 20 May 1657. 'You will present it to Monsieur Servien in such manner as the Attorney-General will instruct, taking care that no one else should know of the affair. This order concerns in part Monsieur Le Tellier; but in consultation with the Attorney-General, you will present it to Monsieur Servien in such a way that the King appears to have resolved to make payment under a general head rather than for the private business of individuals.'[31] In the same letter, the

Cardinal wrote, 'I think this letter will reach you before Marshal de Gramont, who will present you with two promissory notes from me . . . One of them is for payment of 8,000 or so livres that he won from me, a sum you will take from the same source . . .'[32]

The way in which the Cardinal could take Colbert into his confidence over this matter seems almost as extraordinary as the fact that he should have expected the state to pay his gambling debts in the first place. The reason for both lay in the fact that – according to the regime of absolute power that Richelieu had put in place and Mazarin then perfected — the King *was* the state, as Louis XIV himself made explicit when he began to rule in his own name a few years later. If the Cardinal did not wish to be seen to be taking personal advantage from his office, it was simply a question of prudence, not because he thought that he had done anything wrong. After all, he was the King's godfather, wasn't he? If he didn't have the King's backing, then no one did. And to have the King's backing was all the justification that was needed.

The same logic justified those who aided and abetted the Cardinal in his depredations. They were *créatures* of the Cardinal, who was in turn the *créature* of the King, from whom all temporal authority emanated. 'Everyone knows', Nicolas would write many years later, 'that, with the authority of the King, Cardinal Mazarin, in his role as Prime Minister, had absolute power over all the affairs of France, including finances, in such a way that it could truly be said that he was the first and foremost mover of policy, and I acted only under his orders.'[33]

7

Saint-Mandé

For many years now Nicolas's life had been a matter of attending to one crisis after another. First there had been the civil wars of the Fronde, then the pressing challenges that faced him as the new Superintendent of Finances. But now that he had eclipsed Servien and won the Cardinal's confidence, he felt secure enough to give rein to his imagination.

Nicolas had more than one Paris residence at his disposal. There was his own house off the rue Matignon, there was an official residence in the Louvre and there was an *hôtel* in the Marais which was part of his wife Marie-Madeleine's dowry. But finding all these dwellings too cramped for the new, more expansive lifestyle he had in mind, Nicolas began in 1654 to acquire a number of contiguous properties in the village of Saint-Mandé to the east of Paris, conveniently close to the Château de Vincennes, where the Cardinal and the Court often resided. Here he undertook an ambitious construction programme, hastening to put some long-postponed dreams of splendour into practice.

Behind the unremarkable, rather ordinary façade of the original buildings, a labyrinth of new wings and courtyards began to take shape. The centrepiece was a great library, which, taking the form of a long gallery, opened out on to newly land-scaped gardens.

Saint-Mandé was the fruit of Nicolas's wish to promote who

he was and what he wanted to be. Up to this point he had been too much the prisoner of immediate circumstances to be able to think about the future. But now he was free at last to assert his own will, in an expression of positive values that mirrored a wider mood among France's ruling élite. Spain hadn't been defeated yet, but France clearly had the upper hand and it was at last possible to begin to imagine what peace might be like.

A chief inspiration for him in anticipating the fruits of that peace was his close friend Madame Suzanne du Plessis-Bellière. As soon as the Fronde was over she had turned her house in Charenton – a village not far from Saint-Mandé – into a rural retreat, where a number of the most notable writers and artists of the day were able to find some respite from the turmoil of the city.* The death of her husband, General Jacques de Rougé du Plessis-Bellière, mortally wounded in November 1654 during the Battle of Castellamare near Naples, caused her to dedicate herself all the more to the activities of her little salon. She won an important early success by securing the friendship of the famous writer Madeleine de Scudéry, who had a decade previously been one of the very first of the literary guests to gather in the Blue Room of the Hôtel de Rambouillet.

If it was in the house of the Marquise de Rambouillet – the great society hostess Catherine de Vivonne, otherwise known as the incomparable Arthénice† – that the essential ingredients of the literary salon were established, Madeleine de Scudéry had unquestionably been the brightest star of the gathering, sustaining its high reputation with a charm, wit and refinement

---

* Although today Madame du Plessis-Bellière's guest list – which included such then well-known literary names as Isaac de Benserade, Louis Petit, François de Boisrobert, Jean Loret and Jacques Moisant de Brieux – is unlikely to provoke much more than a flicker of recognition even in France.
†This anagram of 'Cathérine' was typical of the kind of wordplay that the habitués of the salons delighted in.

that more than justified her own nom de plume of Sappho, after the legendary female lyrical poet of Lesbos. The five conflict-ridden years of the Fronde, which split up the salon members between the senseless, often murderous factions of the time, badly dented the façade of a civilised society, but with the return of peace Madeleine de Scudéry was swift to demonstrate her faith in reconciliation.

Enjoying a renewed celebrity with the publication in 1653 of her long, ten-volume romance *Le Grand Cyrus*, she revived the Rambouillet spirit in weekend gatherings that she held at her home in the rue Vieille-du-Temple. Set in 600 BC, *Le Grand Cyrus* was ostensibly about the great founder of the Persian Empire, but its principal appeal lay in the allegorical portraits that it provided of some of the most well-known figures in mid-seventeenth-century Paris. In the final book of the romance de Scudéry describes the salon that Sappho held in Mytilene, the capital of Lesbos. Her portrait offers a vision of how she liked to imagine herself: '[W]hat is admirable in her, this person who knows so many varied things, is that she knows them without pedantry, without conceit, and without disdain for those who are unlearned. Her conversation is so natural and easy, so charming, that she is never heard to say anything but what someone untutored, but of large understanding, might say.'[1] The words seem immodest, but perhaps are best understood as an ideal to live up to. Such were the refined sentiments that she hoped to cultivate at the meetings of her own salon, which became known as 'Sappho's Samedis'. Her mission was to engender an atmosphere of courtesy, delicacy and high feeling, *amitié*, even if the less skilled adherents of this programme tended to lapse into the kind of pomposity and affectation that Molière would later satirise in his play *Les Précieuses ridicules*.

However, there was one detail that hampered Sappho's high-minded ambitions. The eponymous hero of her novel was a thinly veiled, but adulatory portrait of the Great Condé, who, in real life, was scandalising France with one treacherous act after another. This highly visible support for the wrong side during the Fronde was now a deep embarrassment. It meant that Madame du Plessis-Bellière's suggestion that Sappho should from time to time bring her friends to Charenton, where they would benefit from the more relaxed atmosphere of the countryside, provided a particularly welcome opportunity for her to make some gesture of public loyalty.

Attaching herself in this way to a known ally of the Superintendent was one obvious way of signposting her acceptance of the new dispensation, so she gladly encouraged her own coterie of literary names to make the short journey to Charenton. Here in the country she was able to continue the deeper purpose that doubtless lay behind the light-hearted façade of her meetings – restoring some faith in human culture and progress after all the discord, savagery and bloodshed of the past few years.

If Madeleine de Scudéry was clearly the chief jewel of these gatherings at Charenton, Suzanne du Plessis-Bellière employed plenty of touches of her own to embellish the display yet further. She commissioned the artist Eustache Le Sueur to do seven paintings that depicted the lives of the Muses, hanging them up in the gallery where her guests would gather. Delicate, charming studies of Terpsichore, Melpomene, Clio or Thalia gathering together to practise their art beneath a canopy of trees, with the landscape of Arcadia in the background, they offered a standard of intellectual harmony that quietly set the tone for the guests who attended her evenings.

Ten years older than Nicolas, Suzanne was his closest confidante. 'She ruled the Superintendent completely,' wrote Bussy-Rabutin in his memoirs. Whether she was more than a confidante is unknown. The novel *The Man in the Iron Mask* – in which a helplessly admiring Dumas gives Nicolas a notably heroic portrait for an otherwise minor character – depicts them as devoted lovers, but whether or not this was true, certainly Nicolas treated her social and literary endeavours as a model for what he would like to achieve himself and visited her house often – conveniently close, as it was, to Saint-Mandé. There he could enjoy a respite from the wary, guarded mode of his everyday existence, displaying – in a company that existed as much for mutual edification and amusement as personal advantage – a natural spontaneity.

Encouraged by Suzanne du Plessis-Bellière's circle, he delighted in puns, riddles and puzzles, and even made his own attempts at literary composition, which – like Churchill's paintings – perhaps served to divert his restless mind. There was the sonnet, for example, that he wrote to mark the death of Suzanne's parrot. Humour being notoriously difficult to translate, the verse with its carefully devised rhymes does not render itself well into English,* but the essential conceit is easy enough to convey: card players would rather lose all their tricks, drunkards go without their drink, and magistrates pass judgement without their robes than see the poor parrot forgotten. 'Lovable parrot,' he promised, 'your portrait will have a place on my wall for ever.'[2]

If our pastimes offer some measure of our characters, then Nicolas's suggested an ironic but affectionate sensibility, an exuberance and sense of wonder. As Superintendent of Finances, he was necessarily caught up in the dark intrigues of high politics, but he showed a compensating desire to contribute to a more gracious, generous and elegant world.

The clever company, the lively exchange of ideas and the tranquil beauty of the surroundings at Charenton offered an ideal of contentment to Nicolas, but much more significantly – since

* The original French has been reproduced as an appendix to this book. See page 309.

he could never be content simply to while away the hours – strengthened his resolve to found his own salon, which he imagined on an altogether greater scale. At the heart of his vision was the large library he was building. It would be far more than just a meeting place for writers, but a great academy facilitating the study of every discipline, a haven of the world's knowledge attracting architects, engineers, physicians, mathematicians, explorers. Ever since Nicolas's father had died over a decade previously, Nicolas's moral guardian Pierre Deschampsneufs had been responsible for cataloguing the books that Nicolas had inherited. Every now and then at Nicolas's bidding or on his own initiative, he would purchase new books to add to the already substantial collection. But it had been essentially a negligible activity reflecting the personal taste of two bibliophiles who had very little time to exercise their passion. While Deschampsneufs laboured away on his translation of the Psalms of David, Nicolas had been equally preoccupied with meeting the endless demands of Mazarin.

But, as the library of Saint-Mandé neared completion, Nicolas encouraged Deschampsneufs to buy books that might appeal not only to them but also to the scholars whom Nicolas intended the new library to serve. For most of Nicolas's adult life the Jesuit priest had made a point of counselling restraint to his young protégé; but now, making the most of the licence to spend, Deschampsneufs began to appreciate the peculiar exhilaration of excess. When the family of the late Archbishop of Toulouse, Charles de Montchal, put up for sale his collection of rare Latin and Greek manuscripts, he did not waste his time painstakingly poring over each individual volume, as he would have done in the past, but simply bought up the entire library. The death soon afterwards of René Moreau, Professor of Medicine at the Collège Royal, who had assembled the largest medical library in France, offered another opportunity for this chequebook librarianship, as

– pre-empting rival buyers – Deschampsneufs agreed an extremely generous settlement to prevent the executors from breaking up the collection.

The cartloads of books that arrived daily at Saint-Mandé made a mockery of the priest's previous efforts at cataloguing. If Deschampsneufs took pride in the vast house of wisdom that was being assembled, he must nonetheless have found it hard at times not to feel some niggling sense of despair. The knowledge of the world might be descending on Saint-Mandé, but amid the growing mountains of yet to be listed books how would it ever be possible to make sense of it? Even before the library was finished, it was too small. To make up for the lack of space, Deschampsneufs resorted to ad hoc solutions, cramming books ceiling-high in his own apartment, as well as any other rooms about Saint-Mandé that happened to be free – a resort made all the more necessary by Nicolas's insistence that, whatever the behind-the-scenes pressures on the library's capacity, it should present a façade of spacious serenity and order. Visitors should feel able to wander without any sense of restraint, the grandeur of the most splendidly decorated surroundings encouraging a sense of limitless possibility. And Nicolas devoted as much care to the newly landscaped gardens on to which the library opened, a delightfully harmonious arrangement of geometric paths and flowerbeds, secluded bowers and statues of the Greek gods. In specially constructed greenhouses Nicolas's German gardener Jacob Besseman grew exotic plants and practised special grafting techniques.

As well as being Nicolas's personal residence, Saint-Mandé was intended to offer a powerful demonstration of the authority of the King's Superintendent of Finances. Through instilling confidence in his office, Nicolas hoped that the opulent display would help to attract the vast sums from financiers that the country's coffers so badly needed. In meeting the costs of building, decoration and refurbishment, he drew on his own resources and his wife's considerable fortune, but also borrowed heavily. As the debts built up, he did not trouble to ask himself whether they were incurred as a private individual or as France's Superintendent of Finances. The important thing was to acquire the necessary money and to spend it well. As Nicolas set about transforming Saint-Mandé, it was second nature for him to involve his family as much as possible. He looked upon them as natural partners in the enterprise, which he regarded as merely an expression of the wider will of the family as a whole. The place quickly became the informal family hearth, to which all the Foucquets gravitated. Nicolas's mother Marie de Maupeou took up residence there, confirming its new importance.

One unspoken motive for her arrival was concern for her son's moral well-being. The reports she had been receiving from Pierre Deschampsneufs had filled her with foreboding. It was true that in career terms Nicolas had reached a pinnacle of success and achievement, but from the spiritual point of view his willingness to flaunt the trappings was a dangerous sign. Many years ago Deschampsneufs had promised Nicolas's parents that he would take responsibility for their son's moral welfare, but now he found himself being as easily dismissed as any other servant. For the sake of her son's soul, Marie knew that it was time to make her own personal intervention. If it was unrealistic to expect him any longer to listen to her reprimands, she could at least set an example. Taking up residence in a house that was becoming one of the most extravagantly decorated in all France, she duly chose the smallest and most austere quarters she could find, a crucifix on otherwise bare walls providing the only ornament.

While Deschampsneufs was close by accumulating – among other subjects – one of the largest collections of religious books in France, Marie contented herself with just two: the Holy Bible and Saint Juve's *Treatise on the Knowledge and Love of God*. In her little cell, scarcely eight feet square, she spent most of her day either praying or making up anagrams of religious devotion: *'J'AIME DE PUR AMOUR; DIEU POUR MA VIE'* (I love with a pure love; God for my life).

Clearly Nicolas would have to make serious efforts to convince his mother that Saint-Mandé was more than simply a case of worldly pride. An important ally in this endeavour was a young Jesuit-trained physician called Jean Pecquet. He was able to indulge Marie Foucquet's fascination with cures and potions, having already won her approval through lengthy medical researches, which the Foucquet family had supported. After attending the Jesuit college in Rouen, Pecquet had during the 1640s come to Paris, where he taught for a while at the Collège de Clermont. It was while he was there that he met Nicolas's older brother François, who was then the Bishop of Agde.

François provided important early support for Pecquet's medical studies, in 1648 inviting the young man to join his staff at Agde in the Languedoc. With the help of François's patronage, Pecquet received his doctor's degree from Montpellier University, but even before qualification had already published his first treatise, *Experimenta nova anatomica*, in which he became the first person to describe the lymphatic system correctly. François met the costs of its publication.

When after the Fronde Pecquet wanted to return to Paris to continue his research, François arranged for him to meet his brother, the Superintendent of Finances. Nicolas took him on as his personal physician and had a laboratory built for him at Saint-Mandé. Here Pecquet was able to immerse himself in his medical experiments.

Maybe if Pecquet had remained in his laboratory Marie would have been impressed, but she had little sympathy for those who allowed their intellect to stray. After the example of the Jesuits,

Marie's faith caused her to embrace reason, which she believed was the best way to reach a true understanding of God. Yet at the same time the pursuit of knowledge clearly required an extra measure of discipline. In the daily growing grandeur of Saint-Mandé she saw how easily such knowledge could come to be undertaken for its own sake, when it was the Christian's duty never to forget the Prime Mover.

It would have bothered her how easily Pecquet passed from describing the wonders of the new laboratory Nicolas had built for him to admiring the verses of whichever writer happened to be present on a particular night. It would have bothered her too the way the physician and his new patient happily lost themselves in the most temporal of distractions. Whether it was literature, painting or poetry, whether it was the circulation of the blood or the great discoveries being made across the westward ocean, the two egged each other on in their debate, airing endless questions about pretty well everything in God's universe, although paying very little attention to God himself.

If finally Marie Foucquet found it more a source of disquiet than comfort to see Pecquet join Nicolas's inner circle, even more disturbing must have been the example Nicolas was setting for her youngest son, Louis. Ever since Nicolas had, *in loco parentis*, carried Louis to his baptism in the church of Saint-Nicolas-des-Champs twenty years ago, he had had a responsibility to look after his brother's spiritual welfare, but Marie could only lament what that meant in practice, as in the summer of 1655 Nicolas sent Louis on one of the greatest shopping sprees of the century.

The twenty-year-old had become a young counsellor in the Parlement, but he still wasn't sure about what he really wanted to do in life, and he was happy to accept Nicolas's suggestion that a trip down to Rome would broaden his horizons. While he was there, it would also be an excellent opportunity for him to undertake some business for Nicolas, acquiring some paintings, statues and ornaments for Saint-Mandé, as well as Nicolas's other houses.

Louis's contact in the Eternal City was the painter Nicolas Poussin, who had of choice spent nearly his entire working life in Italy. Although in the last years of the reign of Louis XIII, Cardinal Richelieu had lured Poussin to Paris with the title of 'First Painter to the King', the great painter – of Norman peasant stock – was so disgusted by the intrigues and petty jealousies of the artists in Paris that he gave up his commission of painting the Great Gallery of the Louvre and returned to Italy after two short years. But even in Rome he found there were very few painters whom he could respect. The great days of Raphael, Leonardo and Michelangelo were long over.

Poussin's unsparing attitude made him a rather forbidding combination of consultant and mentor as the young Louis sought to acquire the basic expertise and judgement he needed to carry out Nicolas's wishes responsibly. Soon after his arrival in Rome, he came upon several pictures that seemed to his untutored eye to surpass anything that he had seen back in France, but Poussin dismissed them as a third-rate pandering to the vulgar tastes of the market.

The old painter's ferocious condemnation of the latest generation of Italian artists caused Louis to doubt his own taste so much that during his first few weeks in Italy he refrained from buying any paintings at all. The only ones of incontestable quality were those that Poussin had painted himself, but they were so expensive that Louis hesitated to commit his brother's money to such extravagant expenditure. Instead, swayed by Poussin's passionate praise for the great sculptors of Rome's imperial past, he put most of his early efforts into acquiring ancient statues. 'They'll provide much better decoration for your houses than these silly paintings that hardly anyone seems able to determine the true quality of,' he advised Nicolas.[4]

Poussin helped him get hold of twelve good-quality ancient statues, but also agreed to sketch several designs for new ones, which were then carved by a team of craftsmen in Rome under Poussin's supervision. It was a gesture of friendship that the old painter – who had long ceased trying to please anyone – accorded to only a very few people. Warming to his young visitor, Poussin even offered, in addition to the statue sketches, to paint any subject that Louis might choose. 'Some say his latest work is not so good because of his trembling hand,' Louis wrote to his brother, 'but that's nonsense. He paints as well as ever.'[5]

Mistrustful of easy flattery, the painter could not help but bask in Louis's obviously genuine admiration. The boy's open-hearted enthusiasm made for a refreshing contrast with the conceit and grand airs of the cardinals and bankers who usually took up of his time. One of Louis's most engaging qualities was that he never claimed knowledge he did not have. Free of preconceptions and prejudices, but with boundless curiosity and good nature, he recognised his limitations, even if – true to the family motto – he was determined to push them back as far as he could.

A few weeks after his arrival, when he had been overwhelmed by endless viewings of artworks, he wrote to Nicolas:

I would be delighted, sir, if I could learn in Italy to become as expert and intelligent in painting as in sculpture and other subjects. I know that such knowledge would stand me in good stead, and that I can gain much to my advantage by helping you in such matters. But, quite apart from the fact that long, hard study is required to become competent and this business is very new to me, it is also necessary to have a certain natural aptitude, which I don't think I have. All the same, I can certainly assure you that my eye is much better than it was when I first came to Rome. The extraordinary number of things I've had to look at means that I have a much more refined taste now, and I'm doing my best to make it even more so, not just because of your instructions, but because it's a good thing for me anyway.[6]

In the weeks that followed he won Poussin's trust and, just as critically, the protection that the artist was able to provide from the circling sharks of Rome's art dealers, who were always happy to prey on a rich, clueless ingénue from the other side of the Alps. With his growing confidence Louis was soon not only searching for artworks that Nicolas could display in his houses, but also seeking expert advice on the houses themselves. The architectural plans he gathered of various Italian monuments, palaces and fountains helped to stimulate Nicolas's thinking, in particular influencing his ambitious plans for a new chateau he was planning to build on his estate at Vaux-le-Vicomte. Art buyer, research assistant and project manager all rolled into one, Louis circulated Nicolas's skeleton proposal for the building among the architectural and engineering experts in Rome, relaying back their comments on its feasibility.

As Louis became more and more assured in dealing with these important people, he even began to cast aside his previous reluctance to spend. Dropping his reservation about paintings, he tried to look for those that had been executed on a large enough scale to suit the majestic new spaces that Nicolas's building programme would soon make available.

By the new year of 1656 Louis was despatching by sea to Marseilles sizeable consignments of paintings and ornaments, which were then conveyed northwards in a convoy of wagons. But he had also accumulated a priceless store of ancient statues and busts, as well as marble pedestals, tables and other furniture, that were far too heavy and vulnerable to risk a long land journey. These he sent by ship through the Straits of Gibraltar and up the Bay of Biscay to the northern Breton port of Saint

Malo, from where the journey to Paris was comparatively short and less punishing. The torrent of treasures soon became so great that Nicolas had to take some steps to stem the flow. Was a Polish amber tabernacle really a necessary purchase, he asked in one of his periodic letters of instruction. It had no obvious use and would only be one more over-precious item that needed special care. In the months ahead there would be many more such queries.

Nicolas was much more positive about Louis's suggestion that Poussin be invited to paint two subjects of his own choosing once he had finished supervising the completion of the statues, which Roman sculptors continued to work on through the first half of 1656. Nicolas did everything he could to encourage Poussin. Using his influence with Cardinal Mazarin, he had the young Louis XIV reconfirm his father's award to Poussin of the title 'First Painter to the King'. If such an honour was still not enough to lure the artist back to France, as no doubt Nicolas had hoped it might, Poussin was nonetheless eager to show his gratitude.

'You cannot imagine the efforts he's making on your behalf,' Louis wrote to Nicolas in April 1656, 'nor the great affection with which he undertakes such work.' Indeed, young Louis Foucquet and the painter had become such firm friends that they began to dream of fantastic new schemes that they could work on together. 'He and I have discussed certain things that I'll soon be able to explain to you in detail,' Louis wrote to his brother. 'Things that, if you choose to pursue them, will give you rewards from Monsieur Poussin that not even kings enjoy, and that no one will be able to match in the centuries to come.'[7]

Given the consistent determination of Louis to involve his new mentor as much as possible in the decoration of Nicolas's houses, the most plausible interpretation of this comment is that together they had hatched up some scheme for how the painter might play a leading role in the Superintendent's ambitious plans. Nicolas had made it clear that he intended the new house he was planning to build at Vaux to eclipse all possible rivals. At any rate Poussin – who had been so relieved to leave behind all the plots and intrigues of his two years in Paris – would surely have been surprised to find that three centuries later a host of best-seller writers were latching on to these remarks as proof of his part in some fantastic conspiracy involving the Knights Templar, old scrolls and secret signs in his paintings. His own admiration for Leonardo da Vinci lay in a shared respect for the classical past, not in any enthusiasm for hidden codes.

One of the many new sculptures to decorate the garden of Saint-Mandé had been carved out of limestone by the sculptor Michel Anguier. It depicted the goddess Charity cradling a sleeping child in her arms, while three more children sat at her feet. The figures bore the features of Nicolas's wife Marie-Madeleine and their young children. During these early years of marriage most of Marie-Madeleine's time had been taken up in childbirth and motherhood, although she had also to contend with the loss that was sadly so often an accompaniment, when – towards the end of 1656 – the eldest of her children, François, died. Until then she had been too overwhelmed by the delirium of babies and young children to be more than a passive presence, but henceforward the poets of Saint-Mandé would increasingly single her out as an ideal of maternal, chaste and artless beauty, praising an outgoing young woman who was determined to play a full part in her husband's life as well as the circles he frequented. 'Her eyes, in spite of their modesty, rival the most beautiful women whether in town or at Court, daily inciting their jealousy,' wrote the poet Philippe Quinault. Even Nicolas's old schoolteacher Father Vavasseur was moved to pick up his pen: '*Forma sine arte decens, matrisque simillima formae. / Candida, cum modico mixta rubore, nitet.'*

No woman could have been more suited by both temperament and background to stand at the Superintendent's side. Taking charge of a domestic sphere that was too grand to treat entirely as their own, negotiating with her engaging but decorous manner the often awkward boundary between the public and the private, she complemented the Superintendent's life perfectly. At Saint-Mandé, she was one half of a golden couple that seemed to live a blessed existence.

---

* 'She was both attractive and motherly without contrivance. / She stood out for her blend of beauty and modesty.'

8

Vaux-le-Vicomte

All the most memorable patrons of the arts, whether de'
Medici, Rockefeller or Getty, have possessed great fortunes,
but equally important to their long-term reputation has been the
discernment with which they have bestowed their patronage.
Necessarily busy managing their wealth, they did not in practice
exercise such discernment alone. In each case, if we were able to
see behind the scenes, we would find some *éminence grise* or
consigliere who stood in the shadow of the fabled name, providing
the advice and practical assistance to realise the patron's vision.

Paul Pellisson-Fontanier was perhaps too well known and
widely admired a figure – especially in the literary salons of Paris
– to be considered to be in anyone's shadow, but such was the
role that he undertook for Nicolas. He was a Protestant from the
town of Béziers in Languedoc. As a law student in Toulouse, he
was a gifted scholar, who wrote a commentary on the
jurisprudence of the Emperor Justinian, but what came to
animate him every bit as much was a more general passion for the
Greek and Roman writers of antiquity.

His first visit to Paris in 1645, when he was just twenty-one,
was made in order to find a publisher for his book on Justinian.
His influential connection there was fellow Protestant Valentin
Conrart, who was secretary of the recently formed Académie
Française. Conrart helped Pellisson to get his book published,

but with his privileged position at the very heart of the capital's literary set, he also played a significant part in encouraging the young man to venture far beyond his early studies in juris-prudence. He let Pellisson sit in on the meetings of the Academy, which took place in his house, and introduced him to some of the many literary clubs that, after the example of the salon of the Marquise de Rambouillet, had sprung up all over Paris.

Cheerful and outgoing, Pellisson possessed the warmth, good humour and wit that were an asset in such society. He had intended to stay in Paris three months, but was so fêted and in demand that he was still there three years later.

The trip made a decisive impact on him. When he finally returned to his native Languedoc in 1648 to commence a career as an advocate in the town of Castres, he founded a salon there to facilitate the kind of literary debate he had known at the Academy. Determined to become a writer himself, he embarked on a translation of Homer's *Odyssey*, sending back the chapters for comment to Conrart and his friends in Paris.

In the summer of 1650 he caught smallpox. The disease chewed up his face and nearly blinded him. There could hardly have been a greater blow for someone whose whole life had been built around a social existence, yet at the same time what happened revealed just how very important books and poetry were to him. They sustained him through his solitude when, unable to endure the looks of revulsion that his appearance occasioned, he took refuge in the depths of the countryside, and they gave him the courage to seek out his old friends once again. In November 1650 he returned to Paris, where he continued his convalescence in Conrart's well-stocked library.

In this familiar surrounding he would often meet the members of the Academy, who, making light of his appearance, showed every bit as much regard for him as before. With their support, slowly he found the confidence to resume his previous salon life.

Indeed, the ready acceptance that they offered encouraged him to write an account of the Academy's early days. He called it a history, but it was as much a tribute to the friendship they had shown. He described the institution's informal origins in the group of writers and scholars who used to meet every Monday at Conrart's house. He explained how the late Cardinal Richelieu invested them with an official function, asking them to codify the rules of the French language and to prepare a dictionary. A constitution for the new body was established and statutes were drawn up. Richelieu's support gave it huge prestige, but it was of the informal nucleus that had existed beforehand that Pellisson wrote most fondly:

> They would meet without the least ceremony and discuss every possible subject from current affairs to literature. If anyone had recently written something, as was often the case, he would make it known and his companions would freely tell him what they thought of it. Afterwards, they might take a walk together or have a meal.
>
> In this way they continued for three or four years and, as I've heard many of them say, these meetings were so very useful and rewarding that when they look back on this first phase of the Academy it seems like a Golden Age: in all the innocence and freedom that accompany new beginnings, and without fuss, ceremony or any rule whatsoever other than that of friendship, they enjoyed together all the charm and pleasure that such intellectual exchange can offer.[1]

The members of the Academy were so pleased with the affectionate, but nonetheless accurate portrait that Pellisson provided of them, that they asked him to read his work aloud in their presence. When a year later their oldest member, Porchères Laugier, died at the age of ninety-two, they invited Pellisson to take his place – they had to wait until then because Richelieu's charter forbade them to have more than forty members.

Pellisson's appetite for literary conversation soon brought him in contact with Madeleine de Scudéry. A regular visitor to her salon, he was given the name of 'Acante' and, although 'Sappho' was nearly twenty years his senior, the two became inseparable companions. Since she had been born with as hideous an appearance as the pox had given him, they made rather unlikely lovers, but they shared a perfect romantic understanding, which they prized above the physical relationship that their friends continually speculated about but could not be sure actually existed.

The degree of both their ugliness and their devotion to each other was enough to give Sappho and Acante a life in legend. According to one story, Pellisson was walking along one day when a lady grabbed his hand and led him off to a painter's studio. 'That's the way to do it! Exactly like him,' she told the painter before hurrying off again. The painter told Pellisson to sit still and, when asked to explain what was going on, told him, 'Monsieur, this lady has commissioned me to paint the Temptation of Jesus Christ in the desert. We've been arguing for hours over what the devil should look like, and now she has found the perfect model!'[2] Sappho herself sat as a model for the celebrated engraver and portraitist Robert Nanteuil. 'With his inspired art, Nanteuil has, in drawing my image, revealed his great ability: I hate my eyes in the mirror; but I love them in his work.'[3]

If it was difficult to decide which of the two was the ugliest, the question was of no account to Sappho and Acante themselves. One verse of the time went, 'Pellisson's face is terrifying; but although this wretched boy is uglier than a monkey or a devil, Sappho thinks he's good-looking! That doesn't surprise me, because everyone likes his own kind.'[4]

The symbiotic dependency was such that when on some occasion Nicolas made a generous gift to Madeleine de Scudéry, Pellisson wrote – in verse – to offer his thanks on her behalf. Nicolas was so charmed by 'Le remercîment du Siècle à M. le Surintendant Foucquet'* that he wrote back a thank you for the thank you. A firm friendship was established and it was soon afterwards that Pellisson was invited to become Nicolas's private secretary. It didn't matter that one was a Protestant, the other a Jesuit-educated Catholic whose family had been zealous supporters of the Counter-Reformation – what mattered was the meeting of minds.

Like his new employer, Pellisson may have loved to discuss art and literature and philosophy, but he had an equal appetite for practical affairs, which he treated with every bit as much respect. Even as he was finishing his history of the Academy, he purchased for himself the office of *secrétaire du roi*, a position that required him to draw up and edit government decrees. De Scudéry marvelled at this facility for spontaneous and varied creation. 'He is capable of so many different things,' she wrote. 'I have seen him in one day concoct great speeches, business letters, love notes, epic poems, romances . . . He can write them even in the midst of a great gathering, as if he is hardly giving them any thought at all.'[5]

Such qualities made Pellisson an indispensable ally for Nicolas. His sensitive yet industrious nature provided the basis for a natural affinity that developed into a relationship of total trust. With his remarkable versatility he was able to integrate the different worlds that Nicolas inhabited from politics and finance to the arts, widening the scope of Nicolas's already huge ambition. At the very hub of Nicolas's activity, he was the essential figure imposing an overall coherence, co-ordinating and often

*'The Century's Thank you to Superintendent Foucquet'.

finding the people who would turn Nicolas's endless schemes into reality.

It is perhaps no accident that Pellisson began to work for Nicolas in 1656 just as he unveiled the project that remains his most enduring testament. For it required someone with Pellisson's gift for both the practical and the inspirational to marshal the team of talents that would build the 'great pleasure dome' that Nicolas decreed. The old castle at Vaux, which had been left to moulder ever since Nicolas had bought the estate over ten years earlier, was now pulled down to make way for an edifice of stone flanked by two pavilions. The project, which was to include a landscaped park, was of a scale and complexity that dwarfed anything Nicolas had previously attempted.

Nicolas signed the drawings for the new chateau in August 1656. Beneath his simple, compact signature was the far more florid one of his chosen architect, Louis Le Vau, branching out into an extravagant assembly of loops and curls that made the five letters of his name seem to take up the space of fifty. But the particular piece of showmanship that had most recommended Le Vau to Nicolas was the magnificent Château du Raincy, which the architect had designed just before the outbreak of the Fronde for the then Intendant of Finances, Jacques Bordier.

With its network of moats and pavilions clustering around a great central dome, Raincy offered the model of majesty that set Nicolas's own ideas in motion. It offered a starting point, which – together with the regular notes and observations on Italian buildings that he continued to receive from his brother Louis in Rome – swelled his sense of architectural possibility.

The engagement of Le Vau was really as much the commencement of a dialogue as a commission. Less interested in what the Château du Raincy was than what it could inspire, Nicolas was pleased to discover that Le Vau, who had recently designed several houses for private clients on the Île Saint-Louis, was an enthusiastic, flexible and pragmatic professional. Happy to discuss the possible modification of all sketches and perspectives, Le Vau took Nicolas's talk of Italian architects not as a threat, but as a welcome challenge and inspiration.

At Raincy, Le Vau had worked with the painter Charles Le Brun and the landscape gardener André Le Nôtre. Both were invited to join Nicolas's new team. Le Brun would already have been warmly recommended to Nicolas by Poussin, who regarded him as a rare worthwhile exception among contemporary French painters.

A son of a sculptor, Le Brun had been a famous child prodigy, who began to draw at the age of three with dead coals plucked from the fire. By the time he was nine, he was already modelling in clay and confidently carving heraldic eagles and griffins in wood. He became an apprentice of the painter Simon Vouet, who was known as the 'French Raphael'. But unable to hide his contempt for his master's shortcomings as a painter, he soon left Vouet's studio to study the paintings of the real Raphael at Fontainebleau.

Barely fifteen years old, the young Le Brun astonished the Court when he copied Raphael's *Holy Family* with such fidelity that the only way to distinguish his work from the original was its smaller size. Soon the boy was taking on commissions for Cardinal Richelieu. When the Cardinal showed the finished paintings to Nicolas Poussin – during the brief, bitter stay in Paris that made him decide to spend the rest of his life in Italy – the great painter told him: 'If these are the work of a young man, then he will one day be a very great artist.'[6] Indeed, Poussin was so impressed by the prodigy that when he set off back to Rome in 1642, he took Le Brun with him, over the next few years providing the guidance that would help his prediction come true.

In Rome Le Brun studied the great master's style closely, but also immersed himself in the treasures of the city, familiarising himself with its ancient monuments, making endless drawings and notes. When he returned to Paris three years later, he acknowledged only Poussin to be his superior, although – his ambition having no limit – he was determined one day to surpass even him.

Becoming the founder of the Royal Academy of Painting, he delivered its opening lecture in early 1648. Not yet thirty, he had achieved countless splendid commissions, received every accolade, so that no task seemed beyond him – not even to paint the Queen's dream. The image of a cross surrounded by angels had long haunted Anne. The vision gave her such a powerful sense of divine prophecy that it seemed a sin to keep it to herself. So she asked Le Brun to paint what she had seen. The result was so exact that she had the canvas hung in a place of honour in the Louvre.

It seemed that there was no feat of the brush beyond Le Brun's capability. But for all he had already accomplished, the sheer scale and complexity of Vaux-le-Vicomte made it the most important commission of his life. He must have known too that Nicolas Foucquet had been in close touch with his old teacher Nicolas Poussin, to whom undoubtedly he would have entrusted the assignment if only he had been able to lure him back to France. It was one of those rare occasions on which Le Brun was made to feel overshadowed and second-best. Usually his clients were overwhelmed with gratitude when he accepted a commission, but Nicolas made him feel as though he were still an apprentice.

One of the early preparatory sketches that Le Brun drew for his new client was a *Rape of the Sabine Women*; his mentor Poussin had made two attempts on the subject nearly two decades previously. Le Brun's sketch failed to make Nicolas feel that there was any need for a third: with amused but withering irony, he observed that Le Brun's women looked as though they were enjoying themselves. The painter snatched up the sketch after

Nicolas had left the room and tore it up, throwing the pieces into a bin. The gesture may have been a mark of his anger, but it was also an acknowledgement that he knew Nicolas was right.

Nicolas had got behind the shield of outward brilliance to take the measure of Le Brun, as perhaps only Poussin had managed to do before. It meant that in the work Le Brun undertook at Vaux, there remained behind the surface swagger a sense that he still needed to prove himself. The resulting degree of doubt brought to his painting an invaluable extra human dimension.

The third member of Nicolas's team had neither rival nor reason to feel overshadowed by anyone. Yet the nature of his profession was such that he is remembered more for his modesty than his pride. The great landscape gardener André Le Nôtre offered yet another example of the all-round skill that was such an appealing feature of the seventeenth century. Following in the footsteps of both his father, Jean, and grandfather, Pierre, André Le Nôtre would became a royal gardener at the Tuileries. His career was a case of natural progress within a world that had been familiar to him since birth. His reputation as France's greatest gardener resulted less from ambition than from growth in the most ideal conditions. One of the plants he cared for in the royal hothouse could easily serve as a metaphor for his career. When the King invited him to choose his own coat of arms to celebrate the noble title that his garden landscapes had won for him, he asked for three snails and a head of cabbage, remarking: 'It is due to my spade that I am recipient of all the kindnesses with which Your Majesty honours me.'[7]

In a garden there may be many snails, but otherwise the plants and flowers live and grow peaceably together within their prescribed borders. It's perhaps difficult to appreciate in Britain, where a profusion of Capability Brown landscapes marks the nation's passion for the more romantic and wild aspects of nature, but in the seventeenth century the measure of a gardener's skill was the extent to which he could suggest an inherent order and pattern.

The chestnut trees that Le Nôtre planted in Vaux's gardens were as much an example of careful design as the great mile-long man-made canal that they flanked. Still saplings, they may have lacked the majesty they would later assume, but their very slenderness allowed one to perceive a growth that observed strict principles, sending forth first a symmetrical splay of twin branches along one axis, then, duly following beneath, the second at right-angles to the first, and so on, so that if you could look down from the top of the tree you would perceive a continuous cross-pattern through the succession of branches. The leaves were no less disciplined, each spray forming a perfect fan of seven.

The very essence of Le Nôtre's job lay in bringing such harmony to every part of Nicolas's domain. Indeed, the extent to which this harmony was a working principle for him, both governing and extending the inter-relatedness of things, really made a nonsense of the term 'gardener'. His craft called as much for the skills of a painter, architect and mathematician. This was evident in the careful geometry of the parterres; in the complex array of fountains with their spectacular but carefully organised water displays; in the way the gardens cohered seamlessly with the house, so inseparable that both appeared to be the product of one mind; in the dispensation of grass, hedges, woods and flowers like colours on an artist's palette. The nurseries and potting sheds of the Tuileries had been only a part of Le Nôtre's training; equally important was the time he had spent studying draftsmanship with Simon Vouet, or structural engineering with Jacques Le Mercier.

Once building began at Vaux, it proceeded at an extraordinarily rapid pace. Nicolas, who had achieved a position of pre-eminence through his magician's ability to conjure large sums of money out of nothing, took a similar attitude towards houses. Unlike the endlessly dithering Cardinal Mazarin, he had a capacity for swift, spontaneous action. Once an idea had been conceived, his restless temperament spurred him on to give it reality.

By September 1657, little less than a year after the plans had been approved, the stonework had been completed. Concerned to conceal the huge expense of the project and perhaps also – like any good showman – wishing to preserve the surprise of the eventual unveiling, he discouraged visitors while the works were in progress. In February 1657 Nicolas wrote this note to his servant Bénigne Courtois: 'A gentleman in the neighbourhood told the Queen that he has spent the past few days at Vaux and counted 900 men in the workshop. To stop this kind of thing, we must carry out our plan to employ guards and to keep the gates locked. I'd be happy if you could speed everything up as much as you can ahead of the time when everyone goes to the country, and as few workers as possible should be visible.'[8] A few months later the head of Nicolas's household, François Vatel, passed on another anxious note from Nicolas: 'He would like to know when Monsieur Colbert visited Vaux . . . where he went, who looked after him during his walk and even what he said.'[9] Of all the visitors the Cardinal and his secretary were by far the least welcome. Every week they plagued him with new demands for money – demands that he knew would become all the more pressing if they could see how free he was with the purse strings at Vaux. He feared, too, that they would make the most of any excuse to turn against him.

But it was unrealistic to imagine that the extraordinary scale of the works could be hidden. There were times when there were not just 900 workers labouring at Vaux, but 2,000. In any case it was becoming day by day more and more apparent as the works progressed that Vaux-le-Vicomte was turning into an extraordinary jewel that far exceeded even Nicolas's hopes. If it was important to discourage visitors for a while longer, he still wanted to show it off just as soon as possible.

In the meantime he asked Pellisson to find a writer who could quietly chronicle its marvels. Gathering nightly in the library at Saint-Mandé, there was no shortage of promising candidates for such an assignment. 'Everyone knows that this great statesman is as much the Superintendent of literature as he is of finances, that his house is as open to poets as it is to businessmen,' wrote the great dramatist Pierre Corneille, in gratitude for Nicolas's support.[10] But rather than turn to Corneille or de Scudéry or Paul Scarron or even the precocious Charles Perrault, a young man in his twenties who would one day achieve worldwide fame with his fairy tales *Little Red Riding Hood*, *Sleeping Beauty* and *Cinderella* – and with Pellisson's encouragement had begun to work on a *Dialogue de l'amour et l'amitié* – he chose an obscure friend no one had heard of – which was like giving the glass slipper to someone who hadn't even attended the ball.

Nicolas, who had complete trust in his secretary's judgement, was more intrigued than dismayed. Used to Pellisson's knack of turning what often seemed unlikely beginnings into the most glorious solutions, he was only too happy to wait to be surprised. So although on the day – some time in 1657 – that Pellisson first ushered the unknown poet into Nicolas's office at Saint-Mandé – there would have been very little to suggest his future reputation, Nicolas was sure that it would be a very great one.

A large, slightly shambling figure in his mid-thirties, Jean de la Fontaine had good reason to feel embarrassed by how little he had written. The only work he could boast of any length was a translation of *The Eunuch* by the Roman poet Terence. It hadn't even been performed, although at Pellisson's pleading Conrart had at least managed to find a publisher for it.*

*A. Courbé, Paris, 1654.

In the absence of any real achievement, the writer was heavily dependent on Pellisson to make a good case for him. The two had met more than ten years previously when, on his very first visit to Paris, Pellisson was making his name among the many literary clubs that were thriving before the outbreak of the Fronde. One such club that Pellisson attended was known as the 'Round Table'. He soon recognised Jean de la Fontaine to be its most talented member, even if this particular knight was generally considered to be something of a slacker.

Endlessly distractable, La Fontaine was a born drifter. When he was twenty he drifted into the Church, fancying that he had a vocation. It required only a brief spell as a novice in the austere order of the Oratory to realise that, although he had a very real knack for contemplation, it was not of the religious kind. Dropping out, he drifted into law, but quickly became a truant, instead of his legal studies writing verses to amuse his fellow knights of the Round Table, or disappearing home to Château-Thierry.

A small town on the River Marne, about fifty miles to the east of Paris, it was here that La Fontaine was brought up. It was the one fixed point in a life of flux. He tolerated Paris for the company he found there, but he was happiest in the countryside around Château-Thierry.

Pellisson would surely have stressed to Nicolas the importance of trying to imagine the place. Nestling in the wooded river valley, it was an oasis of calm, which somehow even the battles of the recent Fronde had spared, although it would not be so lucky 300 years later. No one could have imagined the ruined husk of a town it would become in the 1914–18 war, when a song would tell of 'battle-weary Château-Thierry'. A strategic hub of the Second Battle of the Marne, it acquired a new reputation as one of the many symbols of twentieth-century carnage.

But in the seventeenth century there were few better places for a sylvan poet. The trees that twentieth-century munitions would reduce to shattered stumps still stood tall. Flanking both sides of the river, a fairy-tale forest ran up to the ramparts of a castle that belonged to the duc de Bouillon.

La Fontaine had been born in one of the houses that stood in the castle's shadow, on the rue des Cordeliers. His father, Charles de la Fontaine, was warden of the region's waters and forests. The job entailed managing the woodland, supervising the fisheries and maintaining the bridges along the river. On many days Jean would accompany his father into the woods. Owls and foxes and crows and squirrels were his childhood companions, and glades that seemed enchanted his natural habitat.

It required no great leap of the imagination to write of the goddesses, muses and nymphs who lived in such places when he often fancied that he could already see them. But although the knights of the Round Table could see from the scribbles that La Fontaine brought along to their meetings that writing of such things was obviously his vocation, too often he would lose himself in idle trifles. The challenge was somehow to get him to commit himself to the sustained effort that would produce something of real consequence.

When Pellisson became secretary to the Superintendent, unlocking the genius of Jean de la Fontaine was at the very top of his list of priorities. He had a hunch that the wonders of Vaux would provide the key. Nicolas was spending more and more of his precious time dwelling on the project, slipping away from Paris whenever he could to inspect the works. The enthusiastic tales that he brought back from the building site, as well as his comments on how he imagined its future, emboldened Pellisson to suggest that La Fontaine, for all his lack of accomplishment, might well be the writer Nicolas was looking for.

So he dug up some of the amusing but light-weight pieces that La Fontaine had brought to the Round Table, which demonstrated naked talent if not staying power. Showing them to Nicolas, he proposed a trial, in which La Fontaine would write a long poem on a subject of his choosing, but in an epic style suitable to celebrate an achievement of Vaux's scale. It would be a test of the poet's discipline. Only then, if the Superintendent liked the poem enough, would La Fontaine be invited to write about Vaux-le-Vicomte itself. With his usual confidence in Pellisson, Nicolas did not hesitate to give his agreement.

Nicolas wanted Vaux to be a monument to all that he had achieved. Yet at the same time it was a façade of serenity, which masked all that he feared to lose. Among his guests at Saint-Mandé, he remained a picture of outward calm, impressing them with an apparent ease of manner and confidence, but in the privacy of his office he had to grapple with a whole host of worries. At the forefront of his mind was the conviction that the Cardinal was seeking to undermine him. Theirs was a relationship that had always been based on mutual advantage rather than liking. The niggling mistrust that had been a constant element in their dealings meant that Nicolas often felt more like Scheherazade than the powerful minister whom the artists and scholars at Saint-Mandé courted – only safe so long as he continued to provide the Cardinal with regular funds.

The burden of keeping Mazarin satisfied soon caused him to forget all about Vaux and poetry. The expectations of a final victory over the Spanish made such peacetime pursuits seem irresponsibly previous, as the opening of a new campaigning season in early 1658 doubled an already impossible load. With the war at a critical stage, the Cardinal's demands for money became even more insistent. Nicolas had to struggle to meet exceptional military expenditure while at the same time coping with the unrest that the privations of war were causing.

Through the spring there occurred one crisis after another. In

March there was a mutiny of the garrison at Le Havre. Then in April the Toulouse Parlement blocked the payment of royal revenues, even arresting some of the King's officials. It provided a pretext for some elements in the Paris Parlement to begin their own intrigues, raising the spectre of renewed civil war. To add to the growing chaos, in May there was a revolt in the Sologne against army levies on the land.

Accompanying the King to northern France, where a 20,000-strong French army was about to take on the Spanish, Mazarin left the chief responsibility for dealing with these emergencies on Nicolas's shoulders, yet at the same time did not hesitate to send regular letters from Calais begging for ever more funds. Even a decisive victory over the Spanish at Dunkirk failed to bring about a respite. On the contrary, it served only to make the Cardinal's importuning all the more urgent. He wrote that every gain would be reversed if Nicolas didn't promptly provide the necessary finance. Adopting his favourite tactic of abject desperation, he declared, 'I don't know where else to turn. I don't have a penny that I can call my own, nor the means of borrowing from my friends.'[11]

Although the Cardinal knew well enough how overworked Nicolas was, the more help Nicolas gave, the more help Mazarin seemed to expect. But then, just a few days after the victory at Dunkirk had been declared, Nicolas's household announced that he had succumbed to a dangerous fever. Over the next few days the reports became more and more grave. He was close to death, it seemed, in his few waking moments only able to find the lucidity of mind to clarify certain details concerning his estate that were vital to resolve while he was still alive. The idea of attending to any other business was impossible.

Basile Foucquet, who was often with the Cardinal in Calais, confirmed the bad news. Mazarin was so disturbed that he sent his own envoy to Saint-Mandé. Monsieur Toucheprez was to communicate the Cardinal's heartfelt desire for the Superintendent's speedy recovery, but at the same time gently enquire when the next instalment of badly needed funds might be expected. Too impatient to wait for an answer, and doubting the ability of Toucheprez to be suitably insistent, he soon afterwards sent his secretary Colbert off to Saint-Mandé too.

As the Cardinal's written letter of instructions makes clear, Nicolas's parlous state of health made it all the more necessary to get to the point. 'Please tell the Superintendent that I have never been so pressed for money as I am now . . .'[12] If there were any potential financiers that Nicolas hadn't been able to see because of his illness, Colbert was to offer to speak to them in his place.

The Cardinal's panic was such that it must have been tempting for Nicolas to keep to his sickbed a little longer. But he had made his point. In July he returned to his office after a miraculous recovery and the funds began to flow again.

9

Behind the Façade

One of the more pleasant surprises of Nicolas's convalescence – if indeed he ever had been ill – was to receive the promised poem from La Fontaine. It had a charm that made Nicolas read it through without interruption, even though after so many days of inactivity a longer queue of people than usual would have been waiting to see him. The subject La Fontaine had chosen was Venus and Adonis. The story was as follows.

Adonis resides on the slopes of Mount Ida, home to the Muses. Here, under the leafy shade of trees whose branches seem almost to touch the sky, he pursues an idyllic, carefree life. Far from the cities, he spends his days hunting the animals of the forest, enjoying quiet repose in Ida's meadows, taking refreshment from its cool streams.

Most beautiful of all men, he wins the admiration of even the immortals. The goddess Venus falls in love with him and, enlisting the wiles of her son Cupid, causes Adonis in turn to fall in love with her. For a while they live together in the forest. Happy in each other's company, they enjoy the most perfect peace, but then Venus is compelled to return to the heavens to dispel rumours that she is neglecting her responsibilities.

Nicolas admired the conceit of the poem, which had been cleverly tailored to capture his concerns through veiled allusion: just like Venus, he too was about to return to onerous responsibilities. La Fontaine had fashioned a poem that was timeless in its Arcadian setting, yet at the same time evoked contemporary issues with ease. It was universal yet personal, demonstrating a combination of wit and genuine feeling that Nicolas found immensely pleasing. As he read on, he must already have known that here was the poet to do justice to Vaux.

Venus begs Adonis to be true to her while she is gone, to think only of her and not to dally with any of the nymphs in the forest. Above all, she begs him not to risk his life hunting the fierce beasts that roam the woods in case she should lose him for ever.

Weeping, Adonis watches Venus's chariot regain the heavens and when he awakes the next morning she seems no more than a deceiving dream. Without her, Ida's forest glades and mountain pastures, once so clement, become for him a desert and his solitude an aching, unbearable void.

The only respite he can find from his loneliness is his former pastime of hunting, which he forgets that Venus had warned him against. A giant boar has been rampaging through Ida's forests and plains, causing havoc in the local farmers' orchards and fields, destroying their crops and attacking their livestock. Summoning together the young hunters of the area, Adonis decides that it is time to rid the land of this menace once and for all.

They track the beast to his lair – a cesspool of stagnant water deep in the forest – and send in the hounds. Hurtling out, the crazed creature instantly gores to death two of the dogs, then turns on the horses and their riders. Sinking his teeth deep into the flank of the first horse he reaches, he brings it tumbling down and sends its rider scrambling for the safety of a tree. Hurrying to take their revenge, the other hunters close ranks to cut off any possible escape. They unleash arrows and plunge their spears deep into its side, but against all reason the beast will not die. The blows seems only to stir it to an even greater ferocity. Whirling round, it scythes down men, dogs and horses indiscriminately.

The nymphs of the forest – who are able to see into the future – look on with dismay. The violence of the animal's attack provokes presentiments they would prefer not to have. Hoping that Adonis might yet escape his destiny, they use their magic to make him take a path away from the battle. They silence the hunters' horns, even wipe the day from Adonis's memory, returning him to that tranquil time before the goddess had come down to Ida, when he was still able to enjoy the peace of the forest.

But one of the hunters, Palmyrus, badly wounded in the fighting, is carried to the same glade and set down where Adonis can see his broken body. Angry and ashamed, Adonis rejoins the fray. In his rage only one thing matters now – that the animal should pay for his comrades' blood. He even implores Venus not to be offended that, against her instructions, he is now risking danger, but to help him kill the creature.

As Adonis catches up with his enemy, Venus, looking on from heaven, guides his arrow home, driving it deep into the boar's side. Reeling, the beast twists round and, turning back on itself, charges down its assailant. Rearing up, it tears open Adonis's chest with its tusks, as in the same moment Adonis plunges his spear deep into its guts. Triumphant, he watches the creature slump down, rejoicing in its death even as his own life's blood trickles away. Then at last, closing his eyes, on the very cusp of oblivion, he gives a long, grief-stricken sigh as he recalls the goddess who loved him.

Nicolas was astonished by this poem because La Fontaine had, by some miracle, described the refuge of enchanted glades and fountains that he had wanted to create at Vaux, yet at the same time fathomed his deepest desires and fears. Venus represented the serenity he longed for but cheated himself of daily. And the boar charging through the forest, dealing death and destruction –

well, that wasn't difficult to figure out either. Just look at the chaos beyond his office door – war, revolt, illness, debt, Mazarin. He strove to create an illusion of perfect order, but he lived permanently on the edge of disaster. He might build Vaux, but would he ever be able to enjoy it? Sooner or later some menace would come rampaging through his life to snatch it away. Somehow La Fontaine had sensed this, that what he was building was not a palace, but a dream. At least now he had the poet he needed to chart this dream. For with *Venus and Adonis* La Fontaine had shown that he already knew what Vaux was all about before he had even visited it.

La Fontaine wanted to turn round to take in once again the sight of the dome – solid, massive, yet ethereal, seeming about to float up to the heavens. It was the perfect image of how La Fontaine had always imagined authority should be – commanding, yet serene, inspirational in its own confidence – an emanation of the Superintendent himself, the man who had brought Vaux-le-Vicomte into existence.

André Le Nôtre's gardens contained their own genius, yet in their unfinished state still demanded imagination. The hillside that rose up beyond the newly dug canal was of raked earth, waiting to be laid with turf. The trees that would flank this gentle slope had yet to be planted. Even when they were, it would be at least twenty years before they were high enough to suggest the Arcadia that Le Nôtre had intended. His greatest ally was time, which would bestow upon Vaux a beauty that his own generation would not witness. Vaux-le-Vicomte, it was clear, had been created not just for one time, but for all time.

Seeing Vaux in its unfinished state, and realising that even after the last sapling had been planted, many more years would be required for it to achieve maturity, La Fontaine decided that in order to capture the truth of the place he would have to rely not on the naked eye but the mind's eye. 'So I pretended that one spring night I nodded off and implored the god of sleep to allow me to see Vaux in a dream . . .'[1]

If this chapter takes similar licence in imagining La Fontaine's first visit to Vaux, it is not to depart from the truth but to get closer to it. In the spring of 1659 the poet *did* travel to Vaux to fulfil the commission that he won with the success of *Venus and Adonis* to write about the chateau. The works were then nearing completion, but the estate was still a turmoil of builders, decorators and landscapers.

In the house La Fontaine would have found Le Brun directing the decoration of the state rooms, which with their magnificent ceilings of mythological allusion offered a counterpart to the poet's verse. Possibly even Le Brun himself – who for the duration of the assignment had been camping with his wife on the first floor – gave the poet a guided tour. In any case, we know what La Fontaine saw from the verses he later wrote. Of all the splendid chambers that he described, he devoted special attention to one that enjoyed a prominent position on the garden side of the house.

About forty feet square, it boasted a high vaulted ceiling. Eight of the nine muses gathered in pairs at each corner: Melpomene, the muse of tragedy, sitting back to back with her sister Thalia, the muse of comedy; in the next corner, Erato, of lyric poetry, and Polyhymnia, of elegy; in the third, Urania, of astronomy, and Calliope of epic poetry; and in the last, Euterpe, of music, and Terpsichore, of dance. The ninth muse, Clio, the muse of history, occupied the ceiling's central, octagonal panel, helping Faith to ascend into the sky.

The muses were 'so well painted that I thought I was looking at the divinities themselves', wrote La Fontaine.[2]

I was completely fooled, even I who never stray far from Helicon.[3] This place I found them in, so different from their usual abode, caused me to cry out to them: 'What are you doing here, my divine mistresses, so far away from your mountain home? What charms can these panels and cornices hold for you who used to love the silence of the forest. What has curbed your taste for solitude? How come it is palaces that please you now?'

La Fontaine had many more such questions, but, he noted, 'Not one of the nine sisters deigned to reply.'If Charles Le Brun had been there to explain on their behalf, he might perhaps have told La Fontaine that the muses had lent their names to a room that Nicolas wanted to rival the celebrated Blue Chamber in the Hôtel de Rambouillet. Called the Salon of the Muses in honour of its permanent residents, it was intended to give all those who cared about art and progress the maximum of comfort and inspiration. Nicolas's privileged guests would be able to sit in armchairs of Chinese velvet and stretch their legs out on the Persian carpet underneath. On the walls, they would be able to admire eight finely woven tapestries from the famed Mortlake workshop in London. The handiwork of Flemish weavers who had fled endless wars for the comparative peace of England, these tapestries had been imported from London to expedite the chateau's decoration, but soon Le Brun hoped to be able to replace them with new tapestries based on his own cartoons. For Nicolas had recently established under the painter's direction a tapestry factory in a ruined convent in the nearby village of Maincy. No expense, no effort, was to be spared in the quest for perfection.

Perhaps it was here, among the muses, that one could find the truest measure of what Nicolas was trying to achieve. La Fontaine expressed his delight to see the daughters of Jupiter given such a place of honour in 'one of the most beautiful rooms in the house',[4] but the tribute was as much to all those who worked in the muses' name.

Looking up to the ceiling, La Fontaine would have seen the

winged muse Clio helping the goddesses Prudence and Virtue to bear Fidelity aloft to the heavens. A golden scroll unfurling from her left wrist bore the familiar words of the Foucquet motto, '*Quo Non Ascendet?*' In her right hand Clio holds a trumpet with which she seems about to herald this ascension, while behind her Apollo, a calm and deadly rearguard, fires arrows at a horde of pursuing monsters. Under the god's terrible onslaught, these creatures of destruction seem on the point of tumbling earthwards, just as Fidelity and her companions, on their arduous but sure path to the heavens, reach a sunlit opening in the dark clouds.

There was an easy, obvious way to read the picture to the glory of the chateau's owner. But its true power lay in the possession of not one meaning but many. Yes, certainly, it was the story of the royal servant who had remained loyal to his sovereign through the bitter years of the Fronde, with his wisdom, faith and courage dispelling the forces of darkness. But it contained as many interpretations as the number of visitors to behold it. Nicolas's Jesuit education had instilled in him an appetite for myth, enigma and allusion. In this golden age for the practice, he fully encouraged the use of allegory among the artists who worked for him. But they all knew that such allegory possessed charm only so long as it was allowed to wander free of strict association.

La Fontaine himself captured the attitude in a preface he wrote to explain the verses that he wrote in celebration of Vaux. In the *Songe de Vaux* (Dream of Vaux) he imagines himself, after his visit to the chateau, strolling along to nearby Maincy, where Nicolas had built his tapestry factory. Here, in a meadow lined with weeping willows, he sees Cupid sing to a group of nymphs who dance in the moonlight. Cupid's song is about two beautiful maidens, Aminte and Sylvie, who boast that they can capture even Cupid's heart. But who are Aminte and Sylvie supposed to be?

The reader, if he wishes, can believe that Aminte is a specific person; or, if he wishes, that she represents the beauty of women in general; or even the beauty of all kinds of things. He can accept whichever of these three explanations he prefers. Those who look for a hidden meaning in everything and consider that this kind of poem should be allegorical can embrace the last two explanations. But nor do I mind if people want to imagine Aminte to be this person or that person: it makes the work all the more engaging without taking away anything from its style.[5]

What was true of La Fontaine's poem was equally true of Le Brun's painting. And to the extent that we can think of them in the Salon of the Muses looking at the picture together – these two artists who accorded as much importance as Nicolas to the Muses – it would surely be only natural for them both to look upon the work as a metaphor of their own artistic creation, although this is not to deny all the other possible meanings that the picture might have had for them.

Clio, then, the Muse of History, was La Fontaine, recording for posterity one of the great collaborative feats of *Le Grand Siècle*, while Providence, Virtue and Fidelity embodied all the cares, inspiration and faith that sustained Le Brun, Le Vau and Le Nôtre in their partnership to build Vaux into something greater than any single one of them could have hoped to achieve alone. All three possessed the imperfections of mortals, but together, under Nicolas's protection and with Nicolas's inspiration, they achieved something perfect, something that they would never ever again equal. For who else can Nicolas be in this artists' inter- pretation of the picture other than Apollo, the Muses' god who inspires all artists?

Apollo unleashes his arrows in the background with a calm that might easily cause one to overlook the violence of the winged monsters' pursuit. In Vaux-le-Vicomte Nicolas may have created a vision of perfect harmony, but he was no less embattled and harried than before. The circumstances of its creation, against a background of misfortune, conflict and suspicion, make it seem less like one of the great monuments to civilisation than an exercise in wishful thinking – an illusion of permanence where none really existed.

The great challenge in a precarious existence was to put down roots. At the end of 1656 Nicolas and Marie-Madeleine were mourning the loss of their firstborn, François. In a letter of condolence, a Jesuit friend of the Foucquet family advised the bereaved couple that they should learn to love death, as the only realistic response to the nature of things.[6] But there was also some comfort to be found in the extended family. Just a few weeks later, on 12 February 1657, the Foucquets gathered together in the church of Saint-Nicolas-des-Champs for the marriage of Marie, Nicolas's daughter by his deceased first wife. Sixteen years old, she was marrying a captain in the King's Guard, Armand de Béthune, the marquis de Charost. It was surely a promising new branch. But fate so often had some nasty surprise in store. If it wasn't disease, then one was as likely to succumb to the simple malice of men. This is what Nicolas most feared in 1657.

By the summer the walls of the house had been nearly completed, but the increasingly impatient behaviour of the Cardinal made Nicolas wonder whether he would be around to see the end of the project. Aware of Mazarin's criticisms of him, which, however, were never made directly to his face, Nicolas did not hesitate to be direct in return. In June he fired off this angry letter: 'I was very upset to learn from several different quarters of the continuous complaints Your Eminence has made concerning lack of money and the poor administration of the finances. I had hoped, on account of the great care I take to satisfy you and the promptness with which I have paid all the sums Your Eminence has demanded from the beginning of winter to the present day, that I would not only be spared these reproaches but even deserve a few words of gratitude . . .'[7] Beneath Nicolas's indignation lay the suspicion that people were scheming to turn the Cardinal against him. He went on, 'If Your Eminence would be so good as to reflect upon my conduct . . . you will agree that it is not reasonable that, as soon as the King is away from Paris, I should be exposed to the attacks of my opponents and envious people who would not dare to behave in such a manner in front of me and so instead take advantage of their access to Your Eminence.' Nicolas then addressed the specific complaints that had been made against him, one of which was that he spent far too much time in the country. 'Since my estate is ten leagues from Paris and in the past three years I haven't spent more than eight days there all included, I don't think one can say that I take too much holiday. As for Saint-Mandé, I don't consider that to be being away from Paris, since I go there only to avoid those who beg me for money, and to work solidly with the least interruption, it being difficult to say what I occupy myself with other than continual work.'

Soon afterwards Nicolas received a warning from his friend the Marquise d'Asserac, which suggested that he had been right to be on his guard. She had heard from two well-connected informants that some members of the Parlement and even figures close to Nicolas's own circle were plotting against him. 'Be careful! Overlook nothing,' she wrote. 'Great fortunes tend to lead to envy: the more yours rises, the more your enemies will hate you and work against you.'[8]

Convinced that the time had finally come to take some precautionary measures, Nicolas sat down in his office at Saint-Mandé one evening to draft an elaborate contingency plan.[9] In a lengthy preamble, he spelt out not only the character failings of the Cardinal but also the nature of the larger situation that meant he was somebody particularly to be feared. Mazarin, Nicolas argued, was quick to form unfavourable impressions of people – particularly those who held important posts and enjoyed general esteem. He was dangerous not only because of his jealousy and 'natural timidity', but because 'the complete sway he enjoys over the King and Queen makes it easy for him to undertake whatever he wishes'. If ever he felt threatened, he would use his position to destroy his perceived enemy completely.

Indeed, Nicolas believed that the Cardinal would already have acted against him had it not been for his fear of the Foucquet family's extensive connections – two brothers bishops, a mother who was a friend of the Queen, and many in-laws who occupied important offices or wielded influence within the merchant and banking community. Nicolas's family possessed tentacles that reached deep into the establishment. Furthermore, in the Parlement Nicolas still held the office of Attorney-General, which gave him immunity from prosecution. His wide network of alliances provided yet another layer of protection. In the provinces either he himself or his friends possessed strongholds where it was possible, in taking refuge, to buy time and rally sympathetic forces in opposition.

All these reasons, Nicolas believed, would cause the Cardinal to leave him in his post for the meantime, yet quietly work to bring about his sudden, swift and total downfall. 'From my own familiarity with his thoughts and from what I've heard elsewhere, he will not move against me so long as he believes there is the slightest chance that I might survive such an attempt and that he might be left exposed to the resentment of dangerous opponents.' The 'knife in the back' was of course a tactic that Mazarin had used in the past, arresting the Great Condé just days after sending him a letter expressing his devotion.

The possibility of such a surprise attack, which would leave him no time to react, caused Nicolas to set out his response in the most exhaustive detail. 'First, in the case where I am imprisoned and my brother the Abbé isn't, then his orders are to be followed, assuming that he is free to act and retains the regard for me which he ought to have and which I have no doubt he still does have. If we are both imprisoned but can issue instructions from our place of captivity, then once again our orders are to be followed and this document will be redundant.'

But if such communication was made impossible, then his friends, servants and family were to act as he now dictated in writing. They were to urge his gaolers to allow him to have a valet, preferably Vatel. They should let a few days pass, and then, expressing concern that the prisoner was not eating his food, ask that he be allowed to have his own cook. Next they should ask that he be provided with books and permitted to resolve any pressing domestic business. After some more days had gone by, they should say that he was ill and ask that his doctor, Jean Pecquet, be allowed to stay with him in prison.

Nicolas spelt out every little wile, every little trick, that was to be used on his behalf. After the initial requests had been made, a few months should be allowed to go by in which only his close family should show any concern for his welfare. Meanwhile his allies would work in secret to rally and prepare his supporters. 'Madame du Plessis-Bellière, in whom I have complete trust, and from whom I have never kept the slightest secret, is to be consulted in all such matters and her orders followed, if she is still free. It may even be necessary to entreat her to withdraw to some safe place. She knows all my true friends . . .'

A catalogue then followed of the true friends, with details of the garrisons they would command, the towns they would fortify and the ports they would blockade. It amounted to a meticulously organised rebellion against the Cardinal's authority. The simple, but calculated manner of the planning found an echo in the image of Apollo on the salon ceiling coolly letting loose his arrows at the chasing fiends of discord, mounting this rearguard action as if it were a natural part of everyday existence. Had we been around to share Nicolas's worries, had we been one of the 'true friends' whom he felt able to bring into his network of resistance, here is one more meaning we might have found in the picture.

The ubiquity of discord was such that Nicolas had to fear it even in his own family. Basile, long since his chief brother-in-arms, was to be obeyed, he had written in his plan, 'assuming that he . . . retains the regard for me which he ought to have and which I have no doubt he still does have'. But with hindsight, these words suggest the very ambivalence he sought to deny. The relationship between the two brothers was coming under increasing strain. Basile's blind loyalty to the Cardinal, for whom he continued to work as a quasi-chief of secret police, meant that he would only have contemplated turning against him with extreme reluctance. He would certainly not have welcomed Nicolas putting him into a position of having to choose. Meanwhile Nicolas was growing more impatient with having to tolerate his brother's ever embarrassing antics. There was not only his stormy, long-running and highly public affair with the duchesse de Chatillôn, but also the general pleasure he seemed to take in giving offence, often among the most influential of people. The latest example that summer was Mademoiselle de Montpensier, who had been officially forgiven for siding with Condé during the Fronde and welcomed back to the Court. She was furious to discover that Basile had spread the rumour that she had left her fortune to Condé – who was then still a rebel fighting with Spain against his own country – and that she would probably be sent back into exile. The Cardinal ordered Basile to apologise, but predictably his insincere manner of doing so only made the Great Mademoiselle even more angry. It required Nicolas, whom she considered to be 'a wise and sensible man',[10] to settle the matter.

So passed the strange summer of 1657. By day, Nicolas pored over the latest drawings for arguably the finest house ever to be built in France, slipping away whenever he could to inspect progress in person; but at night he imagined an alternative scenario in which he had lost everything. It was the mindset of a time in which extreme reverses were common. Just a year later the pendulum had swung back again. After the victory over the Spanish at Dunkirk and his recovery from serious illness, Nicolas felt confident enough to put away his contingency plan. The Cardinal seemed to appreciate once again how indispensable he was. In this reality of dramatic, continual changes of fortune, the only really certain thing was the house. That summer saw the crowning moment of its construction. The great dome was put in place, as if to mark the victory over Spain and Nicolas's recovery. Its weighty but elegant mass offered a rare glimpse of permanence. The pendulum would turn again, but Nicolas knew that whatever happened the dream of Vaux-le-Vicomte had been realised, even if he would not be around to enjoy it.

The lesson of life was that you had to make the most of the pre-vailing weather. So now that the sun was shining again, Nicolas gave rein to a whole host of adventurous schemes. With the Cardinal's blessing, in September 1658 he bought Belle-Isle from the Gondi family. The largest island off the north-west coast of France, Belle-Isle lay about ten miles out to sea from Quiberon in Brittany. With its important strategic position – not only com-manding the trade routes across the Bay of Biscay but also giving access to the New World over the ocean – Mazarin's approval of the purchase was a mark of his renewed trust in Nicolas.

The price of 1.3 million livres was a colossal outlay when Nicolas was still pouring money into Vaux-le-Vicomte. But it did not deter him from breathing life into the island. He renovated the principal harbour at Le Palais and improved its fortifications. He had boats made for the island's fishermen and started work on a residence at Roserière, just north of Le Palais. With the aid of Vincent de Paul, he founded a hospital. Now that Spain was in retreat at last, it was time to revive Richelieu's dream to turn France into a great sea-trading empire. With a group of merchants, he founded a company based on the island that would trade silk and spices in the Indies. He even bought his own personal fleet of ships, one of which was called *The Squirrel*. His ambitious plans to turn the island into the centre for an ocean-going fleet seemed set to guarantee it a splendid and prosperous future. The wind was in his sails again.

Nicolas knew all too well from past experience that he had to make the most of the good times to prepare for the bad. Looking forward, he realised that he could not depend on the Cardinal's continued support for long. But also it was clear that the young King was fast developing a mind of his own. Prudence dictated that he should make some effort now to discover what that mind contained. Soon the turn of European politics offered him a promising opportunity.

The recent victory over the Spanish underlined the fact that Louis XIV – who had celebrated his twentieth birthday on 5 September 1658 – was the most eligible bachelor in Europe. As a Spanish princess herself, the fervent wish of the King's mother was that Louis should close the rift between Spain and France by marrying the Infanta Maria-Theresa, daughter of Philip IV, but Cardinal Mazarin, who as ever wanted to postpone a decision until the last possible moment, was considering another contender. Twenty-three years old, Marguerite-Yolande was the sister of Charles-Emmanuel II, the Duke of Savoy. Her mother, Christine of Savoy, had been promoting her virtues as a possible spouse to Louis for some time.

A pleasing serendipity made it possible for Nicolas to plant a spy in this household that could well turn out to be of huge importance to the King's future. Madame du Plessis-Bellière had a young niece from Brittany called Mademoiselle Carné de Trécesson, who had recently fallen head over heels in love with him. Nicolas had encouraged the infatuation, inviting her several times to his private office at Saint-Mandé. She was ready, she declared, to do anything for him. So Nicolas took her at her word and sent her away to the Court of Savoy, using his connections to get her appointed as a lady-in-waiting to the Duke's mother.

Taking up her post in Savoy, she soon won the confidence of not only Christine of Savoy, but also Princess Marguerite and her brother the young Duke Charles-Emmanuel. The Duke 'makes the most of every opportunity to woo me', she wrote back to Nicolas. 'He has music played for me, treats me to dinners and takes me out horse riding. He always lets me have his most beautiful horses and provides me with the most splendid retinue.'[11] But, she assured him, 'I work hard to keep my reputation as pure as my heart, which, I promise, is as faithful as ever.'

Taking the hint, Nicolas despatched to Savoy a carriage full of garments and finery, but the young Duke more than matched the extravagance. He showered Mademoiselle de Trécesson with pearls and diamonds, which she wore on every possible occasion, so that everyone assumed that she must be his mistress. Alarmed by the reports, Nicolas warned his spy to be careful. 'I swear that the memory of your little office means more to me than all the things "Monsieur de Savoy" can do to show that he loves me,'[12] she replied. The Duke might be impetuous, but she knew how to guide him along her chosen path without yielding to his passions.

At the beginning of November 1658 the young princess Marguerite-Yolande set off with her mother for Lyons, where she was to meet Louis XIV for the first time. Mademoiselle de Trécesson was part of the royal retinue that made the long and difficult journey across the Alps. With the prospect of a royal marriage seeming more likely, she used the occasion to pen a long character profile of the young Princess, which she sent back to Nicolas in Paris. 'I do not think she is foolish enough to dare go against the Cardinal's wishes,' she concluded, 'but she will always love those to whom she has pledged her friendship, and never forget the gratitude she owes to some people. She is extremely generous and kind, but very reserved. So much for matters of importance you need to know about. I'd be ashamed of my atrocious handwriting if I wasn't able to give the excuse of having to compose this letter on the edge of high cliffs that fill me with fear.'[13]

When the party from Savoy arrived in Lyons on 28 November, the French court rode out to welcome them, Louis XIV galloping ahead to catch the first glimpse of his prospective bride. Rejoining his own party, he confided to his mother how pretty he thought Marguerite-Yolande looked.

The Princesses were invited to climb into the royal carriage for the grand entrance into the city. The King, who was in high spirits, sat down next to Princess Marguerite-Yolande and regaled her with all his favourite subjects – his Household Cavalry, the exploits of his musketeers and their commanders, the numbers of his troops, and so on. Marguerite might not have said a lot in return, but the young couple seemed to be getting along well.

Later in the day, however, the Cardinal took the Princess's mother aside. He had just received some unexpected news, he explained. Philip IV had written to express his desire for a peace agreement and to offer his daughter's hand in marriage to the King of France. Suddenly the visit of the Royal House of Savoy had become an embarrassing ordeal. The best the Cardinal could offer was that maybe if the proposed marriage to the Infanta fell through, then Louis would go ahead and marry Marguerite after all. The princess behaved with commendable dignity, but it must having been humiliating for her, after having come all this way, to find herself treated as a little regarded backup. The King no longer even bothered to talk to her about his soldiers.

When her brother the Duke, who had travelled separately, arrived in Lyons a few days later, a ball was held in his honour, but he too received mostly indifferent and frosty treatment. After only a brief stay, he left again with the words, 'Goodbye, France, for ever. I am not sorry to leave you.'[14]

All these developments of course ruined Nicolas's plan to secure a well-placed confidante who would be able to report on the King's intentions, but Mademoiselle de Trécesson still continued to report on the disaster as it unfolded. She had hoped that she would be able to return to Paris as one of Marguerite's ladies-in-waiting, but the collapse of the marriage plans meant that she would now have to spend another year in Savoy, putting up with the Duke's attentions, which were fast beginning to pall. Even worse, many of the members of the French Court at Lyons had recognised her as the niece of the Superintendent's close friend Madame du Plessis-Bellière. It became obvious that she must be one of Nicolas's spies.

'I am more concerned and upset about this than I can possibly explain,' she wrote to Nicolas, who had at the outset of this adventure told her that it was vital to keep her relationship with Madame du Plessis-Bellière a secret. 'But if things turn out in such a way as to harm you, I implore you to sacrifice my interests entirely to your own. I will not complain and will be happy, even if it means sacrificing my life, just to be able to prove that no one has ever had more gratitude and respect for you than me.'[15]

The letter came close to being an apology. But it was Nicolas who ought to have known better. It was a reckless misjudgement to imagine that Mademoiselle de Trécesson's relationship with Madame du Plessis-Bellière could ever have been kept a secret. As soon as there was any gathering of French courtiers, she was likely to be exposed. Yet the very unpredictability of life meant that it was natural to take a chance. He might have lost this time, but he still hoped he would win the next.

Pax Mazarina

The embarrassing débâcle over the House of Savoy inevitably fuelled the Cardinal's unease over Nicolas. He understood the need for spies, but he expected them all to report to him. This evidence that the Superintendent was building up his own network was yet another sign of his worrying independence. Whatever agenda he may have had, it clearly wasn't the Cardinal's. For his part Nicolas realised that now he had to be especially careful. He had become too visible, too prosperous, too powerful not to be challenged. The setback impressed upon him the necessity of renewing his insurance. So he took out his old escape plan from behind the mirror in his office where it had been hidden and updated it, designating the newly purchased Belle-Isle as his preferred place of refuge. From here he could take a fast boat to anywhere.

The death of Nicolas's Co-superintendent Abel Servien in February 1659 offered a portent of the trouble ahead. The Cardinal's secretary, Colbert, who was becoming increasingly influential, complained of Nicolas's extravagances and urged the Cardinal to appoint another Co-superintendent. It was a particularly provocative suggestion because Servien had undertaken no practical duties for some time. At first Mazarin announced that he himself would take the job. But he quickly changed his mind when Nicolas explained that as Mazarin's prestige and fortune

Nicolas Foucquet in a pose of sober but cheerful industry somewhat at
odds with the extreme extravagance for which he is more
usually remembered.

The Dauphiné, scene of Nicolas's first adventure and first disgrace.

Not for the first or last time in its history, Paris is turned into a battle-ground during France's bloody civil war, the Fronde. Nicolas's loyal service to the Crown helps to assure a royal victory and a spectacular rise into the very highest echelons of government.

The mother of Louis XIV, Queen Anne of Austria, and …

… the man that some scurrilous tongues suggested was his father, Cardinal Mazarin. As great a statesman as he was a rogue, he effectively ruled France during the King's minority.

Nicolas's greatest achievement: Vaux-le-Vicomte, the
most beautiful building in all France.

An allegory of loyalty and faith, depicted on the ceiling of
Vaux's 'Salon of the Muses'.

The Foucquet team: architect Louis Le Vau (top left), gardener André Le Nôtre (top right), artist Charles Le Brun (centre left), poet Jean de la Fontaine (centre right), and orchestrator of the talents Paul Pellisson.

The King's mistress Louise de la Vallière, dressed as Artemis, the goddess of Chastity - an aspect of her character that Nicolas was foolish not to respect.

Louis XIV being crowned by Victory, one of many eulogizing
portraits that fed his determination never to be usurped.

Nicolas on trial for embezzlement and high treason.

Pignerol, the Alpine fortress in the furthest corner of the Kingdom, where Nicolas was incarcerated for the remainder of his life.

Nicolas's final resting-place, Saint Mary of the Visitation, on the rue Saint-Antoine in Paris.

were even greater than his own he would come under pressure to use them on behalf of the state. Finally agreeing that Nicolas should carry on alone, the Cardinal sent a letter in the name of the King to confirm the arrangement. It would have been necessary, he wrote, to find someone to replace Servien were it not for 'the confidence that we have in your loyalty – which you have proved in the role of Superintendent over the past six years – as well as your ability, zeal, assiduity and vigilance'. Indeed, the letter went on, Nicolas's qualities were such that his sole administration of the finances was likely to ensure that the royal government was 'even better served, and the people with us'.[1]

But the reality was as usual one of private unease behind the public approval. The fulsome terms of the letter amounted to an extracted vote of confidence that masked an underlying dissatisfaction. It was a necessary document, Nicolas would have argued, not only to make him feel secure in his position but also to guarantee the continued support of the financiers. In their truce the Cardinal feared Nicolas's obvious ambition, but realised that his ability to generate money made him essential, especially so long as the war with Spain continued.

But the Cardinal was working hard to bring the war to an end once and for all. A ceasefire had been agreed. And in June 1659 he set off for the border town of Saint-Jean-de-Luz, in the Pyrenees, to begin negotiations with the First Minister of Spain, Luis de Haro. Just before his departure he was entertained by Nicolas at Vaux-le-Vicomte, where only the interior of the house remained to be completed. In the past Nicolas had tried to discourage the widespread and sometimes compromising gossip about his extravagances, but his confirmation as the sole Superintendent emboldened him at last to reveal his new treasure.

Encouraged by the Cardinal's exclamations of genuine admiration and wonder, Nicolas even took him out to see the tapestry factory at Maincy, where his mother had recently established a hospital for sick workers. The tour was a dangerous but irresistible display to an appreciative, but treacherous fellow connoisseur. No one was better equipped than Mazarin to understand the scale of Nicolas's achievement, but equally no one was more likely to question how he had been able to afford it. Nicolas, who knew him far too well not to be able to read the darker thoughts behind the praise, understood that some gesture would be necessary to disarm his suspicion and jealousy. So amidst all the gasps of appreciation, he assured the Cardinal that he had only to say the word for the chateau and garden to be his.

It's easy to imagine the pained expression with which the Cardinal turned the offer down, but at least he had a small consolation present, since Nicolas insisted that he take a few tapestries with him to decorate the house where he would be staying in Saint-Jean-de-Luz. Stopping off at nearby Fontainebleau, where the Court had gathered for the summer, Mazarin was so full of what he had seen that the King, the Queen and his younger brother decided to see the chateau for themselves. Receiving them on 17 July, Nicolas wrote to the Cardinal, 'It was a lovely day. And their Majesties appeared very pleased with the place and showed me much kindness and civility.'[2] The Cardinal wrote back to praise Nicolas's 'application and zeal', and assured him that he made the most of every opportunity to sing his praises: he wasn't at all surprised that the King and Queen had treated him with such warmth.

The Cardinal's habit of flattering both his friends and enemies alike made him impossible to read. The new cordiality he enjoyed with the Superintendent only fanned the jealousy of Nicolas's enemies, who had been whispering against him ever since the Court's visit to Lyons. Once the Cardinal had set off for the Pyrenees, they redoubled their efforts to turn him decisively against Nicolas, a difficult task with someone who almost made it a point of policy not to be decisive about anything.

On 22 July the Controller-General of Finances, Barthélemy Hervart, who had the difficult duty of keeping track of expenditure, wrote to the Cardinal, 'I must warn Your Eminence that as soon as you left, the Superintendent returned to his old ways . . . He does all he can to hide his activities from me and confuses the past with the present so that I cannot distinguish between what is owed and what is not, and so that no one has a clear picture of the finances other than himself and his friends . . .'[3] The following month Colbert added to the pressure, expressing his view that the time had come to investigate the whole question of finances.

To counter such moves, Nicolas sent Jean Hérauld de Gourville to the Pyrenees to warn the Cardinal of the conspiracy that was forming. Knowing Mazarin well enough to appreciate the point of maximum pressure, Gourville laid stress on the fact that the harmful gossip about the Superintendent was damaging his ability to raise money. But the Cardinal was much too pre-occupied by the peace talks with Spain to give much thought to such matters. He merely listened to both sides and tried to encourage them to bury their differences.

On 28 September 1659 Nicolas set off for Saint-Jean-de-Luz himself. Colbert feared that once he was able to see the Cardinal face to face, he would talk him round into supporting him once again, as he had done after Servien's death. So he began to draft a memorandum that listed in great detail the Superintendent's supposed transgressions.[4] 'Your Eminence', he began, 'will find attached a memorandum I couldn't help writing, although I know it contains only a pale shadow of Your Eminence's understanding. If it displeases you in any way, I beg you to toss it on the fire at once. I should also add that Your Eminence will appreciate how important it is that this document should remain secret . . .'

Even in a time where flattery was routine, Colbert's letters to the Cardinal were extraordinary for their habitual self-abasement. He took care to behave as though he had no wishes, no plans, no ambitions that were not also those of his master. The hesitance with which he began his letter stood in stark contrast to the explicit nature of the accusations it contained. Here he did not mince his words. The Superintendent had failed to give a proper accounting of his financial transactions in order to misappropriate funds on a massive scale. In the past two years, Colbert estimated, the Superintendent had embezzled some 10 million livres. 'Everyone knows,' wrote Colbert, 'that the Superintendent has lavished money not only on himself, not only on his brothers, not only on his relations and friends, not only on all those of his staff who have approached him, but also on the most distinguished people in the kingdom and others he has wanted to win over.'

Rather than seek to clear up the financial chaos that decades of war had caused, Colbert went on, Nicolas had sought to encourage it, knowing that he could profit from the confusion. If the Cardinal wished 'to put the King back in control of his revenues', he must sack Nicolas and establish a special court to try him and his accomplices. Colbert even suggested the names of the most suitable officials to be put in charge of this court. He had thought of every detail. Nothing had escaped his attention. Knowing as well as Gourville the cash considerations that would most be exercising the Cardinal's mind, he stressed that it was vital that Nicolas should not discover what they were planning. For it would take some time to assure the continued flow of royal revenues after his departure. In the meantime, therefore, the Cardinal should praise him and do everything he could to make him feel secure, so that he would continue to meet the state's expenses.

Colbert, who had spent two days labouring over the memorandum, sent the twenty closely written pages to Mazarin

in Saint-Jean-de-Luz on 2 October 1659. But since the Superintendent of the Post, Jérome de Nouveau, happened to be in
Nicolas's pay, the letter was swiftly diverted to Nicolas in
Bordeaux, where he had stopped off on his way down to the
Pyrenees. With him was Gourville, who in his memoirs recalled
an anxious Nicolas showing him Colbert's letter. 'I tried to
reassure him a little,' he wrote. 'He then told me that the letter
had to be returned quickly to the person who had supplied it but
that he wanted to keep a copy. So he placed the letter between us
and we both began to copy it, he one page and I the other, and so
on until we had got to the end.'[5]

When Nicolas met the Cardinal in Saint-Jean-de-Luz two
weeks later, neither he nor Mazarin let slip any knowledge of
Colbert's memorandum, although it must have been at the forefront of both their minds. Nicolas complained of the whispering
campaigns that were undermining his ability to fulfil his duties as
Superintendent. Not only was he aware that Colbert had been
talking to Hervart behind his back, he told the Cardinal, but he
had also noticed that Colbert no longer seemed to be as friendly
to him as in the past, even although he, Nicolas, still held him in
the warmest regard and longed for his good opinion. Such
scheming was entirely unnecessary, he went on, because the
Cardinal had only to say the word and at once Nicolas would not
only resign as Superintendent but also give up the office of
Attorney-General in the Parlement. The assurance amounted to
a veiled threat. Both men knew that Nicolas's sudden departure
would cause financial disaster. And they knew, too, that Nicolas
had plenty of compromising details he could give about the
Cardinal's own misuse of state funds.

The Cardinal replied that he was astonished to hear what
Nicolas had to say since it was the first time anyone had given
him the slightest inkling of such intrigues. On the contrary,
Colbert had always spoken of Nicolas as one of the people he

most admired. But Nicolas was insistent. He spoke on good authority and if the Cardinal hadn't yet received any complaints from Colbert concerning the finances he soon would.

'He was very definite,' Mazarin wrote to Colbert in a letter, dated 20 October, which described the meeting.[6] 'And you can easily imagine how surprised I was. But I recovered myself enough to convince him that you had sent me nothing against his interests.' The Cardinal went on to urge Colbert to bury his differences with Nicolas, 'because I can see that he has a fervent desire to get on with you and to profit from your advice'. The Cardinal had many qualms about Nicolas, but still feared him too much, and valued his ability to raise money too much, to wish to turn against him. In any case he didn't mind rogues, as long as they were useful.

Indeed, after their meeting, Nicolas travelled on to Toulouse, where he negotiated a generous contribution to the royal exchequer from the estates of Languedoc. On 7 November 1959, after months of talks, Mazarin finally signed the long-awaited peace treaty with Spain, but amidst the celebrations he still found time to send Nicolas a note of congratulations on his achievement. 'I have no doubt that you had to do some extraordinary things to persuade the estates to find two and a half million livres . . .'[7]

The Peace of the Pyrenees was a personal triumph for the Cardinal, bringing to an end a war that had lasted nearly a quarter of a century. If getting Nicolas and Colbert to like each other was a much less straightforward matter, Mazarin was still adamant that they should do so. Expedience required that, in spite of their mutual contempt, they too should drop their feud. Such was the *Pax Mazarina*.

So that there should not be any danger of misunderstanding, the Cardinal wrote to Colbert a second time to reiterate his wish that he make his peace with the Superintendent.

I have done, it seems to me, what I had to do in the present circumstances. And I'm satisfied from my meeting with him that he will pay due regard to my wishes. I told him that I want to be kept informed of the smallest matters even during my absence, which he solemnly promised. I also told him that I wanted him not only to get on with you but also to do all he could to win your friendship and to put his complete trust in you, confiding in you as he might in me. I beg you therefore to see him when he gets back to Paris and to do whatever you can to make him appreciate that there's nothing to prevent you from being his sincere friend, since quite apart from the regard you have for him, you know that I desire that this should be so, and that I have complete confidence in him.'[8]

But how much of this did the Cardinal really believe? He used sentiments so often as tools of policy that words like 'faith' or 'trust' or 'friendship' had about as much meaning as 'yours sincerely' at the end of a letter.

Colbert, who had based his entire strategy for advancement on being the perfect *créature*, had no choice but to do as the Cardinal wished, even though any genuine friendship with Nicolas was now impossible. 'As for the desire he has shown Your Eminence to get on with me, that shouldn't be too difficult, because either he will change his conduct or Your Eminence will accept the conduct he already follows, or Your Eminence will excuse him on account of the present state of affairs, and perhaps find that his good qualities outweigh and even make up for the bad. Whatever the case, I will have no trouble in conducting myself entirely according to what I recognise to be Your Eminence's intentions, since before God I can swear that they have always been and always will be the rules that guide me.'[9]

At the beginning of January 1660, Colbert visited Nicolas at Saint-Mandé to make friends as the Cardinal had instructed.

Afterwards Nicolas wrote to Mazarin, 'Monsieur Colbert left content with me. But since he is in your service, I take the liberty of entreating Your Eminence not to renew any little complaints from the past that might alter this sentiment.'[10]

Nicolas and Jean-Baptiste Colbert had made up. But they both knew it was just a temporary truce, contingent on Nicolas's continued support from the Cardinal, which was in turn an uncertain thing dependent entirely upon expedience.

Soon after Colbert's visit, Nicolas wrote to a powerful protector, the Queen Mother, whose support he enjoyed naturally through his family connections but had also cultivated by giving generous pensions to her appointees. He complained that the damage Colbert and Hervart had done to his reputation had made it even more difficult for him to raise money. He wanted to put the finances on a stable footing, but all the interference he received prevented him from taking the necessary measures. 'If I shake everybody up with some initiative, everyone complains and His Eminence instantly blames me for causing him problems. If I try to do things quietly, without drawing attention, His Eminence says I want to take charge of everything myself. The lack of support and protection makes it impossible for me to do my job properly.'[11]

Of Colbert he wrote that he had done the best he could to patch up their differences, but finally, if his aim was to steal away the Superintendent's office for himself, there was nothing Nicolas could do to satisfy him.

The letter displayed a winning openness. 'It is true,' he confided, 'that I have a weakness for great deeds beyond my station. I love to entertain important people and make them my friends. I have some success in this because I am liberal, and love to do whatever I do with style. I spend a little too much; and although I have cut back on entertainment, gaming and other such expenses, it is still true that the building and the gardens of

Vaux have cost me a lot, and it would have been wiser not to have undertaken them. I offered to give them to the Cardinal and I would have been delighted if he had accepted because to give something of this kind is an even greater gesture than to build it in the first place . . .'[12] He went on to explain the acquisition of Belle-Isle, giving precise details of its cost. He was well aware that Vaux and Belle-Isle represented an excess; but he cited in mitigation that he had worked in the service of the King for many years without respite and had at every critical moment willingly risked his own fortune and that of his friends. In such circumstances, 'one must be able to stand out a little from other men, because simply to invest money or to pile it up uselessly in coffers would be for me a wretched way to live quite at odds with my nature . . .'[13]

The chief purpose of this letter was to enlist the sympathy and understanding of an influential ally, whose support he might later need. So he sought to anticipate any criticisms from his enemies and to show that he had nothing to hide. But it also amounted to an unrepentant testament of what he was about.

Outwardly, Nicolas was one of the most celebrated personages in the kingdom, only too eager to show off his prestige, hoping to rise yet higher, but those who were closest to him watched his progress with dismay. At about the same time as Nicolas wrote his letter to the Queen Mother, he received a gift from Pierre Deschampsneufs. After many years the Jesuit father had at last completed his translation of the Psalms of David. Published under the title *Suspiria Davidis* (the Sighs of David), it contained a dedication to Nicolas. There was nothing unusual in this; many of the great writers in France had similarly written dedications to the patron who had supported them so generously. But in place of the usual high-flown eulogies, the words Deschampsneufs wrote contained a warning:

You now enjoy honours that few people dare dream of, let alone achieve, but I hope that you will still occasionally find some time to share the thoughts of David, and contemplate matters that are of far greater importance than the affairs of this world. The recent death of your colleague has exposed you to the perils of vanity. Your assumption of the entire responsibility for the country's wealth has been greeted with great joy. If people celebrate on behalf of King and country, then that is right and fitting. But those who choose to praise you are not your friends. As for me, the more I rejoice for the public good, the more I worry about you.

Our order prays that you will not allow yourself to be tempted by the fleeting riches of this world, but instead devote yourself to the eternal ones of the next. And I, who have been so closely associated with you over the years, add to these prayers my own heartfelt wishes. Plenty of people will toast your good fortune, not enough people repent it; yet such repentance ought to impose some measure on all mortal joy, which otherwise delivers men to misery.[14]

Deschampsneufs placed all the more trust in the book's power to guide its new owner because he was given so little opportunity these days to see Nicolas in person. But if Nicolas even read the dedication, he would have had very little time to dwell on its implications, so busy was he chasing precisely the kind of glory that Deschampsneufs had warned him against. The small volume was duly passed on for the old priest himself to catalogue and shelve in the Saint-Mandé library.

Marie de Maupeou was so worried for her son that she visited Father Vincent de Paul at Saint-Lazare, which was the principal seat for his order. Here, in the house that he had opened up to some of the poorest people in Paris, she confided her fears for one of the wealthiest. 'Entrust mother and child to Our Lord,' he said. 'He will look after them both.'[15]

11

You Can't Take It With You

The marriage of Louis XIV to the King of Spain's daughter Maria-Theresa at Saint-Jean-de-Luz in June 1660 confirmed the diplomatic triumph of the Peace of the Pyrenees. But the difficult negotiations had taken their toll on Mazarin's health. By the time of the wedding he was so ill that his attendance surprised everyone. Although he was required to stand for the entire length of a long ceremony, somehow he managed to get through the day, but the ordeal had exhausted him.

The memoirs of Louis-Henri de Loménie, the comte de Brienne, offer a vivid eyewitness account of the long, slow decline that followed. The son of the then Minister for Foreign Affairs, Henri-Auguste de Loménie, he was in his early twenties at the time. Through his father, he had already known the Cardinal for many years, but he developed an especially close relationship after writing a short eulogy that Mazarin – who was even more happy to receive flattery than to give it – found particularly pleasing. On the strength of this seven-line verse, the young Brienne also received a salary from Nicolas Foucquet for two years without any obligation to write anything else. Later he was appointed a minister in the same department as his father.

Brienne recalled how after the wedding the increasingly feeble Cardinal took to his bed, and he used to sit with him. One day the Queen Mother dropped by to ask how the Cardinal was feeling.

'Awful,' came the reply and, throwing aside his bedcovers, Mazarin showed the Queen his emaciated limbs covered with sores. 'See these legs, which have sacrificed their repose for the sake of France!'[1]

The Queen let out a cry and wept to see him in such a pitiful state. Brienne thought he looked like Lazarus raised from the dead – only there was no doubt that the Cardinal was clearly heading for his tomb, not escaping it. From this day onwards the rest of Mazarin's life, in Brienne's words, was 'no more than one long death'.[2]

He made the exhausting journey back to Paris in several stages, lying flat on his back on a mattress that had been specially fitted into his carriage. On the few occasions that he attempted to walk he had to be supported on both sides. The slightest physical effort seemed to risk expediting his demise.

Nicolas made the most of the opportunity to steal the limelight. The young King and his new bride were due to make a ceremonial entrance into Paris in August, but they were Nicolas's guests first, visiting him at Vaux-le-Vicomte on 24 July, soon after their return to Fontainebleau from the Pyrenees. The Court gazetteer, Jean Loret, reported the occasion: 'On Monday the sole Superintendent of Finances Foucquet, well-loved by the Great, generously treated the Royal Court to a splendid feast in his beautiful house at Vaux, where through his care, labour and noble expense, a hundred wonders have appeared.'[3]

Meanwhile, far too ill to get to his feet this time, the Cardinal languished in his Louvre apartment, no doubt brooding over the impudence with which Nicolas seemed to be making an early claim to step into his shoes. The summer passed in a fever of speculation. 'Although the Cardinal appears a little better,' wrote Guy Patin on 17 August, 'there's still ceaseless talk about who will take his place. The four favourites are the Marshal de Villeroi, Monsieur Le Tellier, Monsieur Foucquet, the Superintendent of

Finances, and Lord Ondedei, the Bishop of Fréjus.'[4] As a doctor with Court connections, Patin followed the progress of the Cardinal's illness closely. Three months later he reported the patient's growing frustration at his condition. 'He says the doctors offer only words, but no cure . . . He says that he is completely fed up with the way he's still in such pain, although they always promise to relieve his suffering.'[5] Finally in the new year he learned from one of his contacts 'that Cardinal Mazarin has resigned himself to death; that he believes himself lost and that he cannot recover from this illness'.[6]

In these last days Nicolas took the trouble to see the Cardinal as often as he could, hoping that his presence would help quietly to confirm him as the most obvious successor. But one of these visits led to an embarrassing encounter with his brother Basile that served only to undermine him. Having many times come close to it, the two had finally fallen out – doubtless over the latest of Basile's many indiscretions – and not spoken to each other for months. When Basile chanced upon Nicolas in the Cardinal's antechamber, he began to hurl insults at him, seemingly oblivious to the many people who were present to report the incident. Nicolas was a thief, he cried. He'd squandered France's wealth, wasting millions on his buildings. Not only that. He was a liar, a fraud, a womaniser. Basile even listed the names of all the women at Court his brother was supposed to have slept with. While it would have been better to maintain a dignified silence, Nicolas angrily weighed in with an even longer list of Basile's failings. As the Abbé de Choisy put it, the two brothers 'declared to each other publicly what all their enemies had thought in private'.[7] Lying on his deathbed next door, the Cardinal was able to hear every single word.

The Cardinal's dying had become such a familiar part of Court life that it was hard to imagine him ever actually being dead. But then a terrible event occurred that drove home – to the Cardinal himself at least – the fact that this day must soon arrive. In the early hours of 7 February the Louvre caught fire. Brienne, whose lodgings were on the other side of the Seine, rushed to the palace and met Mazarin just as he was being carried from his apartment by his captain of guards. 'He was trembling and exhausted,' Brienne remembered. 'Death seemed to be painted in his eyes, whether it was fear of being burned in his bed that had put him in this state, or because he regarded the inferno as a divine warning.'[8] Pale and defeated, the Cardinal was too shocked even to be able to speak. While the Swiss Guards formed a chain down the stairs to pass up buckets of water, he was escorted into a chair and carried away by four porters. Behind him, his apartments were already engulfed in flames.

When he reached his own palace the Cardinal at last found his voice, summoning his team of twelve doctors. Before, they had always tried to reassure him. But now the most distinguished doctor of them all, Guénaud, admitted the bleak reality of the situation. 'There's no point, Your Eminence, in giving you false hope. Our remedies can give you a few extra days, but they can't address the chief cause of your illness: you will definitely die from this disease.'

The Cardinal received this news with an uncharacteristic calm. 'How long have I still to live?' he asked.

'Two months,' replied Guénaud.

'That's enough,' said the Cardinal quietly.[9]

But this kind of composure did not last long. Some days later Brienne found himself alone in a gallery within the palace where the Cardinal displayed many of his treasures. Hearing the sound of Mazarin approaching, dragging himself painfully along in his slippers, Brienne hid behind a tapestry.

'I must leave all this behind!' lamented the Cardinal to himself aloud as he gazed at the tapestry. 'I must leave all this behind!' He then turned round to behold some new object. 'And that too! What trouble I've had collecting these things! . . . Where I'm heading, I'll never see them again!'

At this point Brienne coughed in spite of himself.

'Who's there!' called the Cardinal. 'Who's there?'

'It's me, Your Eminence . . .'

'Come close, come close!' The Cardinal was wearing a nightcap and, noticed Brienne, was naked under his dressing gown. 'Give me your hand. I am very weak, I don't have the strength . . .'

'Maybe Your Eminence should sit down.'

'No,' he said, 'I want to walk, and I have things to see to in my library.'

As Brienne gave him an arm to lean on, Mazarin made it clear that he did not want to talk about state business. 'I'm no longer up to it. Speak to the King. Do what he tells you. I have other things to worry about.'

With that familiar way of his, he then took Brienne into his confidence. 'Look, my friend, do you see this beautiful Correggio picture? And there, Titian's *Venus*, and Annibale Carraccci's incomparable *Flood*? I know how much you like paintings, and know about them too. Well, my poor friend, I must leave them all behind! Farewell, dear pictures, which I've loved so much and which have cost me so much!'

'You're less ill than you think if you still love your pictures,' replied Brienne, trying to offer some comfort.[10]

The Cardinal's taste for spectacle was so renowned that perhaps it was only natural that he made such a high drama of his own death. On another occasion Brienne found him asleep in an armchair before his bedroom fire but shaking violently. He jerked from side to side and rolled backwards and forwards, his head almost knocking his knees. Brienne was afraid that he might fall in the fire and summoned Mazarin's valet, Bernouin.

Bernouin took hold of his master and shook him vigorously.
'What is it, Bernouin?' said the Cardinal, suddenly waking up.
He then let out a tormented cry: 'It was Guénaud who said it!'

'To the Devil with Guénaud and whatever he said,' replied
Bernouin. 'Must you keep repeating that?'

'Yes, Bernouin, yes. It was Guénaud who said it. And he says
only the truth. I must die. There is no escape.'

When Bernouin told him that Brienne was there, the Cardinal
asked Brienne to come near. Taking his hand, he kissed it,
saying, 'My poor friend, I am dying!'

Brienne, who had become very fond of the Cardinal, could not
help but shed a few tears for this strange churchman who he
noticed never read his breviary. Mazarin embraced him tenderly,
but his breath was so pestilent that Brienne nearly fainted.
Noticing, the Cardinal popped a throat pastille and gave one to
Brienne as well.[11]

Some days later the drama moved on to the Château de
Vincennes. Here the Cardinal could spend his last days in more
peace than his palace in Paris had made possible. His chief
occupation now was to do whatever he could to ensure a tidy and
blameless departure. He had several long meetings with the
King, advising on the necessary steps to take for a smooth
transition of power. He was especially careful to assess the virtues
and failings of the King's chief ministers.

Keen to know his latest standing, Nicolas sounded out the
very few people who – like himself – still had access, but the
accounts they offered were frustratingly contradictory. Not even
approaching death seemed enough to make the Cardinal
completely candid and Nicolas was left to extract what comfort
he could from tantalising titbits.

One of the ministers on the King's Council, Hugues de
Lionne, wrote; 'His Eminence told me that you had had a chat
with him, which he found extremely satisfying. Unfortunately

the Chancellor then walked in and interrupted the interview . . .
However, I think it counts for a lot that what you said pleased
him.'[12] But other reports were less encouraging. An anonymous
informant warned Nicolas of rumours that the Cardinal had
advised the King not to trust him. 'It's being said that . . . if he
does not die, you're lost.'[13]

Thankfully, however, the medical bulletins suggested that he
very soon would die. 'Pellisson told me,' wrote yet another one
of Nicolas's spies, 'that you would not be upset to learn the Abbé
de Maure's opinion of the Cardinal's state of health . . . He
doesn't think he can pull through or even continue much longer
the treatments he's already being given.'[14] In other words the
Cardinal would either die from his disease or be bled to death.

Meanwhile the closely observed invalid preoccupied himself
with his will. His confessor, Angelo Bissaro, wore the white
socks of the Theatines, an order whose strict austerity prevented
its members from begging or owning property. Wanting to
ensure for the Cardinal as smooth a passage as possible to the
next world, Bissaro touched on the thorny issue of his immense
wealth. Before appearing before God, he should make some
effort to restore any ill-gotten possessions.[15]

'But all my benefits come through my service to the King!'

'Then you must distinguish what the King has given you and
what you have given yourself.'

'In that case, I must give everything back!'

But his ever dependable secretary, Colbert, suggested a way
round this difficulty. The Cardinal should make a public gesture
giving all his possessions to his godson the King, who in his good
nature would almost certainly give everything back again. So on
3 March the Cardinal formally made over to Louis his entire
fortune of more than 50 million livres.

The King did not hurry to set his godfather at his ease. 'My poor
family will have nothing to eat!' the Cardinal was heard to cry two

days later.[16] But at last, on the third day, the King, as Colbert had predicted, turned down the gift. Assured that his family would not be destitute after all, Mazarin was able the next morning to receive Extreme Unction in a state of comparative grace.

But even then he retained his knack for surprises, as he rallied with the strange renewal of vigour that often occurs in people on the threshold of death. He shaved off his moustache and put rouge on his cheeks. And although spring had barely arrived, he paraded about the gardens of the chateau. 'I was never so surprised than when I saw this sudden and complete metamorphosis,' commented Brienne, 'from the deathbed where I had left him, to this rejuvenation that seemed more genuine than that of Eson.'[17] Yet this *coup de théâtre* deceived no one. The cynical courtiers simply regarded this picture of health as one more example of the Cardinal's trickery, commenting to one another, 'He lived a fraud and now he wants to die a fraud.'

Another mark of Mazarin's tenacious grip on life during these final days at Vincennes had been his appetite for gambling. It was only once the card players had been dismissed from his bedside and the Papal Nuncio granted him the Indulgence of the Pope that the Court realised the last encore really was approaching. From this moment onwards, only his personal chaplain and Jean-Baptiste Colbert were allowed to enter his chamber without special permission.

The Cardinal was in a kind of quarantine, shut away now from any possibility of contagious temptation. Colbert mounted a continuous vigil outside, writing in a notebook the names of the handful of people who were still allowed to present themselves. Finally, in the early hours of the morning of 9 March, one of life's richest players left the stage.

Brienne, who had come to make a last farewell to his patron, saw the King leaving the bedroom of his dead godfather. Sobbing and leaning on Marshal de Gramont for support, Louis said, 'Marshal, we have just lost a good friend.'[18] He then turned to Brienne, telling him to summon his ministers to a meeting of the Council at seven the next morning.

Setting off for Paris, Brienne spotted Nicolas walking towards the Château de Vincennes through the park. He stopped his carriage to pass on the King's message.

'The Cardinal's dead?' said Nicolas, looking surprised since none of his many spies had yet given him the news. 'I don't know whom to trust any more. People are so unreliable. How annoying! The King is looking for me and I should have been one of the first to be on hand. My God! Brienne, tell me everything that happened so I don't make a fool of myself.'[19] When Nicolas finally arrived at the chateau, he was embarrassed to find that Lionne and Le Tellier had already given the King their condolences before him. Also present was Colbert.

At the meeting of the Council the next morning, the King stood in front of his chair and, addressing himself to the Chancellor, Pierre Séguier, said, 'Until now I have been pleased to allow my affairs to be governed by the Cardinal, but it is time that I take charge of them myself. You will help me with your advice when I ask for it. Outside the normal course of state business, which I do not intend to change, I request and order you, Monsieur Chancellor, to seal no orders without my command and without having discussed them with me.'[20]

Addressing his other ministers, he forbade them likewise to sign anything without seeking his authority first.

He then turned to Nicolas. 'And you, Superintendent, you know my wishes: I would like you to make use of Colbert, whom the late Cardinal has recommended to me.'[21]

In recent months Nicolas had heard more than enough of Colbert, but he was confident that now, with the Cardinal dead, he would quietly be able to sideline him. As for the King, it was an impressive assertion of regal authority for a twenty-two-year-old, but Nicolas did not expect his appetite for government to last for long. It was surely only a matter of time until, faced with the temptation of endless amusing distractions, he would grow bored with having to sit at meetings and designate a prime minister to step into Mazarin's shoes.

Meanwhile, Nicolas was content enough to be one of the three ministers Louis appointed to a new Privy Council. Of the other two, Michel Le Tellier, who was Minister for War, had been a secretary of state for nearly twenty years. Conscientious and dogged, he was not the kind of man to take brilliant initiatives, but owed his advancement to the scrupulous way in which he carried out the orders of his superiors to the letter. Hugues de Lionne, in charge of foreign affairs, was sharp and quick-witted, but hopelessly compromised by an addiction to cards. Their presence in the Cabinet seemed only to make Nicolas's own eventual rise to the top all the more certain.

Quietly confident about his prospects, Nicolas spent much of the spring of 1661 thinking about party arrangements. When the time came, he was determined to celebrate in style. And, while he waited, another satisfaction he could dwell on was fulfilling the King's injunction that he should 'make use of Colbert'. There was no shortage of unpleasant jobs he had to offer this jumped-up clerk who had tried to ruin him. But before he could consign Colbert to some dark and airless office, the King intervened once again. He told Nicolas that he would like to appoint Colbert to be an intendant of finances. Not only that, but he would like Colbert to report not to Nicolas as the Superintendent of Finances, but directly to himself.

The King was polite and reassuring about this odd request. He explained that if he really was to take up the reins of power, he needed to know how this important aspect of government worked. He required someone who could teach him. And who better than Colbert, who had been so close to the late Cardinal?

Nicolas may have made light of the matter in front of the King, but he remembered the intercepted letter that not so long ago he and Gourville had copied, in which Colbert had urged the Cardinal to establish a special court to investigate the conduct of the Superintendent of Finances. The unexpected diligence with which the King now held weekly meetings with Colbert to go through the treasury accounts only filled him with more foreboding. It was impossible to imagine that Colbert wouldn't use the occasion to stir up the embers. So Nicolas sought a private interview with the King. He explained how over the years various financial crises had often forced him to overlook the strict letter of the law, although he had always acted with the Cardinal's agreement. He asked the King's pardon for these regrettable but unavoidable irregularities and promised to serve him in the future with renewed care and devotion.

The King continued to be reassuring. He would forget whatever might have happened in the past as long as Nicolas was honest with him now. He said he appreciated Nicolas's qualities and wanted him to continue to play an important role in his government. But he emphasised that he intended to be an active ruler and to have a complete understanding of state business – particularly the country's finances, which were the most important part of state business.

Nicolas may have found Louis's application unsettling, but in those weeks after Mazarin's death the young King astonished everyone with his conscientiousness and calm. The ambassador of Holland, Van Beuningen, who, on behalf of his own country, was following closely the transition of power in Europe's most powerful state, reported, 'Everyone comments on the extraordinary speed, competence, judgement and intelligence with which this young Prince conducts affairs. He shows considerable kindness towards those he has dealings with and great patience in listening to what people have to say, and this wins him enormous goodwill. He expresses himself with confidence and, when necessary, an eloquence that surprises those . . . who have seen the Cardinal so absolutely the master of all in the past.'[22]

In that past, Nicolas used to think of Louis as 'only the King', with little more capacity for independent action than his counterpart on a chessboard – it was the Queen and the bishops and the knights who really ruled. But it was important now to recognise that the King *really* was determined to act and to think for himself.

As for Mazarin, after his death the King gave express instructions that no one should make any malicious comments, but it was too much to expect people not to speak ill of this particular corpse. According to Guy Patin, even the Jesuits were complaining, because the Cardinal had given 400,000 livres to the Theatine order to help get him into Heaven when they would have done it for half the price.[23]

On the streets of Paris, people were making up epitaphs for him as during his life they had made up scurrilous songs. The following was a typical example:

Here lies the second Eminence.
God save us from the third![24]

12

Summer at Fontainebleau

W hat was the King thinking? Until very recently it would have been easy to conclude not very much. Louis was affable and pleasant enough, but seemed to spend most of his time outdoors, hunting and shooting. Tall and athletic, with penetrating eyes and a mane of curly chestnut hair, he was an excellent horseman and keen tennis player. But in the Cardinal's last years he had begun to show a more serious side. Romantic but conscientious, he had, at the insistence of his mother and godfather – and with considerable personal pain – ended a passionate relationship with the Cardinal's niece Marie Mancini, whom he would have married, in order instead to marry Maria Theresa, the Infanta of Spain. The sacrifice perhaps helped to account for an underlying solemnity that became increasingly apparent after Mazarin's death. The King had shown no particular enthusiasm for his other studies, but a sense of pride and duty made him specifically attentive to the Cardinal's lessons in kingship, to which he brought a natural intelligence, excellent memory and common sense. There was enough material in him for 'several great kings and one good man', Mazarin himself often commented of his protégé.[1]

The first days of Louis's sole rule revealed how determined he was to follow the advice and precepts of his mentor. 'One might say what they said of Alexander,' commented Guy Patin of the late Cardinal. '*Etiam mortuus adhuc imperat*' (Even dead, he still ruled).[2] But the self-confidence and authority with which Louis conducted himself suggested that such respect marked above all else a determination to master his brief before striking out in his own direction.

As Nicolas came to terms with the fact that he had no idea what that direction might be, he began to appreciate the inadequacies of his intelligence-gathering organisation. In his efforts to discover the true intentions of the Cardinal, he had neglected to think about the King. It was now vital to make amends. The attempt to plant Mademoiselle de Trécesson in the House of Savoy may have turned out badly, but Nicolas knew that he would have to place greater reliance on this kind of information. For the key to the King's mind lay not in the ministries, but in the secrets and confidences he disclosed among his intimates at Court. The natural recruiting ground for the new kind of spy Nicolas needed was to be found among the young ladies-in-waiting, whose combination of innocence, ambition and vanity made them particularly susceptible to the fine words, jewels and perfumes he was able to offer in abundance.

Nicolas had already taken the first steps to exploiting this rich resource some months earlier. As soon as he realised Mazarin's days were numbered, he contacted Madame Brigitte Laloy, a high-society laundress on the rue Saint-Honoré, who sold soap and other toiletries to the ladies-in-waiting at Court. Many of the girls treated her like a favourite aunt in whom they confided all their most intimate secrets. Pleased to be associated with someone of the Superintendent's importance, she gladly agreed to act as both recruiting mistress and procuress for him.

Soon Madame Laloy found a promising candidate in one of the ladies-in-waiting to the Queen Mother. Mademoiselle de Menneville was reputed to be the most beautiful of all the royal maids of honour. Already twenty-five years old, she was anxious to find a wealthy husband, but her chances had been compromised by her lack of a dowry. She had recently received a promise of marriage from the elderly duc de Damville, but now he was wavering. Having listened to the girl's sob story with her usual sympathy, Madame Laloy arranged a discreet meeting for her with the Superintendent. The secret romance that soon ensued was underpinned by some mutual practical benefits. Nicolas gave Mademoiselle de Menneville the money that would help the Duke change his mind, while she provided precious information from inside the Court.

Louis's early departure for Fontainebleau, on 20 April 1661, was a hopeful sign that he was at last ready to enjoy himself, leaving the governance of the realm to his elders. Circumstances seemed to be coming together nicely to ensure his profitable distraction. The mourning for the Cardinal came to an unofficial end on 31 March with the wedding in the chapel of the Palais-Royal of Louis's younger brother Philippe to Henrietta Stuart, sister to Charles II of England. An unusually warm spring followed, which Nicolas hoped would encourage the two newly married young Princes to stay with their wives in the country.

Previously Louis had always found his English cousin – now sister-in-law – a rather irritating child he had been obliged to feel sorry for. Ever since the execution of her father Charles I in 1649, Henrietta had spent most of her life trailing from palace to palace in France with her mother Henrietta Maria. Dependent upon the charity of their French royal relations, the indigent pair were an uncomfortable example of the sort of turmoil that Louis had so narrowly escaped himself. But ever since the change of fortune that had just a year earlier restored her brother Charles to the English throne, it had become easier to appreciate her qualities. At seventeen years old, she had grown into a young woman of extraordinary wit, charm and beauty. The Queen Mother, who had long sung her praises, made the formal request that she should marry her younger son at about the same time as Louis's marriage in June 1660 to Maria Theresa. The offer was accepted, but the wedding itself was deferred while Henrietta returned with her mother to London to enjoy the first few months of her brother's reign.

Here, to the alarm of the French Court, the young Duke of Buckingham, George Villiers, fell passionately in love with her. Pressed with almost daily letters from her fiancé Philippe to return to France, Henrietta and her mother set off back to Paris in the new year. The English Court accompanied them for the first day of the journey and then returned to London. But the love-lorn Buckingham begged the English King to be allowed to accompany Henrietta all the way to Paris. Only a stern rebuke from the Princess's mother persuaded him to leave them alone at Le Havre. But Buckingham was just one of many admirers for a Princess who had become used to being adored.

In France she went on to bewitch French society with equal ease, both men and women singing her praises and doing whatever they could to gain her favour. Nicolas commissioned Jean de la Fontaine to write an ode in her honour.

The universal worship she received encouraged her to have high expectations of her new husband, which unfortunately he had not been well equipped to meet. The Queen Mother called Philippe 'my little daughter'. It was said that she and Cardinal Mazarin had deliberately brought him up as a girl so that he would not be a threat to his older brother. 'He was fond of play,' wrote his second wife, Elizabeth-Charlotte of Bavaria, 'of holding drawing rooms, of eating, dancing and dress – in short, of all that women are fond of.'[3] Philippe showered Henrietta with countless gestures of care and respect, but not the kind of love a young woman expected of a husband.

When the Princess arrived at Fontainebleau, she brought with

her good cheer and amusement, but her underlying dissatisfaction was all too apparent to her brother-in-law, who felt
equally thwarted. After a strange fashion, the two cousins might
have been made for each other. Louis was tired of his plain, dull
wife, whom he had been made to marry for reasons of state, while
Henrietta grew increasingly impatient with a husband who
behaved more like one of her ladies-in-waiting. Both had grown
up in an atmosphere of continuous insecurity – Henrietta the
exiled daughter of a beheaded king, Louis the child-king whose
reign had been one long succession of wars and rebellions. While
Henrietta had passed most of her life under the close supervision
of her mother, Louis had had to submit to the equally watchful
eye of Cardinal Mazarin. But now the Cardinal was dead and
Henrietta's mother had returned to England. The sudden absence
of parental authority awoke in them both a determination to
make the most of their new-found freedom, which their disap-
pointment in their partners caused them to enjoy increasingly in
each other's company. It was hardly surprising if in the relaxed
surroundings of Fontainebleau a romance quickly blossomed.

Every morning, looking for some respite from the heat of that
summer, Henrietta – or 'Madame' as she was known – would set
off through the forest of Fontainebleau to bathe in the Seine.
Accompanying her were not only the young people at Court,
'gaily dressed, with countless feathers in their hair',[4] but also the
King, who found himself conveniently single since Maria
Theresa had been confined to her apartments, pregnant with their
first child. Making the outward journey in her carriage, Henrietta
would return in the evening on horseback, as if the river had
washed away all the formalities and restrictions of Court life.

After supper she and the King, surrounded by their favourite
courtiers, would climb back into their open-top carriages and
drive down to the Grand Canal, which stretched nearly a mile
into the forest. Here, to the accompaniment of music from the

King's Twenty-four Violins, they would promenade into the small hours.

Soon the King was spending as much time with Henrietta indoors as outdoors, secluding himself in her rooms with only her maids of honour to provide other company. Alarmed by the inevitable Court gossip, the Queen Mother lectured her son and daughter-in-law on the impropriety of their conduct, but to little effect. The lovers simply took more care to keep their passion for each other secret. They devised a stratagem: the King would deflect attention by pretending to bestow his favours elsewhere. In a court that was brimming with the ladies-in-waiting of not only Madame but also the King's wife, Queen Maria Theresa, and the Queen Mother there was no lack of choice. Soon he was flirting with Mademoiselle de Pons, Mademoiselle la Chemerault and Mademoiselle de la Vallière . . . Rehearsals for the 'Ballet of the Seasons', a summer show in which most of the young courtiers and maids of honour took part, offered plenty of opportunity for further gallantries. The King – an excellent dancer – intended to take the part of Spring, while Madame, to the Court's amusement, was to appear as Diana, the Goddess of Chastity.

Nicolas arrived in Fontainebleau at the beginning of May, to find the place rife with gossip concerning the bewildering catalogue of love trysts and intrigues that seemed to involve the King. He must have welcomed the host of distractions that kept Louis so far from his desk, but at the same time he wanted to know exactly what was going on. So while he moved into the Superintendent's quarters in the palace itself, he arranged to have Madame Laloy appointed as the concierge of Half Way House, a little run-down lodge situated on the Grand Canal some distance from the palace. Built by Catherine de' Medici, it offered a bucolic escape from the more formal life of the palace, with a cowshed, dairy and barn, as well as a little garden of its own with fountains. From here it was possible discreetly to observe the King as he strolled along the canal in the company of his courtiers or took to the waters, as he sometimes did, for an on-boat dinner. It was also a perfect out-of-the-way place to meet maids of honour who might have useful information.

To provide a plausible pretext to visit the lodge Nicolas arranged to have his brothers Louis and Gilles take rooms there, while Madame Laloy invited the mother of Nicolas's chief informant, Mademoiselle de Menneville, to stay above the dairy. But any hopes Nicolas might have had of mixing business with pleasure were compromised by the fact that the Menneville girl had fallen deeply in love with him. It was no longer a romance, but an infatuation. 'Certainly, Monsieur, I am convinced that she loves you without limit,'[5] wrote Madame Laloy. 'As we were talking, she began to cry, and told me how miserable she was to be so attached to you and yet to find so many obstacles.'

Nicolas tried to cheer her up with lavish gifts, buying her jewellery and a gown for the 'Ballet of the Seasons', but found her too lost in her passion for him to be any use as a spy.

A much more reliable informant was Mademoiselle Bénigne de Meaux du Fouilloux, who was a close friend of Fontainebleau's unofficial queen of gossip, the late Cardinal's niece Olympe Mancini, the comtesse de Soissons. It was through her that Nicolas learned the truth of Louis's decoy system. And as usual it was Madame Laloy who passed on the critical information: 'She told me that on Tuesday the King secluded himself with Madame, the comtesse de Soissons, Madame de Valentinois and Madame's maids of honour. He wanted no other man or anyone else to be present. She told me that they got up to all sorts of silliness, even throwing wine over each other . . . She assures you that the King is not interested in La Vallière, but reserves all his tenderness for Madame . . .'[6]

It occurred to Nicolas that the La Vallière girl could provide a valuable source of further intelligence, since in her role as decoy for Madame she was spending as much time in the King's company as anyone. Seventeen years old, Louise de la Baume Le Blanc, duchesse de la Vallière, had come to court from the château de Blois, where her stepfather had been maître d'hôtel to the King's late uncle, Gaston d'Orléans. A maid of honour to Henrietta, she was pretty, but rather simple and lame in one foot. Doubtless this was why Henrietta was happy to encourage her to amuse the King.

Nicolas asked Madame Laloy to make an approach on his behalf, but was surprised to find his offer of help angrily rejected. 'To secure her good will,' explained Madame Laloy in a hastily written note, 'I complimented her on her beauty – which to be perfectly honest isn't that remarkable – and let her know that you'd see to it she'd want for nothing and would give her 20,000 pistoles. But she turned on me, saying that not even 250,000 livres would persuade her to do anything unworthy. I did everything I could to calm her down, but she repeated it over and over again with such pride that I'm seriously worried she'll tell what happened to the King.'[7] Nicolas decided to speak to Louise de la Vallière directly. Singing the King's praises, he said that he hadn't intended to compromise her, but his reassurances were to no avail.

When she complained to the King anyway, suddenly it became clear that Madame had been superseded. If Louise de la Vallière had been a decoy once, she was certainly no longer one now; she and the King really were in love.

13

A Thing Apart

L ouise de la Vallière's reaction was a shock. Nicolas had wanted only information, yet here she was behaving as if he had seduced her. On the other hand, he thought he had wanted only information from Catherine de Menneville, yet suddenly he found himself falling as much in love with her as she had with him.

He tried to pretend that he gave her no more time than any of the other ladies-in-waiting, whom he cultivated strictly in accordance with the quality of intelligence they had to offer. He took comfort, therefore, from her complaints that he neglected her, just as it reassured him that she was always seeking his advice over how she might finally get de Damville to marry her. For surely here was the evidence that, whatever amusements they might find in each other's company, whatever love they might profess for each other on the surface, their relationship was finally no more than one of mutual advantage.

Yet the more they talked about de Damville the less he seemed to matter. He was just a pretext that allowed them to continue to see each other, the absurdity of which became apparent in the colossal sum of 150,000 livres that Nicolas gave Catherine to persuade de Damville to honour his promise to marry her. The gesture, which it was impossible to keep secret, only strengthened his reputation for recklessness at just the time when he most needed to show prudence and discretion. And as the rumours of his extraordinary generosity spread around the Court, the effect of such an obvious love gift was only to cause de Damville to hesitate even further.

But Nicolas himself was much too blinded by love to realise that he was in love. He may have spent much of the summer putting off meetings with Catherine in order to see other ladies-in-waiting who could offer better intelligence, but when Catherine in turn began to find more and more reasons why she could not slip away to see him – whether it was a cold or some Court engagement – he felt unaccountably upset.

Even more surprising was the sudden stab of jealousy he suffered when he saw her in the company of a young courtier called the marquis de Puyguilhem. He sent a note to Madame Laloy to ask what was going on. She wrote back that actually the young man was in love with another lady-in-waiting – Mademoiselle de Beauvais – and that, while it was true Mademoiselle de Menneville was often in de Beauvais's company, she never spoke to him. But the need for this reassurance in itself was a sign of how badly smitten the Superintendent had become.

A letter from Catherine herself soon followed. 'After all the signs of affection I've given, you cannot doubt the way I feel about you without causing me the deepest offence. I find it just as upsetting that it is so long since we've seen each other. If there was anything I could do about it, I would at once. But if I were to believe what I hear, I'd have to conclude that our relationship doesn't mean nearly so much to you. I tell myself over and again that this isn't true, because it would be too awful if you didn't feel the same way I do.' Although it was partly a note intended to test Nicolas's feelings, she didn't trouble to conceal the depths of her own, ending with the assurance that she would try to see him soon. 'Farewell,' she signed off, 'I am yours without reserve.'[1]

It was one of those affairs that fed on a wilful disregard for reality. Nicolas's wife Marie-Madeleine occupied a prominent and much respected position at Court. Indeed, that very summer, while Nicolas was enjoying his romantic tête-à-têtes in Fontainebleau's gardens, she was confined to their stuffy rooms in the palace, about to give birth to their latest child.* Nicolas would have been dangerously skirting scandal anyway, even if Mademoiselle de Menneville's intention to marry the duc de Damville hadn't been one of the most prominent items of Court gossip. The timing made it only all the more extraordinary – that Nicolas should risk compromising himself just as he was working so hard to win the King's favour. He was a man of obvious flair and brilliance, but he possessed too many failings for it really to make any sense to speak of an 'Achilles' heel'. Making up a very long list were impetuosity, naïveté, extravagance, vanity, overambition, but perhaps at the very top was this fondness for women. He may have liked to think that they were 'a thing apart' for him, but in truth they had dominated his existence for just about as long as he could remember.

When he was growing up, women were a notably strong influence in his life. His mother, Marie de Maupeou, had twelve children to raise, but refused to be confined to the usual domesticity. Instead, she pursued her charitable causes with an extraordinary energy and purpose that defied conventional notions of the 'weaker sex', whether it was preparing her medicinal cures or visiting the poor. And with most of Nicolas's sisters of an age to be his childhood companions, it was natural for him not only to regard women as confident and resourceful, but also to find in them a familiar, reassuring presence.

But Nicolas's immediate family provided only the nucleus of a much larger female community. His parents had been important benefactors to the convent of the Visitation, his father was buried

*Louis Foucquet, born July 1661.

211

in its chapel and its director, Vincent de Paul, was his mother's close friend and spiritual guide. Long before his sisters joined the order, therefore, Nicolas was accustomed to looking upon the convent as a kind of home from home. Situated in the heart of Paris, its cloisters also happened to offer an unusually valuable platform for future social connections. True to the principles of its founding, the convent of the Visitation was a place that sought to be a part of the world, encouraging the daughters of the privileged who stayed there to learn about society rather than to retire from it. Indeed, there was probably no better place to meet and to keep in touch with Paris's most well-connected and wealthy young women. Even Mazarin's Italian nieces had spent some months there when they first arrived in France from Rome.

Nicolas's experience of the opposite sex, then, was a series of widening circles, from his family, to the convent of the Visitation, to the Royal Court, in all three of which – through long habit and circumstance – he felt perfectly comfortable and at ease. This gregarious existence could not have helped to encourage him to accept the more exclusive terms of a marriage.

On the occasion of his wedding to Marie-Madeleine, he commissioned Charles Le Brun to paint a picture of his new wife as 'Beauty Clipping the Wings of Cupid'. As Marie-Madeleine purposefully sets about her task, next to her stands Hymenaios, the God of Weddings, illuminating the operation with his traditional bridal torch, while Minerva, the Goddess of Wisdom, pins the cherub firmly down. Perched on top of a cornucopia that Hymenaios holds up in his other hand, a Foucquet squirrel watches the bride – perhaps a little anxiously – as she snips away. In the background a plume of thick black smokes rises from a plinth, where Cupid's burning quiver of arrows lie abandoned.

When they married, in a union that had been arranged foremost to cement an alliance between two powerful families, Marie-Madeleine was only sixteen, twenty years Nicolas's junior. Little more than a child, she lacked the sophistication to compete with the clever women whose company Nicolas so treasured. When he really needed a confidante's advice he relied not on his young wife but on Madame du Plessis-Bellière. While Marie-Madeleine passed the first years of their marriage in repeated pregnancy, he preferred the company of the women who shone in the literary salons.

Marie de Rabutin-Chantal, marquise de Sévigné, was a young widow who had returned to Paris from Brittany with her two small children at about the same time as Nicolas's marriage to Marie-Madeleine. Her late husband, Henri de Sévigné, belonged to a distinguished old Breton family, but had been too busy womanising and gambling away his inheritance to care about either her or their children. Few people could have been surprised when he was killed in a duel over his mistress, Madame de Gondran, known as the 'Belle Lolo'.

In Paris, Marie took a house close to her uncle and former guardian, the Abbé de Coulanges, who helped her to put her life back together again. Since she was the granddaughter of Jeanne de Chantal, the founder of the Visitation, the Foucquet family already knew her very well. In a gesture of family friendship Nicolas offered to help her sort out her debts, but soon fell for the charm, wit and beauty that was winning her enormous popularity in the literary salons. Madame de Sévigné's correspondence with her cousin the comte de Bussy-Rabutin reveals how assiduously Nicolas courted her, but also how careful she was not to compromise her good name, as she made it clear to him that their relationship could continue only on the basis of friendship. 'I am relieved to hear you so pleased with the Superintendent,' wrote Bussy-Rabutin. 'It does him credit the way he has let reason prevail, and no longer takes everything so to heart.'[2] Nicolas's fundamentally compassionate and sensitive nature meant that he preferred a respectful, chivalrous retreat to conduct that might be perceived as unpleasant or overbearing. But although he continued a relationship of perfect propriety with Madame de Sévigné, who valued his warmth and intelligence as much as he did hers, he remained ever liable to wager his heart on the next attractive woman who came along.

His perpetual dalliances and crushes, which were too numerous to be kept hidden, must have caused Marie-Madeleine considerable pain. But rather than allow herself to be intimidated by the beautiful and stylish women who surrounded her husband, she decided to offer them some unbeatable competition of her own. Determined to understand her husband's world, she made friends with his secretary, Paul Pellisson, got to know the poets and writers who frequented the library at Saint-Mandé, and even, took drawing lessons from Charles Le Brun. Open-minded and adaptable, she found no subject too dull or grim. One day she was even overheard patiently discussing various arcane theories concerning the pox with Nicolas's doctor Jean Pecquet.

She became a familiar presence not only at the salon of Saint-Mandé but also the gambling parties that during this period were a regular feature of Court life. She laid down her cards with such good humour and cheerfulness that she was reputed to be one of the two women the young King Louis himself most liked to play against.[3] (The other was Mazarin's niece, Olympe Mancini, the comtesse de Soissons.)

Determined to make the most of the title 'Madame la Superintendante', she turned herself into the kind of hostess who would show the many rivals for her husband's affections that, whatever passing triumphs they might enjoy, the future belonged to her. It was perhaps too much to hope to be able to clip his wings completely, but she tried hard to save him from temptation, making every effort to be at his side. Her solicitude had tragic consequences when, in December 1659 during the peace negotiations with Spain, she accompanied Nicolas on a long and difficult journey to Toulouse, although she was pregnant. On the way back the rolling and bumping motion of the coach caused her to miscarry.

La Fontaine wrote a poem to console her for the loss:[4] 'Miserable to be parted from your beloved husband, / And seeing him set out on such a long journey, / You wanted to follow him, and he couldn't stop you: / Such was the price you paid for the purity of your love.'* La Fontaine was too discreet to suggest that the journey was partly a result of Marie-Madeleine's wish to keep an eye on a husband she couldn't trust to be faithful, but for all Nicolas's many infidelities, the couple enjoyed a strong relationship that had clearly grown over the years into one of mutual love and affection.

When they married in 1651, Marie-Madeleine was no more than a schoolgirl whom Nicolas – twice her age – had little reason to take seriously. But he compensated for any initial indifference with his ready recognition of talent and delight in nurturing it: he watched her grow and, praising her progress, gave her confidence. Rather than shut her out, as many powerful men in his shoes might have done, he willingly encouraged her to play a full part in his life. They became a team. She presided over his salons and, winning the devotion of the writers who surrounded him, even began to set their assignments and supervise the payment of their pensions.

There seemed no end to the blessings Nicolas enjoyed – a loving wife, a beautiful mistress and the most magnificent house in France. But even these were not enough. Now he wanted to add to them the office of first minister to the King. In the quest, he had expended great efforts to discover what the King was thinking, but it is difficult to escape the conclusion that, for all the

---

*'Ne quittant qu'avec peine un mari par trop cher, / Et le voyant partir pour un si long voyage, / Vous le voulûtes suivre, il ne put l'empêcher: / De vos chastes amours vous lui dûtes ce gage.'

apparent attempts at gathering intelligence, he was far too much in the grip of his own wishes and desires to understand those of Louis – someone whom experience and circumstance had made uniquely guarded.

While Nicolas freely pursued his passions, Louis had been taught by the late Cardinal to suppress his true feelings. For the greater good of the state he had sacrificed the love of his life, Marie Mancini. The words of his godfather, who had ruthlessly broken up the relationship, would still have been ringing in his ears: 'Remember what I often told you when you asked how to become a great king: most important of all is not to allow yourself to be ruled by your passions. For when this misfortune happens, it becomes impossible, however many good intentions you may have, to take the right decisions.'[5]

To treat love as a thing apart. Whether it was pride, fame or ambition, Nicolas had far too many other desires for love ever to be his whole existence, yet at the same time it was too important in his life for him to be able to learn the Cardinal's lesson.

14

The Party

During that warm and languid summer, Fontainebleau may have had the outward appearance of an enchanted haven, but behind the scenes the fierce battle for hearts and minds continued. A powerful source of support that Nicolas had long counted on was the Queen Mother. He had not only been scrupulous in paying out the large pensions to her and her retainers, but had also shown considerable sympathy and understanding for her position. Since Cardinal Mazarin's death, Anne had found herself excluded by her own son from a role in the government of the country, but Nicolas promised to change all that when he was appointed prime minister. Anne's fundamental attitude to Nicolas had been one of admiration and approval, even if she had few illusions about his weaknesses: he was a crook, but – like the late Cardinal, who had been a crook too – still the most capable minister France had. As Mazarin had once confided to her: 'If only one could knock women and buildings out of his head, he'd be perfect.'[1]

But while he was still at Fontainebleau Nicolas began to receive alarming reports that Anne had turned against him. In June the Queen Mother had paid a visit to her friend the duchesse de Chevreuse, who lived at Dampierre with her new husband the marquis de Laigues. The elderly Duchess, who had been involved in countless schemes against both Richelieu and

Mazarin, had a flair for intrigue that many years in prison or exile had failed to quench – Mazarin had once observed of her that France had only been quiet when she wasn't there. Although she had no reason of her own to dislike Nicolas, the fact that her husband bore some unknown grudge against him was enough of an excuse for her to take up her favourite pastime. She had already warned Anne's confessor, Father Philippe Le Roy, against Nicolas's influence; and at Dampierre she was able to speak to Anne herself.

Nicolas's other enemies had joined the conspiracy. In an urgent note to Nicolas, one of his more reliable informants, Madame d'Huxelles, sought to impress on him the gravity of the situation. 'Many things have been said about you that seemed to me to be unimportant; but I now find myself obliged to send this message by courier to warn you that M. . . . has teamed up with the Queen's confessor . . .' The blank space she had left was for none other than Nicolas's own brother Basile. 'He is going all out against you,' she continued. 'He has sent reports to the Queen, which claim that you have wasted a fortune.' She put the most damning news in invisible ink. Nicolas had to warm the note over the fire to make the words legible: 'The Queen has forbidden her confessor to have any dealings with you. She says that you have spent a million on corrupting people . . .' She ended the letter with a final plea: 'Take care of your safety more than you ever have done before.'[2]

Rather than take the letter seriously, Nicolas dismissed it as needless scaremongering. It was only to be expected that, as he came closer to achieving his ambition, his enemies would redouble their efforts against him. But what finally counted was the King. He had worried that the embarrassing incident with Louise de la Vallière might have compromised him, but in fact it was an example of why the King was more reliant on him than ever. Struggling with his complex romantic life, Louis needed someone to whom he could safely delegate. He summoned Nicolas at all hours of the day and decided all sorts of issues on Nicolas's advice without consulting the other ministers. Even if he had yet to abandon the childish notion that he would rule France by himself, he was already treating Nicolas as a prime minister-in-waiting.

Another encouraging sign was the deference and respect with which Nicolas's arch-enemy Jean-Baptiste Colbert had recently begun to treat him. Nicolas didn't delude himself that Colbert had suddenly become a willing friend, but this change in attitude did suggest that Colbert too had taken note of the trust the King was placing in Nicolas.

Indeed, the King had come to depend on Nicolas so much that he asked him to give up his office of Attorney-General in the Parlement. Nicolas promised not only to sell the office, but also, as a pledge of his total loyalty, to hand over the proceeds of a million livres to the King. At the same time he enthusiastically welcomed – maybe even suggested – the proposal that the King should travel to Nantes, where Nicolas would use his influence to persuade the Estates of Brittany to raise a levy on the King's behalf. Owning great swaths of land there, and with friends who were governors of some of the principal towns, Nicolas was proud of his family's roots in the province. The King's visit there would be one more mark of his favour.

Through July 1661, Nicolas worked on the complex negotiations necessary to effect the sale of one of the most important offices of state. But then he received another letter from Madame d'Huxelles. This time she wrote to warn him to hold on to the office, since being Attorney-General entitled him to valuable rights and immunities. She had learned that selling the office was precisely what his enemies wanted him to do. Nor should he even trust the goodwill and support he had received from the King, who it seemed was now feeding the hopes of the conspirators.

'Madame de Chevreuse has been here,' she wrote, 'and my sources have promised to give me some vital information concerning her visit, the trip to Brittany, some secret resolutions of the King and other measures that have been taken against you.'[3]

But Nicolas ignored the letter. On 10 August 1661 he finally sold the office to an old friend, Achille de Harlay, and handed over the proceeds to the King, depositing them not in the Treasury, but at Louis's request in a cellar in the Château de Vincennes. He ignored, too, the advice of Paul Pellisson, who had the task of sifting through the countless reports concerning his safety. He told him that he had no wish for any protection, support, wealth or honour that was not by grace of the King.[3] It was the characteristic response of a man who, for all his gift of intellect, had built his career on confidence rather than logic, and courage rather than caution. It may often not have been apparent amid all the scheming and deceptions and trickery, but the ruling principle of Nicolas's life was to have faith in the future. So he resolved to pay no heed to all the prophecies of doom. Instead, he decided to hold a party at Vaux-le-Vicomte that would express his belief in not only the young King's reign but also the leading role that he had expected to play in it.

The seventeenth of August was a swelteringly hot day. Queen Maria Theresa, who was many months pregnant now, had had a sleepless night and decided to stay behind at Fontainebleau. The rest of the Court set off in a long procession at about three in the afternoon, the King travelling in an open-top carriage with his brother Philippe, the comtesse d'Armagnac, the duchesse de Valentinois and the comtesse de Guiche. Arriving at Vaux-le-Vicomte about three hours later, the procession passed through into the vast forecourt, which was flanked on both sides by stables and other outbuildings that, elsewhere, might almost have passed for palaces themselves. Nicolas and his wife greeted the members of the royal family as they descended from their carriages and escorted them up into the house. Here they were taken on a tour of the newly painted rooms, where Charles Le Brun was on hand to explain the symbolism of the allegorical paintings that adorned the walls and ceilings. Maybe it was just the fancy of hindsight, but some courtiers had the impression that one of these pictures caused the King to give a little start of annoyance. It featured Louise de la Vallière dressed as Diana the Huntress. But if so, the King quickly retrieved his veil of regal composure. Having gossiped about Nicolas's ambitions for months now, the courtiers couldn't also help but remark on the Superintendent's coat of arms that decorated every room: the squirrel climbing to the summit of a tree and those words that had perhaps never seemed quite so triumphant and presumptious before. *Quo non ascendet?*

From the house, the courtiers passed through the oval grand salon and out into the gardens. Here a vista of fountains, sculptures and ponds stretched ahead of them. They then passed down a broad central path, a hundred jets of water on each side making it seem as though they were walking between two sheer walls of water. Reaching a terrace, most of the Court, who had not visited Vaux before, would have been surprised suddenly to see their progress halted by a long canal. From the house it looked as if you could walk straight up to the park on the rising ground in the far distance. At their feet, a cascade bubbled and tumbled down through basins and sculpted shells to the level of the canal, in the words of one eyewitness, 'making such a majestic and beautiful noise that everyone swore that it was Neptune's throne'.[4]

To save the King and his mother any further exertion, Nicolas made available to them a pair of horse-drawn, two-wheeled buggies that took them down to the level of the canal, then along its length and round to the terrace on the far side. At the foot of the steps that led up to this far terrace were four stone lions, each of these creatures cradling between his paws a great pile of fruit on top of which perched a squirrel gnawing a nut. It wasn't a question that occurred to anyone at the time, but later it would take on considerable significance. Had the squirrel stolen the nut, or had the lion offered it to him?

After their tour of the garden, the royal family and courtiers returned to the house, where a lottery was held. Everyone who took part won something, with prizes that included jewels, swords and pistols. At the supper that followed Nicolas's maître d'hôtel Vatel demonstrated the discreet organisation and effortless generosity that is the key to hospitality on the grand scale. Easily able to find their places at over a hundred tables, the guests feasted on 'pheasants [. . .] and many other delicious delicacies and all sorts of wine in abundance',[5] while Lully's Twenty-four Violins played in the background. They ate not off china, but silver plates. The cruets and sugar bowls were made of gold. As many guests could not resist remarking, not even the King himself could match such splendour.

After supper the guests strolled back into the garden, which had been illuminated by hundreds of candles. Here, under a starlit sky and against a backdrop of fountains and trees, a temporary theatre had been set up halfway down the garden by one of the giant ponds. The playwright Molière, dressed in ordinary town clothes, hurried on to the stage as if he had been whisked totally unawares off the rue Saint-Antoine. In a fine conceit after the serene order of Vatel's carefully planned feast, he apologised for being so unprepared to provide the spectacle that the King seemed to be expecting, but promised he would do his best with what help was available. The King had only to order the show to begin.

When the sign was duly given, a rock on the stage metamorphosed into a shell. A water nymph then stepped forth and

bade her divinities to come out of the stone in which they had
been encased and to devote all their powers to entertaining their
King:

> Young, victorious, wise, gallant, august,
> As gentle as he is firm, as powerful as he is just . . .

The statues and trees on the stage came alive, revealing themselves to be dryads, fauns and satyrs. They then danced the first
of several ballet sequences that interspersed the acts of Molière's
play. Molière had been given less than two weeks to write the
work. But hastily put together though it may have been, *Les
Fâcheux** received warm applause. Its story of a man who finds
his attempts at courtship continually interrupted must have had a
familiar ring for many of the guests after the escapades at
Fontainebleau that summer.

A firework display followed. La Fontaine described the scene
in a letter to his friend Charles Maucroix. 'Imagine seeing a
thousand rockets shoot into the sky at once,' he wrote, 'filling the
sky with lightning, their fiery progress chasing away the night.'[6]
The drums and trumpets of the King's escort of musketeers
counterpointed the sound of the explosions, lending the scene the
aspect of some great battle. As the rockets fell back earthwards,
they formed the shapes of fleur-de-lis. A huge whale advanced
down the length of the canal, disgorging yet more rockets.

When everything was quiet again and the last sparks had
subsided, the King made his way back towards the chateau, from
where, after a light meal, he intended to return to Fontainebleau.
But on the way, while the guests were still marvelling over what
they had just seen and were expecting nothing else, the great
dome of the chateau erupted into a mass of light and flame as yet

---

* 'The Nuisances'.

more rockets took to the sky. 'At first it seemed as though all the stars, large and small, had fallen to earth in order to pay their respects to Madame,' wrote La Fontaine, 'but once the storm was over, we could see that they were where they had always been.'[7]

Frightened by this sudden eruption of noise and fire, two horses harnessed to the Queen Mother's carriage reared up, jumped their traces and fell into the moat of the chateau, where they broke their necks. La Fontaine, who in his letters had the habit of passing freely back and forth between prose and poetry, crystallised the terrible moment in a verse:

> These two horses who once pulled a carriage
> But now draw the ferry of Charon
> Fell into the waters of Vaux
> And from there into the River Acheron.*

'I could not have imagined that this story would have so tragic and pitiful an ending.'[8]

Ces chevaux, qui jadis un carrosse tirèrent / Et tirent maintenant la barque de Charon, / Dans les fossés de Vaux tombèrent, / Et puis de là dans l'Achéron. In Greek mythology the Acheron is a branch of the River Styx, across which Charon ferries the newly dead into the Underworld.

PART THREE

Quo Non Descendet?

(To where will he not fall?)

15

The Birthday Present

Nantes. Why was the King going to Nantes? Only a month
ago it had seemed like wonderful news. But now Nicolas was
having second thoughts. In a terrible dawning everything he'd
once welcomed he now dreaded. But maybe he just wasn't seeing
straight. Ever since the party, he had been suffering from a series
of blinding headaches. When they were upon him, they made it
impossible for him to think or to do anything at all. He simply had
to lie prostrate on a couch and hope that the pain would soon pass.
It was easy to regard these attacks as the result of the
extraordinary tension of the times. His fate hung in the balance,
but the outcome was out of his hands. He had placed his bet on the
King and he had to wait to see what the King would do.

He was on the threshold of power, but never had he felt so
powerless. Unable to do anything, he longed for news. But when
he asked Gourville whether he had heard anything, he received
the usual contradictory predictions of catastrophe and splendid
good fortune: 'Some say you're going to be declared Prime
Minister, others that there's a plot to destroy you.'[1] According to
one report, the King had been consumed with jealousy by what
he saw at Vaux and had told his mother that he would make
Nicolas and his kind pay back all their ill-gotten gains. Another
report suggested that the King had been furious to see the woman
he loved most in all the world put in a picture without his having

any say in the matter. Yet in their face-to-face meetings the King himself continued to treat Nicolas with the usual cordiality and respect.

In this atmosphere of smokescreens and mirrors, Nicolas had to struggle to make sense of the faintest of clues, some of which were disturbing. One day, soon after the party, Louis's favourite courtier, the comte de Saint-Aignan, publicly renounced his friendship with Nicolas after meeting him in the King's ante-chamber. Then, in a meeting of the Council, the King suggested that Nicolas should give up the system of accounting – to which the late Cardinal had been so attached – that made it possible for him as Finance Minister to make certain secret payments. With the self-defeating spontaneity that from time to time let him down, Nicolas cried out, 'Do I count for nothing, then?'[2] Realising at once that he had said the wrong thing, he tried to recover the situation with the comment that some other way would have to be found to hide secret state expenses, but the damage had been done.

With the headaches, it was impossible to think clearly, easy to find plots and schemes in everything. The day before his departure for Nantes, he asked Brienne – who was also travelling to Nantes and for whom the King seemed to have a special regard – whether he had heard anything.

'Not a word,' answered the young man.[3]

Nicolas then agonised aloud over how very exposed he had left himself. He had surrendered the immunity that went with the office of attorney-general in the hope of receiving a far larger prize. But what if it was all a trick? 'No!' he suddenly cried. 'I can't believe that the King means to destroy me!'[4]

But why did the King want to go to Nantes? Nicolas had regarded the trip to Brittany as an opportunity to show off the support he enjoyed in the provinces. But now he saw how easily this trip lent itself to another purpose that suited his enemies.

Nantes was close to Belle-Isle. From Nantes, Louis could quickly despatch forces to take control of the island – if he was so minded.

'Well, what should I do,' Nicolas mused. 'Run? Hide? Not easy, though. What country would dare give me sanctuary?'[5]

Breaking out of his reverie, he said to Brienne, 'You see how I worry. Please let me know if you hear anything.'

Brienne noticed that as Nicolas wished him farewell he had tears in his eyes, and he couldn't help but shed a few tears too. It was as if they both had the same sense of impending doom.

All those close to Nicolas shared the presentiment. On the eve of his departure Mademoiselle de Menneville sent him this note: 'I beg you not to allow your affection for me to diminish with your absence. As for the affection I feel for you, I can assure you it will last my whole life. Farewell. Believe me when I tell you that I love you with all my heart, and will never love anyone other than you.'[6] She wrote as if she knew she would never see him again.

Nicolas had arranged that he and Marie-Madeleine should travel to Nantes with Hugues de Lionne. Making use of the Superintendent's relay of horses, the party's carriage completed the fifty-mile journey to Orléans in just a few hours. Here, they boarded the spacious barge, equipped with galley and living quarters, that was to take them down the Loire to Nantes. Nursing his persistent headache and worried about what might await him at Nantes, just about the very last thing Nicolas would have wanted to think about were the splendid, sometimes rather forbidding royal chateaux that stood like sentinels high above the gently winding course of the Loire, with their histories testifying to the routine treachery of French politics.

Just a few hours downriver from Orléans was the chateau of Blois, where Henri III had taken refuge in 1588 after the uprising of the Catholic League, and where he had his enemy the duc de Guise assassinated. A few miles further on was the imposing chateau of Amboise, perched on a massive outcrop overlooking the river. Here, just a hundred years previously, over a thousand Protestants who had plotted against François II had been executed and strung from the city walls, from trees lining the river and even from iron hooks on the castle. There were plenty of other castles along the Loire that could teach similar lessons in the merciless retribution of the Crown.

At Nantes, Nicolas's barge glided quietly past the ramparts of the castle, where the King was due to arrive the next day, and continued along the Quai de la Fosse some distance downriver to a small tributary called the Chézine. Here the Loire began to widen out to give some hint of the ocean miles beyond. His lodging at the Hôtel de Rougé had been carefully chosen. Belonging to the family of Madame du Plessis-Bellière, it looked out over the narrow banks of the Chézine, but was connected by an underground aqueduct to the Loire. In case of any danger, Nicolas hoped to make a swift river-bound escape to the open sea and to the island of Belle-Île beyond.

The next day the King, who had just settled in at Nantes castle, sent Brienne to enquire after the Superintendent's health. In his memoirs Brienne recalled finding Nicolas in his dressing gown shivering with fever, but nonetheless oddly calm, almost cheerful. Propped up on a pile of green damask pillows, Nicolas asked him what news there was from the castle.[7]

Brienne confessed that the only thing anyone seemed able to talk about at the moment was his imminent arrest.

'No,' said Nicolas. 'It's Colbert who's going to be arrested. Not me!'

Brienne stared at Nicolas as if he had gone mad, astonished that he could have allowed himself to believe this. 'Are you sure?'

'I myself gave the orders to have him taken to Angers castle.'

'No, you're wrong. Your friends *fear* for you. And the King's up to something. He's locked himself away in a room in the castle, making out secret orders, which are brought to him by the dozen from Le Tellier. Saint-Aignan and Rose have been posted outside with instructions not to let anyone in without letting him know first. Any time anyone enters his rooms, no matter who it is, they have to ring a little silver bell.'

'It was my idea,' replied Nicolas. 'A ruse to hide our schemes.'

'If only it were so,' Brienne sighed. 'But I doubt it.'

Nicolas continued to perspire and tremble with fever, but he invited Brienne to stay a while, proposing a toast of hot water mixed with sugar and cinnamon to his health.

Later in the evening Brienne dropped by again.[8] This time he found Nicolas out of bed and dressed, drinking wine and in the process of polishing off a whole roast chicken. It was as if he had never been ill. But his mood had swung yet again. Nicolas had noticed that there were musketeers posted outside in the street. He told Brienne in a grave voice that he'd heard that the Captain of the Guards, Chevigny, was on his way to Belle-Isle with a company of men to seize the island. Gourville was urging him to make his escape through the underground viaduct.

'But I'm going to stay here,' he said firmly. 'I *have* to take the risk. I just can't believe the King has turned against me.' Half confiding, half thinking aloud, he told Brienne how he'd confessed to the various irregularities that had occurred under the Cardinal, and how the King had forgiven him. The idea that the King might be as capable of deception as anyone else seemed inconceivable to him. 'I just *can't believe* that the King has turned against me.'

Jittery and nervous, Nicolas must have had trouble getting to sleep that night. If he ever succeeded, it is difficult to imagine that his dreams would have brought him any comfort. The last of the big fortress towns along the Loire, Nantes could tell as terrible a tale of treachery as any of those that had preceded it. The family connection made it likely enough that Nicolas would have pondered the strange echo of circumstances. Thirty-five years ago the duc de Chalais had followed *his* King to Nantes for a meeting at the Estates-General. He thought that he enjoyed the King's friendship, but in the end ruin awaited him. What an irony it would be if now the son of Chalais's judges should suffer the same fate.

The next day, 5 September, was the King's birthday. Nicolas had been summoned to an early morning meeting of the Council because Louis had let it be known that he wanted to spend the rest of the day hunting. Perhaps that explained the presence of so many musketeers in the castle courtyard. In the meeting itself Nicolas was oddly reassured when the King asked for money: 48,000 francs for the navy. When the meeting was over, the King asked him to stay behind a while; there were other matters he wanted to discuss. This extra reliance was reassuring too. But still Nicolas could not dispel from his mind all those warnings that he was walking into a trap. It would have been difficult not to feel nervous as he went back down into the courtyard, only natural to anticipate some hand on the shoulder. But Nicolas passed the musketeers in the courtyard, he climbed into his litter, he went through the castle gates . . . and no one held him back.

The moment, when it came, was strangely casual. On the far side of the castle bridge, the litter turned right and climbed up the rue Haute du Château (known today as the rue Mathelin-Rodier) towards the cathedral of St Peter and St Paul. As he crossed the cathedral square, a number of musketeers overtook him and forced his litter to draw to a halt.

D'Artagnan, the captain-lieutenant of the musketeers, appeared at his side. 'Sir,' he said. 'I arrest you by order of the King.'[9]

'But Monsieur d'Artagnan, are you sure it's *me* you're looking for?' Nicolas replied calmly.

'Yes, sir.'

Nicolas got out of the litter and read the order of arrest. Determined to keep his self-composure, he allowed d'Artagnan to search him for papers. Sighing, he said, 'I used to think the King held me in greater regard than anyone else in his kingdom.'

D'Artagnan then led him off to a nearby house to wait for a carriage. On the way Nicolas quickly whispered to one of his servants, 'Let Madame du Plessis at Saint-Mandé know what has happened.'[10] In the square life continued – as Auden observed, uninterested in this disaster, the passers-by just walking dully along.

Later that afternoon, an escort of a hundred musketeers escorted Nicolas's carriage out of Nantes. At his side sat d'Artagnan. That evening they lodged at Oudon and the next, as they continued back eastwards along the course of the Loire, at Ingrandes. On the third day they came within sight of the sombre grey towers of Angers castle. The seat of the Dukes of Anjou, this forbidding building, which was used as a state prison, would be Nicolas's home for the next few weeks.

It's not clear whether the King actually did go out hunting on the day of Nicolas's arrest. There would surely have been little point. After the capture of the Superintendent, any other quarry – boar, stag or falcon – would have seemed a derisory catch. The King's birthday present to himself was this first major exercise of his power.

Nicolas's arrest was just one part of a much larger operation. Pellisson, who had also made the journey to Nantes, was arrested at the same time and the papers found on him seized. To pre-empt any possible attempt of Nicolas's friends and allies to come to his aid, the musketeers guarded all the roads out of Nantes as far as Saumur. The King was determined that no news of the arrest should get back to Paris ahead of his own imminent return. To prevent Nicolas's wife, Marie-Madeleine, from providing a focus for any possible regrouping in the capital she was banished on the spot to Limoges. No time was allowed for her even to organise her affairs. She was told to set off for her new place of exile at once, although she had no more than a few coins in her purse.

In the evening the King sat down to write a long letter to his mother,[11] in which he described all the key events of the day: the Council meeting in the morning, his announcement that he wanted to go hunting as a pretext to prepare his musketeers, the arrest itself, and so on. He told her how he had now announced Nicolas's capture to his courtiers. 'I told them quite openly that I'd been planning it for four months; that only you had known; and that I only let Le Tellier into the secret two days ago so he could put my orders into effect. I told them, too, that I no longer wanted to have a Superintendent of Finances; that from now on I would supervise financial matters with the help of people I can trust, who would act at my behest, appreciating that this is the best way to restore my fortune and to bring relief to my people.'

The King's chief accomplice in the plot was Jean-Baptiste Colbert. The King did not mention him once in his letter, but Colbert was content enough to linger in the shadows while those with greater nominal authority than himself, like Le Tellier, issued the orders for an arrest that he had quietly masterminded.

16

'Lightning Strikes the Highest Mountains'*

At Angers, where Nicolas arrived on 7 September, d'Artagnan chose a set of chambers in the most impregnable of the castle's eight towers. The King had made available to him his intendant of fortifications, Monsieur de Châtillon, with express instructions that d'Artagnan should have him modify the castle in any way he thought necessary to ensure the complete security of the prisoner. Since the Duke of Angers had received no warning that he would have to put up such an important prisoner of state, the living arrangements were makeshift, with d'Artagnan having to buy crockery, furniture and a new bed in the town.

The possibility that Nicolas might escape was the least of d'Artagnan's worries. Nicolas's fever had returned. He was so ill that d'Artagnan feared that he would die.

Eventually, at the suggestion of Gourville, who had somehow been spared imprisonment himself, Le Tellier persuaded the King to allow Jean Pecquet to attend Nicolas. Pecquet was duly locked into Angers castle along with Nicolas's valet de chambre, La Vallée, both men subject to the same harsh restrictions as Nicolas himself. Worried about Nicolas's extreme weakness,

*'*Feriunt summos fulmina montes.*' The words come from a letter that a shocked La Fontaine wrote to his friend François Maucroix upon hearing the news of Nicolas's arrest. They are a paraphrase of Horace, *Odes*, 2.10.11–12.

Pecquet asked for permission to confer with doctors in both Angers and Paris. He had to write down his questions in the presence of d'Artagnan, who would then, under strict instructions from Le Tellier, take away pen, any spare paper and ink afterwards. His gaolers wanted to keep Nicolas alive, but to prevent any news of him whatsoever from reaching the outside world. From her exile, Nicolas's wife, Marie-Madeleine, sent representatives to Angers to enquire after him, but even they were turned away and warned not to come back.

The one person Nicolas was free to correspond with was Le Tellier. During the first weeks of his imprisonment he wrote to him to request a confessor. 'I am incredibly weak and tired . . . I daydream, I come close to nodding off sometimes, but I've had very little real sleep. I am naturally rather frail. If my fever is the result of melancholy, then this place is hardly going to dispel my sorrows.'[1] He feared that with the approaching winter his health would only get worse. If he did not die first, he might easily lose his mind. In these circumstances, seeing a good priest was urgent. He would not feel at ease until he had made his peace with God. He suggested Claude Joly, who was the priest of his parish church in Paris, Saint-Nicolas-des-Champs, and knew him well. But the curt reply, which Le Tellier addressed to d'Artagnan rather than Nicolas himself, made clear the lack of will to grant special concessions: 'Monsieur Joly will not be able to travel to Angers. If the prisoner wishes to take confession, find an ordinary priest.'[2]

Jittery, despondent and ill, Nicolas wrote the letter when he was at the very lowest point in his fortunes. But suddenly the fever abated. The next time Nicolas wrote to Le Tellier, it was not to prepare himself for the next world but to defend his conduct in this one. He begged Le Tellier to represent to the King all the arguments that his disgrace prevented him from making himself. The King should consider all those who had borne arms against him during his minority and sought to deprive him of his crown, how although they had been guilty of countless acts of hostility, now they enjoyed wealth, honour and good fortune; while, on the other hand, he, Nicolas, who had remained unshakeably loyal, who had rendered – often at great personal risk – more important services to the King than anyone else, who had continued to display such loyalty to the very last, was now the only person to suffer the King's anger.

Although he had yet to be officially charged, in an indignant, combative tone Nicolas sketched out what would be the outline of his defence when he was finally brought to trial:[3]

I oversaw the finances with Monsieur Servien, but in those first years it was he who had the chief responsibility. Monsieur Le Tellier well knows that at the end of 1654 Servien and even the Cardinal himself had run out of money and seemed unable to find the least penny, although the entire kingdom was on the edge of disaster. At this point, I took over Servien's responsibilities and, through my zeal and application – but what is more (and what no one else has ever done, but what proved to be the saving of the kingdom), through my own resources and those of my friends – I restored the state finances and kept them going through crisis after crisis over a period of seven years, so that we not only had all we needed but also prevailed over our enemies . . .

With the return of peace I had reason to hope for some reward; for I can say that without me and the risks I took – risks that have meant that my own affairs are in complete disorder – no one else would have come to the rescue and the state would have fallen. One might have thought that after having steered the ship so well during a storm, I deserved better when the weather was calm again. In these early months of his rule there have been plenty of things for the King to be pleased about, yet in return I am to be destroyed!

I may have done some blameworthy things; I do not seek to excuse myself. But I did what I had to do, since it was the only way to avert disaster. In any case, as far as money is concerned, it was impossible to follow strict rules with the Cardinal. He never gave precise orders. He forbade everything and he allowed everything. He would withhold his approval; then after the impossibility of acting otherwise had been explained to him, he would give his approval. He would speak and write to me with glowing words of praise, but then speak ill of me behind my back, and, as those who deal with financial matters attract the kind of unpopularity he wanted to avoid, he deliberately gave only the most vague indications of what he wanted.

For these reasons, and in order to retain his confidence in face of what people were saying about me, I had to tell the King that if my conduct had displeased him – although I thought I had served him well – then I begged him to pardon all my past faults. The King, very obligingly, gave me his word that everything was forgiven. But now I find myself imprisoned and attacked!

Nicolas went on, in several more paragraphs, to express his incomprehension at the way he had been treated. The sheer volume of words and the detailed recollection of services rendered betrayed a kind of raw hurt. How could a sovereign be so ungrateful to this most faithful of servants! But he knew that no amount of reasoning was suddenly going to restore him to favour and the practical purpose of the letter was to beg the King to be lenient. If the King released him, he would go into exile in Brittany, where he would lead a quiet life. 'There I shall undertake, under pain of death, to preoccupy myself solely with my own personal matters – my health, my conscience and my family.'

But no answer was received.

*

The first person to reach Paris with the news of Nicolas's arrest was his servant La Forêt, who had taken advantage of a relay of swift horses that Nicolas had put in place between Nantes and the capital. Reaching Paris in the morning of 7 September, a full twelve hours before the King's men, he made straight for Saint-Mandé, where Madame du Plessis-Bellière was waiting for him.

Once upon a time, when Nicolas had feared the jealousy and power of the Cardinal, he had written an elaborate escape plan, which set out exactly what his friends and allies should do if he was ever imprisoned. Every measure that might facilitate his eventual release and return to influence had been carefully spelt out. Nothing had been left to chance. But what now? The evidence suggests a few haphazard precautions – La Forêt's relay of horses, the escape passage in Nantes – but the overwhelming impression is of how defenceless he had left himself. While he had conceived of every trick and stratagem to protect himself against the Cardinal, in a strange kind of innocence, a wishful thinking, such measures seemed inconceivable to him in the case of the King.

So now there was no grand strategy of well-organised allies who would save the day. Upon learning the news of Nicolas's arrest, the only help that Madame du Plessis-Bellière was able to muster was that of Nicolas's quarrelsome, unpredictable but now contrite brother. But Basile's suggestion that they should set fire to Saint-Mandé and burn Nicolas's papers was so reckless that Madame du Plessis-Bellière wished she hadn't sought his help at all. Instead, she insisted that they should behave as if Nicolas had nothing to hide and wait for the King's instructions.

The next day the Chancellor, Pierre Séguier, sent officers to Saint-Mandé to seal off the property and to make an inventory of Nicolas's papers. Séguier despatched more officers to Nicolas's other properties, including Vaux-le-Vicomte and his apartment at Fontainebleau. Several of Nicolas's servants were arrested, while Madame du Plessis-Bellière, Basile and Nicolas's other brothers were sent into exile.

Soon after La Fontaine learned the news, he wrote this letter to his friend François Maucroix in Rome:

> I can make no reply to your enquiries concerning my own business, my dear friend. It means so little to me compared to the bad fortune the Superintendent has just suffered. He has been arrested and the King is against him and says he has enough evidence in his possession to make him hang. Oh, if he does that, he will be far more cruel than his enemies, even more so since he does not have any need, like them, to be unjust. Madame [du Plessis-Bellière] has received word that there are fears for Monsieur Pellisson's safety. If justified, then here is yet more misfortune to add to the pile. Farewell, my dear friend. I'd write much more now if only I were in a fit state. I shall make up for it next time. *Feriunt summos fulmina montes.*[4]

La Fontaine's reaction was typical of the sadness and despair that all Nicolas's friends felt. Only his mother believed that this supposed catastrophe was good news in the greater scheme of things. When she learned what had happened to her son, she fell to her knees, exclaiming: 'I thank you, my Lord. I have always begged you to save him. Here is the way.'[5]

The King decided that Nicolas would be put on trial. In theory it was the responsibility of the Chancellor to ensure that correct judicial procedure was observed. But on 19 September, after accompanying the King to see the newly built pavilions at the château de Vincennes, Jean-Baptiste Colbert turned up at Saint-Mandé in person and, although he had no judicial role and was generally known to be Nicolas's enemy, he was allowed to conduct his own search of the house. The next morning he was back again, rifling through boxes, levering off panels, sifting through letters. In the evening, hidden behind a mirror in the Superintendent's office, he came upon the escape plan that Nicolas had drawn up in the days of the Cardinal to take refuge in Belle-Isle should he ever fall into disfavour. Jubilant, he walked off with it unchallenged.

On this occasion Séguier's officers were too taken aback, and probably too frightened, to stop him, but they were well aware of the important issue at stake. When, three days later, Colbert sent a detail of musketeers to fetch some more papers that he wanted to show to the King, the officers refused to yield them up. They invited the musketeers to have lunch while they debated what to do. As they had no proof that Colbert had the King's authority but believed that nonetheless they had to respect the King's wishes, they delivered the papers directly to the King. This set a pattern for Nicolas's trial as a whole: a concern that the notional impartiality and supremacy of justice should at least be respected, but a recognition that finally the King was above the law.

Séguier's chief officer at Saint-Mandé, La Fosse, kept his boss informed of the progress of the inventory. While he strove to be an efficient, impartial servant of justice, he did not trouble to conceal his disapproval of Nicolas. The most trusted servant in the household, he reported, was a German Lutheran, who not only had a staff of other Lutherans under him, but also had converted – the word he actually used was 'perverted' – one of them from Catholicism. 'Add to this, sir, if you please, that Foucquet's chief adviser, Monsieur Pellisson, is a Calvinist!'[6]

But above all, La Fosse's reports expressed simple wonder at the extraordinary contents of Nicolas's house. One day two Spanish monks turned up at Saint-Mandé with a letter of authority from Le Tellier to study in Nicolas's library. In a room that contained hundreds of Korans, Talmuds, Rabbinicals and old interpretations of the Bible, they spent most of the day making notes on a rare book by a Spanish biblical scholar they had been unable to find in Spain. But afterwards they could not resist the opportunity to make a quick tour of the house. Astonished by what they found, they commented, 'The King of Spain has nothing to compare.'

'What would they have said if they had seen Vaux-le-Vicomte!' remarked La Fosse.[7]

Making his own repeated tours of the premises, La Fosse kept on stumbling upon new treasures, many locked away in store-rooms, as if Nicolas hadn't had the time to figure out what to do with them. The master of the house, he wrote to Séguier, was *omnium curiositatum explorator*, an explorer of all curiosities. In a room that had been called 'The Magazine', he came across large barrels full of grenades and other weapons, as well as fifty jars of gunpowder. In a courtyard shed he found among various statues and marble tables two huge Egyptian sarcophaguses. It was not something that the Chancellor's officials could possibly have known, but Nicolas and his friends had often pondered over the fate of the occupants – what sort of lives had they led in Ancient Egypt? – not realising, more than a hundred years before the discovery of the Rosetta stone, that their stories were contained in the strange pictures chiselled along the sarcophaguses' sides. La Fontaine, who nicknamed the pair Kiopes and Cephrim, even wrote a little verse about them, expressing the hope that, 'be they kings or gods', they would find some peace in this strange new land.[8] And, indeed, Nicolas had been meaning to transport them to Vaux-le-Vicomte, where he planned to build a special pyramid to make them feel at home. But now they faced a different fate. They would join the King's booty, eventually to find themselves in the Louvre, where they remain to this day.

La Fosse found no charm in any of his discoveries, just decadence. A particularly shocking discovery for him was a small volume hidden away in Nicolas's office called *L'Ecole des filles*. It was so 'shameless and obscene that we thought we ought to burn it, since it could serve only to corrupt the minds of anyone who found it'.[9] But far worse was a little box of private letters that suggested that such corrupting conduct was more than mere imagination. In a report to the Chancellor, La Fosse mentioned the box as one of the items that were sent straight to the King. The letters were of little legal value, he felt, but could only serve 'to compromise several ladies for having written far too freely'.[10] He and his colleagues felt that, for the sake of the women concerned, the most charitable thing would be to destroy these letters.

But in the event the King showed very little charity. He did not hesitate to name and shame the wayward ladies of his Court. The chief casualty was Mademoiselle de Menneville, who was so vilified for attempting to deceive the duc de Damville into marriage while she was pursuing her affair with the Superintendent that she entered a convent, where she died eight years later. But the box served much more as a general vehicle of royal opprobrium regardless of actual guilt.

Madame de Sévigné was upset when one of her letters turned out to be in Nicolas's box. It was a letter of perfect propriety concerning the marriage of her cousin. 'But I was still shaken,' she confided to her friend Gilles Ménage, 'to find myself named among those whose feelings were less pure than mine.'[11] She couldn't help but wonder how the letter had got there, 'so mysteriously'. Was someone trying to blacken her name by association, trying to warn her that she should be more careful about the friends she chose?

The letters offered scope for endless gossip, brightening up an otherwise rather dreary autumn. The wits and satirists of the time naturally had a field day, making up forged love letters that vastly outnumbered the genuine ones. The more eminent the name the more likely it seemed that it would be borrowed:

Madame de Valentinois was the daughter of the Marshal de Gramont and wife of a Grimaldi, who would inherit the principality of Monaco. She had travelled in the same carriage as the King on that day when the Court had set off for the grand party at Vaux-le-Vicomte. Yet her status did not prevent probably apocryphal reports that her signature had been found on this note to Nicolas: 'I don't know what excuse I can find to see you; I've already passed by your window twice today. Suggest a time when we can meet, and I'll do everything I can to be there.'[12] Then there was the Abbé Hurault de Belesbat, another well-known and much respected figure at Court. He may have been a priest, but that didn't prevent his name from turning up on the following: 'I know a very pretty, very well brought-up young girl. I'm pretty certain she's yours for three hundred pistols.'[13] Surely it couldn't have been the Abbé who wrote this? But mud stuck. No one knew for certain.

Kept in total isolation, neither Nicolas nor Pellisson – in his separate confinement – knew anything of the shame and scandal that mired so many of their friends, which was just part of a larger campaign to foment hatred for Nicolas himself. In late November d'Artagnan despatched a sergeant, with an escort of fifteen musketeers, to bring Pellisson to Angers from Nantes castle, where he had been held since his arrest. In this way Pellisson found himself in the same prison as his old master for a few days, but kept apart on the express orders of the King, who had forbidden any communication between them. On 1 December d'Artagnan then set off with both the prisoners for Amboise. While Nicolas travelled in a carriage with his doctor and valet, Pellisson was led along on horseback some distance behind.

As the large, well-guarded convoy set out on the road for Amboise, it attracted a hostile crowd. The former Superintendent offered a perfect scapegoat for the famine that was then affecting many of the most fertile regions of France and the crippling taxes they had had to endure for years. As the long procession of the King's musketeers passed by, they made fun of the lengths d'Artagnan had gone to guard his prisoner. 'Don't worry about him escaping. If he falls into our hands, we'll hang him ourselves!'[14] Similar scenes occurred when the convoy reached Tours. Such was the extraordinary hatred that Nicolas's presence seemed to provoke among ordinary people, that d'Artagnan became concerned for his safety and decided to travel only in the early hours of the morning.

At Amboise, d'Artagnan entrusted Nicolas into the care of the castle Governor, Monsieur Talhouet, who had cleared the building of all its inhabitants. D'Artagnan then continued on to Paris, where he handed Pellisson over to the Governor of the Bastille.

Nicolas's stay in Amboise turned out to be short. On Christmas Day he, Pecquet and La Vallée were told to get ready for another journey. In the courtyard eighty musketeers waited to escort them back to Paris.

La Fontaine, who was travelling with his uncle Jannart into exile at Limousin, stopped off at Amboise some time afterwards. He was struck by the beauty of the Loire countryside. But as he remarked in a letter to his wife, 'Poor Monsieur Foucquet, during his stay there, wasn't able to get the slightest taste of it. They walled up all the windows of his room and left only a tiny hole at the top.'[15] La Fontaine asked if he could see the room and Talhouet, only too eager to show off the measures he had taken to make Nicolas's prison secure, was happy to oblige.

The sad pilgrimage resulted in this poem for La Fontaine's old patron and friend:

> What need have I to describe
> An imprisonment beyond compare
> A walled-up room, narrow of space

Just a little air to give it grace;
Days without sun;
Nights without sleep;
Three doors squeezed into six feet?
To depict such a chamber
Is to bring forth your tears.
I do it insensibly:
This plaint has for me some charms.*

'Were it not for nightfall, one would never have been able to snatch me away from the place,' he told his wife.[16]

On 31 December 1661 Nicolas's carriage reached the Château de Vincennes, passing his house at Saint-Mandé on the way. As he caught a glimpse of his old home, he smiled and said, 'I'd much rather turn left here than right.' But the carriage turned right and, crossing the drawbridge into the castle precinct, passed between the two new royal residences built by Le Vau and headed on towards the old keep. Over 150 feet high, with walls ten feet thick and its own drawbridge, it was really a fortress within a fortress, which was routinely used to house important state prisoners. The Great Condé was held there after his capture during the Fronde and a little later the Cardinal de Retz. Now it was Nicolas's turn. He was given a large room on the first floor, which he was allowed to furnish with carpets, chairs and tables from his house in Saint-Mandé. Two separate areas of the chamber were partitioned off to make cubicles for La Vallée and Pecquet, and a room next door turned into an improvised chapel.

D'Artagnan, who had three weeks earlier safely delivered

---

* *Qu'est-il besoin que je retrace / Une garde au soin nonpareil, / Chambre murée, étroite place / Quelque peu d'air pour toute grâce, / Jour sans soleil, / Nuits sans sommeil, / Trois portes en six pieds d'espace? / Vous peindre un tel appartement, / Ce serait attirer vos larmes; / Je l'ai fait insensiblement: / Cette plainte a pour moi des charmes.*

Pellisson to the Bastille, was appointed once again to become Nicolas's chief gaoler. 'So that you may take the necessary security measures, it is my intention that you alone should have authority over the keep in my castle, including its gate and drawbridge,' the King wrote in his instructions.[17] D'Artagnan would discharge his duties with a notable humanity, but the months of captivity had already taken a heavy toll on Nicolas. When he had been arrested at the beginning of the autumn, his hair was brown; but now, at the end of the year, it was completely white.

17

Justice

The King ordered the establishment of a 'Chamber of Justice' that would not only put Nicolas on trial but also investigate the administration of the state finances. It was what Colbert had suggested to Cardinal Mazarin over two years previously. Made up of about twenty members, the Chamber was drawn from the key judicial institutions of state. Guillaume de Lamoignon, the President of the Parlement of Paris, was appointed to preside over the new Chamber, but its most powerful and influential member was the old Chancellor, Pierre Séguier.

In his mid-seventies, Séguier had been Chancellor and Keeper of the Seals – with just the occasional interlude – for nearly thirty years. In charge of the royal administration and answerable only to the King, he possessed immense authority, but in this case he was hardly an appropriate representative of impartial justice. It was Séguier who had first sworn in the young Nicolas as a Master of Requests over a quarter of a century previously. Ever since the Chancellor's complaints had caused Nicolas to be sacked and recalled in disgrace from Grenoble, an implacable hatred had existed between the two men. Whether it was true or not, Séguier held Nicolas responsible for his exclusion from the King's Council following Mazarin's death. He also believed that Nicolas had been campaigning behind his back to appropriate his office of

Keeper of the Seals. 'So he wants the seals? I'll give him the seals!'[1] he declared as he despatched his officials to impound Nicolas's properties after his arrest.

Both the King and Colbert knew that they could rely on such a man to ensure that the Chamber would deliver the desired verdict. Quite apart from his enmity for Nicolas, Séguier had never in the past allowed any theoretical concerns over the independence of justice to hamper its effective administration. He had survived as long as he had in high office through the swift implementation of royal policy.

In the spring of 1662 the Chamber officially began proceedings against Nicolas, not only for his alleged financial misconduct but also for treason. On the morning of Saturday, 4 March 1662, two members of the Chamber, Pierre Poncet and Jacques Renard, arrived at Vincennes to question him. Not having seen anyone from outside his little tower since his arrival two months previously, Nicolas at first greeted them warmly. But when he realised the tenor of their questions, he refused to make any formal defence without the assistance of a lawyer and an opportunity to see the relevant documents. He offered only to give certain clarifications on condition that his wife, Marie-Madeleine, was allowed to return to Paris from exile. As the hearings continued over the next twenty days, Nicolas made repeated demands to have access to papers, but without success.

Meanwhile, towards the end of March, a mysterious pamphlet began to circulate around Paris. The *Address to the King by one of His Loyal Subjects on the Trial of Monsieur Foucquet* may have had a rather long title, but the arguments of its anonymous author were succinct and persuasive. He challenged the competence and authority of the Chamber. Appointed by the King, the Superintendent should be answerable only to the King. To accuse him of malpractice was in effect to accuse the late Cardinal, whom the

Superintendent had served. In any case it was impossible to expect him to have a fair trial when his papers had been illegally confiscated and suppressed. Where was the Superintendent's correspondence with the Cardinal, which was essential to his defence?

The pamphlet went on to remind the King how the Superintendent had had responsibility for finance during one of the most difficult periods in France's recent history. If he was extravagant, then he had been the first to admit this. But he hadn't drawn on the royal revenues to pay for this extravagance. He had relied instead on his own wealth and substantial borrowing. It might not have been prudent but it was the conduct of a generous man, who had even offered to give up to his sovereign both the estate of Vaux-le-Vicomte and the island of Belle-Isle.

It was uncanny how much the writer clearly knew. He even seemed to be aware of Colbert exerting his secret influence in the wings, since he ended the address with a plea to the King not to listen to anyone else but to trust the promptings of his own heart. A heavy, rough paper and the many printing errors were the signs of a work that had been hastily produced on a clandestine press. It was easy to trace the authorship back to the one person other than Nicolas himself who could have possessed the necessary inside knowledge. By an appalling oversight Paul Pellisson, who was still a prisoner in the Bastille, had been allowed to have access to books, ink and paper. Probably, he had smuggled out the *Address* through his mother, who had been allowed to visit him. The visits were abruptly ended, the books, ink and paper taken away.[2]

Pellisson took to scrawling his defiance on the walls: 'Double gates, triple doors and hefty locks are hell to wicked souls, but only iron, wood and stone to the innocent.' Besmaux, the Governor of the Bastille, made him pay for his innocence by locking him in with a Basque who played loudly and tunelessly on a set of bagpipes all day long, but refused to speak.*

The *Address* marked a turning point. No one outside Nicolas's own circle had shown any sympathy for him until the pamphlet drew attention to the injustices he had suffered. It also encouraged others to come to Nicolas's aid. La Fontaine may have lacked Pellisson's aptitude for legal argument, but he made just as brave a defence of Nicolas in his own inimitable style. In his 'Elegy to the Nymphs of Vaux' he called on the nymphs who had sung the King's praises when he was their guest at Vaux to plead their master's case with him: 'Try to soften him, to make him brave enough to show pity. / He loves his subjects, he is just, he is wise; / So make him wish to aspire to the title of the All Merciful. / It is in this way that kings can resemble gods . . .'³

The plea, which resulted in La Fontaine having his pension taken away, did not lessen the King's resolve to punish Nicolas, but the public awareness that it helped to ignite put pressure on him at least to pay some lip service to justice. Eventually, after lengthy debate among the members of the Chamber, Nicolas was allowed pen and ink, access to documents and lawyers, even though he continued to refuse to recognise the Chamber.

Another important concession was to allow Nicolas's wife, Marie-Madeleine, to return to Paris from her exile in Limoges. She made the most of the occasion to attempt to expose the

---

*According to Bastille legend, even in these difficult circumstances Pellisson managed to create a little of the *amitié* of the salons. He whiled away his time taming a spider he had discovered in a corner of his window. Each time the bagpiper struck up a tune, he would put out some flies on the window ledge. Gently led into the room in this way, the spider was soon happily scurrying about on Pellisson's knee. One day the governor, Besmaux, dropped by to see how Pellisson was managing without his books. 'Oh, I've found a way of amusing myself,' said Pellisson, proudly showing off his pet spider. Besmaux knocked the creature out of his hand and stamped on it. 'Oh, Monsieur,' cried Pellisson, 'I would have preferred you to break my arm!'

enemy who was hiding in the King's shadow. When in July 1662 the King's Council ordered the Chamber of Justice to proceed at once with Nicolas's trial, she took issue in an extraordinarily forthright petition to the King. 'The only consolation left to the unfortunate is to complain.'[4] The King claimed to defer to the will of the newly appointed tribunal, she wrote, but in practice the tribunal was deferring to what it perceived to be the will of the King. She identified the key culprit in this abuse of justice to be none other than Jean-Baptiste Colbert. 'What has shocked all Paris and what is going to shock all France, and soon afterwards all Europe, is the discovery that Monsieur Colbert himself has had the temerity to participate in the Council where the order was given, as a judge of my husband, although everyone knows that he is behind this prosecution, that for six years he has been my husband's avowed enemy, and that he has done everything he can to inspire false accusations against him: first to His Eminence, when he saw his mistrust and jealousy, and then to Your Majesty.'[5]

She argued that Colbert was determined to destroy Nicolas as the one person who could reveal his own crimes. While every day he purported to explain to the King the true state of the kingdom's finances, in fact his own misbegotten gains over the years amounted to the equivalent of 12 million livres. 'I make no case to Your Majesty here that I haven't already heard made to my own husband, who had the evidence in his office, which, doubtless, Monsieur Colbert has now suppressed.'[6]

Ten days later Louis told the Chamber of Justice that *he* had authorised Colbert to remove the evidence from Nicolas's office, since he considered these documents to be state papers. From that moment on, everyone knew that Colbert was secure in the King's favour.

The Chamber now set out its complex case, encompassing thousands of financial documents, in writing. Two *rapporteurs* had to be appointed from among the members of the Chamber to oversee the depositions of both sides and to ensure the correct process of law. On behalf of her son, Marie Foucquet exercised the accused's right to object to specific nominees. She singled out Le Cormier de Sainte-Hélène, a member of the Rouen Parlement, and Olivier d'Ormesson, a Master of Requests, who had both in the past had uncomfortably close dealings with Colbert. But the King summoned the President of the Chamber, Guillaume de Lamoignon, to the Louvre and insisted that the *rapporteurs* be precisely these two people. 'If Madame Foucquet has expressed doubts over the integrity of these magistrates, then that's precisely a reason for nominating them.'[7]

When de Lamoignon began to explain the legal custom that gave the accused the right to have a choice of *rapporteur* he was happy with, the King interrupted: 'Say it is *I* who have ordered this.' De Lamoignon persisted in his attempt to explain to the young man the correct procedure. But the King cut in again: 'My mind is made up.'[8]

The proceedings were not so much a trial as a showcase for absolute power.

Soon afterwards the King made it known that he would like the Chancellor, Pierre Séguier, to preside over the case, not de Lamoignon, whose fussiness over details was wasting time. In face of such interference, the members of the Chamber divided into two camps – those who sought, as far as they could, to uphold the rule of law in the interests of a fair trial and those who paid more regard to the King's desire for a quick trial. The elderly Chancellor, complaining that the trial might well last longer than he would, as usual sided with the King, but there was a minimum degree of seemliness that even Nicolas's most implacable enemies had to observe.

Armed with pen, paper and ink at last, Nicolas threw himself into preparing his case. The support and bravery of his friends and family had raised his morale. In November 1662 Nicolas's lawyers, who consulted with him three days a week at Vincennes, smuggled out a copy of what he had so far written in his defence, which Marie-Madeleine had secretly printed and distributed. It was the start of an energetic campaign. When the Chief of Police discovered the press, Marie-Madeleine set up another in a house belonging to her family in Montreuil-sous-Bois, where she printed subsequent supplements. In early February 1663 this second press was discovered too, but by now Marie-Madeleine had established a wide network of secret presses, which continued to pour out not only Nicolas's defences but also other pamphlets in his support. When, many years later, all of Nicolas's writings in his defence were gathered together, they made up sixteen volumes.

Of the two *rapporteurs*, Sainte-Hélène turned out to be as attentive to the King's wishes as Nicolas's mother had feared, but Olivier d'Ormesson showed a courageous even-handedness in spite of huge pressure from both Colbert and the King, doing everything he could to ensure that Nicolas received a fair trial. Upon his appointment, he wrote in his diary: 'I've decided to give a precise account of all that concerns Monsieur Foucquet's trial, not just because it is very important, but chiefly because, as a *rapporteur*, I must give a full picture of all the details.'[9] Over the next year and a half, as the Chamber set out its case and Nicolas worked away with his lawyers on his defence, d'Ormesson's chief task was to act as a kind of secretary, checking and cataloguing an ever-growing mound of papers. The dogged conscientiousness with which he carried out this duty offered a serious obstacle to the casual suppressions of evidence that occurred before his appointment, even if it was too late to retrieve what had already been lost.

As everybody settled into a calm working routine, it was easy to forget the gravity of the situation. In the old keep at

Vincennes, surrounded by his furniture, Nicolas could almost imagine that he was back in his office again, burning the midnight oil over state affairs – which in a sense, of course, he was. But while once his reach had extended as far as the Americas, now it ended at the terrace that overlooked the moat surrounding the tower.

But in June 1663 there was a sudden change of domicile as Nicolas, under an escort of 300 musketeers, was transferred from Vincennes to the Bastille. Here, he was entrusted not into the hands of Besmaux, the Governor, but kept under the separate guard of d'Artagnan and a company of forty-five musketeers, who took up positions on each of the fortress's eight towers, in the courtyard and outside Nicolas's suite of rooms. Situated between two towers on the east side of the fortress, they afforded the prisoner a familiar view past the convent of the Visitation and up the rue Saint-Antoine.

In October 1663, when Nicolas submitted the first statement of his defence, he challenged the accuracy of the court transcripts of the Treasury registers, in which were detailed the expenditures he had authorised as Superintendent of Finances. In spite of the opposition of both Séguier and Colbert, the Chamber of Justice agreed by a majority that the registers should be checked against the transcripts in the presence of the accused. With this purpose Olivier d'Ormesson began to pay daily visits to Nicolas at the Bastille with the public prosecutor to the Chamber, Guy Chamillart, and its clerk, Joseph Foucault. The diary he kept offers a first-hand picture of Nicolas's remarkable resilience, fortitude and even good humour.

Of the initial visit, on Saturday, 26 January, 1664, d'Ormesson commented that Nicolas seemed very much like his old self except for rather drawn features and tired eyes. Nicolas greeted the small deputation with civility, but at the same time made it clear that he would not yield the slightest inch in defending himself and that he considered the case against him to be a malicious, politically motivated prosecution.

After they had finished work for the day, Nicolas gave his visitors a tour of his new apartments, far more spacious than what he had known in the narrow keep at Vincennes. Besides a study and a bedroom, there was a dressing room and another little room with a cage of birds in a corner. Nicolas introduced Jean Pecquet, who was not only attending to his medical ailments, but also helping him to write and correct the papers that made up his defence. His lawyers, said Nicolas, were only really good for gathering together the necessary items of evidence and keeping him up to date on developments. The immensely time-consuming task of working out an effective defence for himself was, he felt, taking a great toll on his health.

Nonetheless, d'Ormesson was struck by how very calm he seemed. He spoke with an impressive levity, even laughing from time to time as if the case was just a minor matter they had been discussing, rather than an ordeal that could well cost him his life. His disgrace didn't bother him, he commented, because he had a temperament that was able to adapt to any situation, but he did feel aggrieved by the vindictive conduct of his accusers. Surely, if he was deemed to be too liberal and generous to hold the office of Superintendent of Finances, some other job might have been found for him – perhaps a little ambassadorship somewhere. But to wish for his total ruin – that he couldn't understand. He was particularly puzzled that in spite of many requests Colbert had refused to see him, because he felt that only an hour together was needed to settle their differences.* The trial itself didn't bother him, he said, because while his conduct might at times have been

---

*This example of Nicolas's extraordinary confidence in his powers of persuasion reminds one of Voltaire's comment, 'Give me ten minutes to talk away my ugly face and I will bed the Queen of France.'

over-extravagant, he was convinced that he could show he had never acted fraudulently.

'I'll confess here', wrote d'Ormesson in his journal, 'that I admire the intelligence, openness and calm that he shows in everything he does'.[10]

The situation tested his even-handedness. It was difficult to be impartial when Nicolas's enemies seemed so determined to condemn him regardless of the evidence or due process of law. Only a week before Nicolas had challenged the right of the Chancellor to be one of his judges on the grounds of his persistent hostility. 'Everyone thinks it is unjust that Monsieur Séguier should be a judge of Monsieur Foucquet,' d'Ormesson wrote in his journal, 'and what's really disturbing is how badly this decision reflects on the King. In his desire to order and to decide everything by himself he is causing a lot of resentment.'[11]

With the King's encouragement the Chancellor held to his habitual approach that the correct presumption was one of guilt. If the tedious process of law had nonetheless to be respected, at least it should be hurried up. When d'Ormesson gave a report on his first day's visit to the Bastille, the Chancellor complained of the time that going through the transcripts with the accused would take. 'If everyone listens to Monsieur Foucquet, we'll never finish! I warned all along that letting him look at the transcripts would cause endless delay.'[12]

On Wednesday, 30 January, d'Ormesson and Chamillart visited Nicolas in the Bastille again. Before they began to go through the transcripts, d'Ormesson told Nicolas that the Chamber of Justice had instructed him to say that it was prepared to hear whatever points he wanted to make concerning his defence, but it would not tolerate his drawing matters out. The purpose of these meetings was to check facts, not to talk about anything else. Lingering even longer over his words than before, Nicolas answered that he would always listen to the orders of the

Chamber with respect. But before he could finish, Chamillart cut in, insisting that they get on with the matter in hand. A heated exchange between the two followed, which took up even more time than if Chamillart had said nothing at all.

The afternoon was a good example of the way Nicolas conducted himself. He was combative, taking every possible advantage in his defence, but after the judicial jousting was over for the day and it was time for his visitors to leave, he fell easily into cheerful, good-natured banter, allowing no rancour left over from often previously fierce exchanges to cloud their parting.

'Why haven't you and I met before?' he asked Chamillart.[13]

'I used to live in a monastery,' replied Chamillart. Explaining how he had give up this vocation to join the magistracy, he went on, 'I feel like a man coming out into the sun after years in a dark cave.'

'Don't let your bright new life carry you away,' said Nicolas, laughing, perhaps reflecting on the bright old life he had been forced to leave behind.

'I try always to walk *inter legitimos tramites*,' Chamillart answered earnestly. Along righteous paths.

'That word *"legitimos"*,' Nicolas replied with a smile, 'it's a word everyone interprets in his own way.'

Chamillart continued to interrupt whenever Nicolas's comments wandered away from a strict consideration of the transcripts themselves, but his growing fondness for the prisoner would soon undermine his severity. D'Ormesson noted the change: 'When we finally got down to work,' he wrote in his diary after several days had passed, 'Monsieur Foucquet set off on a long, totally irrelevant digression; the public prosecutor [i.e. Chamillart] didn't stop him this time because when he had interrupted before he had begged Monsieur Foucquet to believe that he had every possible respect for him and would do whatever he could to please him. To which Monsieur Foucquet replied that he would prefer a little less respect and a little more humanity.'[14]

In the end it was impossible to forget the gulf between them. One day Nicolas angrily snapped at Chamillart, 'If you want me to agree to something, say the opposite; because I'm convinced that you want the very opposite of what is in my interest, and that you will do nothing to bring me comfort.'[15]

On another occasion Nicolas accused Chamillart of seeking to put before the court tainted evidence through a meeting with an associate of Colbert called Louis Berryer. Outside Nicolas's rooms the clerk, Joseph Foucault, took d'Ormesson aside and told him that it was true, Chamillart had been seeing Berryer. But he was astonished that Nicolas had found out, because every possible precaution had been taken to keep the meeting secret.

Ashamed, even though he had had no part in such blatant abuses of procedure, d'Ormesson had to acknowledge that a simple sense of justice had turned him into a partisan supporter of Nicolas. 'I must comment here,' he wrote in his diary on 19 February, 'that everyone expects that the Chancellor will die very soon; and that one hopes for it because it is likely to bring some change. Such is the hatred for those who are presently in power that it makes one long for the deliverance of Monsieur Foucquet. It's said that the Chancellor's legs are swollen and he's getting weaker every day. Some people think he'll barely make it past Easter; others, not even next month. All the same, he puts on a good face.'[16]

D'Ormesson's careful verification of the transcripts shed less light on Nicolas's supposed frauds than those of court officials. He was shocked to discover seven or eight lines in the transcripts that were entirely false, with no corresponding entries in the registers. 'I do not understand how anyone could invent such obvious falsehoods and pass them off as true,' he wrote in his journal.[17]

The interpolated lines were eventually traced to Berryer, who was found to have been responsible for some even more crude alterations, scratching out the names of people who had received payments. While his chief purpose had been to incriminate Nicolas, some of the amendments had been made simply to save his own embarrassment. For example, the registers recorded a payment that had been made to Berryer of 120,000 livres. By inserting the letters 'SE' (*Son Eminence*), he made it seem as if this sum was finally due to the Cardinal. The falsehoods were so clumsy and blatant that not even Colbert was prepared to defend him. When Le Tellier raised the issue, Colbert replied that he had only just found out what had been going on and that Berryer was a clot.

The prospect of unearthing more such irregularities was not the only reason for Nicolas to linger over the transcripts. With every passing week popular sentiment was now turning in his favour. At the time of his arrest Nicolas was the most unpopular man in France, but now he had become a rather appealing martyr. His behaviour at the Bastille helped to cement the image. When he might have been expected to be one of the keener patrons of the fortress's splendid kitchen, instead he pursued a regime of notable asceticism. Every Saturday he ate only bread and water. During Lent he gave up fresh fish, eating salted herring instead.

Meanwhile, the Chamber of Justice, in its eagerness to impress the King, had brought thirty or forty separate charges against Nicolas when two or three might have sufficed. The sheer number suggested a naked prejudice but also a lack of confidence in its case. The hope was that with so many accusations something was bound to stick, but as matters dragged on the sheer weight of the case actually seemed to be working in the accused's favour. As Le Tellier observed, the rope had now become too thick to hang Nicolas when in the beginning a thin cord would probably have done the trick.

D'Ormesson became the scapegoat for those who believed that Nicolas should have been convicted long ago. Aware that every gesture he made for the accused was being closely scrutinised, d'Ormesson actually welcomed any opportunity that permitted him to make some ruling against Nicolas. But he was so out of step with the official attitude that it was only a matter of time until Colbert made some attempt to bring pressure to bear.

In early May 1664, he paid a visit to d'Ormesson's father, a highly respected member of the Parlement.[18] The King, he told André d'Ormesson, was disappointed that his son was not doing all he could to expedite Foucquet's trial. 'He finds it extraordinary that, when he is the most feared and powerful king in all Europe, he can't bring to an end the trial of one of his subjects.'

'I'm sorry the King is so upset by my son's conduct,' the father replied. 'But I know that he is trying to do his best; and I have always taught him to fear God, to serve the King and to seek justice.'

'But people say he favours the arguments of Monsieur Foucquet more than he does those of the public prosecutor.'

'It is a *rapporteur*'s duty to present *both* sides of the case,' replied André d'Ormesson. 'And I have always taught him to do justice no matter who was concerned, and without regard to rank or fortune.'

'We know very well that he wants to do justice,' replied Colbert, 'but we want him to do it quickly.'

On 23 June the Chamber of Justice was transferred to Fontainebleau, where the King was spending the summer. He was anxious that there should be no further excuses for delay. The next day Nicolas was transported to the castle in the walled town of Moret-sur-Loing, just two miles away from Fontainebleau. If he had chanced to look up as his carriage passed through the fortified gateway, he would have seen engraved in the stone above the two words, *stat spes* (hope endures). It was a timely reminder because the King now once again usurped the powers of the court. He ordered that Nicolas should not be allowed to see his lawyers more than two mornings a week, and then only in the presence of d'Artagnan. When Nicolas made a formal request to the Chamber to have his right of free access to counsel restored, the Chancellor ruled that the plea had to be passed on to the King himself.

So at three o'clock on Monday, 7 July d'Ormesson turned up with his fellow *rapporteur* Sainte-Hélène at Fontainebleau and presented Nicolas's written request to the King. Louis told them that it was too long for him to consider there and then, but that he would read it and let them know his thoughts at the same time next day. When they returned, he had prepared a considered response. D'Ormesson noticed that Colbert was lingering in the background.

Slow and deliberate, the King gave a reply that, doubtless, Colbert had helped to formulate:[19]

I once thought that it was a good thing that Monsieur Foucquet should have free access to counsel because it meant the trial would be swift. But it is now more than two years since it began and I am extremely anxious that it should end. It's a matter of my reputation. This isn't an affair of great consequence – on the contrary, I consider it to be a trifle. But abroad, where it is important that my power be recognised, one might think that I had very little power if I couldn't bring to a close a trial against such a wretched creature . . .

Since Monsieur Foucquet has been at Moret, I have told d'Artagnan to allow his lawyers to communicate with him only twice a week and in d'Artagnan's presence, because I do not want such consultations to carry on for ever, and I know that his lawyers have exceeded their brief, smuggling documents in and out . . . And then there's his plan to overthrow the state – in such a case an accused forfeits the right to a trial and *rapporteurs*. That is what made me give the order, and I believe the Chamber will confirm it. However, I shall defer to whatever it decides to do concerning Monsieur Foucquet's request. I want only justice; and I must consider very carefully what I say to you, for when a man's life is at stake, I do not want to say one more word than is absolutely necessary. The Chamber, therefore, will decide what is to be done in this case.

In this way, having been handed back the authority it had abdicated, the Chamber sat two days later to debate the request. In the light of the King's stated expectation, no one could have been that surprised when it agreed with him. Or when not long afterwards it turned down Nicolas's application to bring a case against Colbert for the wrongful removal of his papers. The Chancellor ruled that Nicolas had no right to bring such a request because it impugned the honour of the King, who relied on Colbert in all the most important affairs of state. 'It's not for me to praise Colbert,' he added, 'but I don't think there's anyone who could have done a better job.'[20] The essence of that job lay in confirming rather than challenging the arrogance of an inexperienced young man.

On 14 August Nicolas was transferred back to the Bastille. Waiting for him in the village of Charenton, which was along his route, were his wife Marie-Madeleine and his children, who hoped to catch a glimpse of him as his carriage went by with its heavy escort of musketeers. Spotting them, d'Artagnan ordered the carriage to slow down without actually stopping, just long enough for Marie-Madeleine to be able to reach the carriage door and to kiss her husband.

18

The Trial

Somewhat to everyone's amazement when the final trial began early on the morning of Friday, 14 November 1664, the Chancellor was still alive. But out of consideration for his fast declining health, it was decided that Nicolas should be examined for no more than an hour each day.*

After raising a few questions concerning correct procedure, the Chancellor asked for the accused to be led into the courtroom. Dressed in simple black clothes, Nicolas saluted his judges and sat down on the defendant's bench. But when the Chancellor asked him to raise his hand to take the oath, he refused. 'Gentlemen,' he said, addressing the judges all together, 'I hope you will not think ill of me if I decline to take the oath. To do so would be to go against my privilege to be tried by my peers in the Parlement, a privilege that I continue to demand.'

'His Majesty has confirmed the competence of this court to try you,' replied the Chancellor.

'But he issued his decree without having heard my objections, which is against all the principles of justice.'

Nicolas went on to apologise for his clothes, explaining that his request to wear the robes of a magistrate, to which he was

*The eyewitness descriptions of both Madame de Sévigné and Olivier Lefèvre d'Ormesson make it possible to give a word for word account of the exchanges at Nicolas's trial. See the endnotes for the appropriate references.

entitled, had been turned down. He had no choice therefore but to appear improperly dressed – although he was sure, he added, that a magistrate's privilege did not depend on what he wore.

After Nicolas refused several more times to take the oath, the Chancellor then asked him to leave the courtroom, while he conferred with his colleagues about what to do. With a courteous bow, Nicolas took his leave.

The judges agreed that the defendant should be asked one more time to take the oath and that, if he still refused, the trial would carry on regardless. When Nicolas was recalled, he continued to insist on his privilege, but once he had made his point that the court had no right to ask him questions, he was content enough – having resisted the oath – to answer those questions.

The first charge brought against Nicolas was that under the fictitious name of Simon le Noir he had, in 1655, raked off for himself a figure of 120,000 livres on the *gabelle*, the tax levied on salt. Nicolas did not deny receiving this sum, but replied that it was Cardinal Mazarin who had authorised the payment to reimburse him for advances he had previously made to the state from his own funds. The name Mazarin would crop up again and again in the course of the trial. The confusion of public and private resources, the extravagant commissions granted to tax collectors and financiers, the byzantine use of fictitious names – Nicolas attributed all these irregularities to the chaos that ruled under Mazarin's cavalier administration. He reminded the court of the complete authority Mazarin had enjoyed as Prime Minister, when he ruled as though he were the King himself. 'I had no right, and even less actual power, to go against his wishes.'

The general opinion of the first day was that while the Chancellor had often mixed up facts and appeared not to be in full command of his brief, Nicolas had displayed an impressive self-possession and calm.[1] When he was brought before the court on Monday, 17 November for the second day's proceedings,[2] the opening ritual of the previous day repeated itself. The Chancellor asked him to take the oath and he refused once again on the grounds that he did not recognise the right of the Chamber to try him.

'All we want is the truth!' said the Chancellor testily. 'And taking the oath will help us to get it.'

'Some men tell the truth without taking an oath,' said Nicolas, 'and others lie on oath.'

'The fact that you've sat down on the bench shows that you recognise this court.'

'To sit here is not a recognition of the court, it's a mortification I receive from God.'

'This Chamber has its authority by decree of the King,' declared Séguier.

'Kings may issue decrees in accordance with the law or contrary to the law,' replied Nicolas. 'If they do the latter, then their decrees are not lawful decrees.'

'Are you saying, then, that the King has failed to do justice here and that he has abused his authority?'

'It's you who say this, not I. These are your words. One may complain of the decrees issued by the King, but that is not to say that he has exceeded his power or abused his authority. You can issue a decree you believe to be just one day, then break it the next. That doesn't mean that you abused your authority on the first day, since you acted in good faith, believing the decree to be just.'

Nicolas had raised an issue that ought to have weighed heavily in a court that had an important opportunity to challenge the absolute monarchy that would dominate France for the next hundred years. But elderly, sick and partisan, the Chancellor was disinclined to explore the implications. Quickly moving on, he stuck to the much safer ground of Nicolas's supposed wrongdoing for the rest of that day's session.

On the Wednesday of that week d'Ormesson arrived at the Arsenal to find that the day's session had been cancelled. The King had asked the Chancellor that the court suspend its deliberations and instead join the rest of the country in saying prayers for Queen Maria Theresa, who was gravely ill after giving birth to a premature child.* Such were the fears for the Queen's life that the previous evening she had received the Holy Sacrament.

Some believed that the suspension was a deliberate attempt to undermine the admiration and sympathy that Nicolas had won for himself in these first days of the trial and to give a much needed breathing space to his enemies. If so, the attempt backfired badly. For among the supplicants who took advantage of the royal day of prayer was the marquise de Charost, Nicolas's daughter by his first wife. Finding the King's mother, Queen Anne of Austria, she gave her a special medicinal plaster that Nicolas's mother Marie had concocted for women after childbirth. The Queen Mother then took the plaster to Maria Theresa. 'I'll put it on,' she declared. 'Madame Foucquet is a saint!'[3] The effect of the plaster was dramatic: two huge blood clots were worked loose from the Queen's insides, each one the size of a fist. In the corridors of the Louvre, people were saying that Madame Foucquet had performed a miracle. But when the Queen Mother tried to tell her son about the extraordinary cure he wouldn't listen. Nicolas's mother and daughter even threw themselves down at his feet, begging him to show mercy to Nicolas, but he ignored them.

When the court reassembled the day after the Queen's miraculous recovery, several of the judges saluted Nicolas as he entered the chamber. Turning on a judge who was a member of the Brittany Parlement, Séguier said, 'I suppose it is because you

*A girl who would survive only a month.

are Breton that you salute Monsieur Foucquet so cordially.'[4] But the real cause for Nicolas's popularity was the impressive calm he had shown since the beginning of the hearing. Madame de Sévigné, who had followed the trial closely, observed, 'Those who love Monsieur Foucquet find this calm admirable, and I am of their number. But others say it's just an affectation. That's the world for you, I suppose.'[5] Several other women shared her fascination. One afternoon during the trial they gathered in a house that offered a view of the Arsenal. From here they could watch the prisoner being led back to the Bastille. Veiled, Madame de Sévigné joined them. 'When I saw him,' she wrote, 'my knees trembled and my heart beat so fiercely that I thought it would stop. As he approached, on his way back to his prison, Monsieur d'Artagnan nudged him and pointed us out to him. He waved to us, adopting that smiling expression you know so well. I confess to you I was terribly shaken when I saw him go back through that little door.'[6]

The capital charge of treason was left until the last day of the trial, on Thursday, 4 December. The details of the Saint-Mandé plan, in which Nicolas had set out the measures to be taken in case he fell out of favour with the Cardinal, were read to the court.

'How can you square these plans of rebellion with your professed loyalty and devotion to the state?' asked the Chancellor.

'Sir,' replied Nicolas, 'these thoughts came to me when I was in the depths of despair that the Cardinal cast me into, when, after having done more than anyone in the world to bring about his return from exile, I found myself repaid with such base ingratitude. I have a letter from him and another from the Queen Mother, which provide proof of what I'm saying, but they were stolen from my papers, along with several others. My great misfortune is not to have burned this wretched document, which is of so little consequence to me that I haven't thought about it for more than two years, had even forgotten that I still had it.'[7]

When the Chancellor continued to press him on the point he went on, 'I admit, sir, that it was foolishness; but it is not treason.' He then turned to the other judges. 'I beg these gentlemen to allow me to explain what treason is. It's not that I consider them to be any less clever than I am; it's just that I've had more time to think about the question. Treason is when, in a position of trust, you possess the Prince's secrets, and then suddenly give yourself over to his enemies and encourage your family to do the same. It's when you open the gates of the town of which you are a governor to the enemy's army and then close them to your real master . . . That, gentlemen, is what one calls treason.'[8]

The courtroom erupted with laughter at this allusion to a notorious episode from the Chancellor's past. Disgraced during the Fronde and relieved of his seals, Séguier had briefly sided with the Princes against the King, persuading his son-in-law, the duc de Sully, governor of Mantes, to give a rebel army passage across the River Seine. The Chancellor sat in his great judge's chair speechless. Suddenly he was the accused.

When there was silence again, Nicolas resumed: 'While I, who have always given loyal service, find even my thoughts turned into crimes in order to hang me. It is Colbert who, through his lies, has pushed the King to this extremity.'[9]

At midday Nicolas was escorted out of the Chamber for the last time. The next morning d'Artagnan, who was curious to discover the mood of his prisoner now that the hearing was over, quietly entered Nicolas's room. For the first time in months, he found him not at his desk labouring over the details of his defence, but sitting by the fire reading a prayer book. Noticing d'Artagnan's look of surprise, Nicolas explained: 'I am a servant for hire now. I have nothing more to do than to pray to God and await the verdict. Whatever it is, I shall accept it with the same peace of mind. I am resolute and prepared.'[10]

Proceedings were now adjourned for a few days while the two *rapporteurs*, Olivier d'Ormesson and Sainte-Hélène, each prepared speeches giving a summing-up of the evidence. The court procedure required that they give their verdicts first. The other twenty judges would then follow.

D'Ormesson finished his speech on Saturday, 6 December. In the evening he met Nicolas's parish priest, Claude Joly, who observed what a favourable omen it must be for the accused that it was Saint Nicolas's Day.

On Tuesday, 9 December he began his address to the court, continuing his summary of the case over the next three days. 'It was a marvellous performance,' observed Madame de Sévigné. 'He spoke with such extraordinary clarity, intelligence and understanding.'[11] But this didn't stop one of the judges, Henri Pussort, who happened to be Colbert's uncle, from interrupting whenever d'Ormesson's interpretation of the facts seemed too favourable to Nicolas. 'Monsieur,' he reminded d'Ormesson, 'it will be our turn to speak next.'[12]

On Saturday, 13 December d'Ormesson gave his conclusion. Although the accused was guilty of improper administration, there were mitigating circumstances. He had been working for Mazarin who, as a foreigner, had a poor understanding of the correct procedures and had routinely confused different kinds of expenditure. Under extreme pressure to find money for the state, the Cardinal's example had encouraged Nicolas to take reckless and unorthodox measures. However, although the evidence was inconclusive, it seemed likely that Nicolas had profited from such disorder and abused his office. Therefore, d'Ormesson recommended that he receive a sentence of banishment for life and have his property confiscated.

'His verdict is a little harsh,' wrote Madame de Sévigné, 'but let's pray to God that it will be followed.'[13]

At the Louvre – possibly because it was obvious what the King wanted to hear – everyone had been convinced that d'Ormesson would recommend the death sentence. Now that his verdict had been otherwise, it set an important precedent for the remaining judges to follow. But the second *rapporteur*, Sainte-Hélène, quickly restored the balance. Having summed up the case in just one day rather than d'Ormesson's three, on Tuesday, 16 December he found Nicolas guilty of both embezzlement and treason. He recommended that he be sentenced to death, but out of consideration for his family beheaded rather than hung.

It was now the turn of the remaining twenty judges to offer their verdicts. On Wednesday, 17 December, after a furious four-hour rant, Colbert's uncle Henri Pussort seconded Sainte-Hélène's verdict of death by beheading. The next day four more judges followed Sainte-Hélène's opinion. But then, just as it seemed that matters were swinging decisively against Nicolas, a fifth seconded d'Ormesson's recommendation of banishment.

'Everyone is engrossed by this extraordinary case,' wrote Madame de Sévigné that evening. 'People talk of nothing else. They ponder its lessons and speculate; they express pity, hope, fear; they curse, they pray; they hate, they admire.'[14]

Meanwhile, Nicolas, who was kept informed of each judge's verdict as it was given, remained quietly in the Bastille, where he observed a strict regime of fast and prayer. He welcomed the sudden appearance of a comet in the sky that week as a favourable omen.

By the end of Friday, 19 December Nicolas's fate still hung in the balance. Seven judges had sided with d'Ormesson, six with Sainte-Hélène. But the next day three more judges, including the Chancellor, voted for the death penalty and six for banishment. By a final total of thirteen to nine, Nicolas's life had been spared.

'All Paris impatiently awaited the news,' wrote d'Ormesson. 'It was quickly spread all over the city and received with extreme joy, even among the most humble of shopkeepers, each one praising my name.'[15]

The King, however, soon removed the smiles, overruling the court to change the sentence of banishment to one of life imprisonment. Nicolas knew far too much to be allowed to go free. He would have preferred to hang Nicolas. But whatever little respect he had for his own judges, he still feared the judgement of God. Nicolas was now to be incarcerated in the fortress of Pignerol, a French enclave in Piedmont that, by one of those ironies, his old adversary Mazarin had acquired for France in 1631 through the Treaty of Cherasco.

Nicolas's escape from the gallows was the favourite subject of the Christmas songs that year, many of which were as notable for their hatred of his prosecutors as their joy that he should have been spared.

> Foucquet's rope is now for sale,
> But there's Colbert, Le Tellier and Berryer,
> Sainte-Hélène, Pussort, Poncet and Séguier:
> There you are, plenty of people to take it;
> Plenty of thieves to hang,
> Plenty of madmen's limbs to bind . . .[16]*

Meanwhile, over that Christmas of 1664, the comet, the size of four normal stars, could still be seen in the night sky, dragging its bright tail from east to west behind it. D'Ormesson stared at it from his attic. A young Isaac Newton remarked it too from his

---

*La corde de Foucquet est maintenant à vendre; / Mais nous avons Colbert, Le Tellier et Berryer, Sainte-Hélène, Pussort, Poncet, le chancelier: / Voilà bien des gens pour la prendre; / Voilà bien des voleurs à pendre; / Voilà bien des fous à lier . . .

place of observation hundreds of miles away in Cambridge: 'a Comet whose rays were round her, yet her tayle extended itselfe a little towards [the] east'. It was the celestial event of the decade. Huge crowds gathered on the Pont-Neuf and in the city squares to mark the comet's passing. No one knew now whether to regard it as a sign of Nicolas's deliverance or Louis's vengeance.

19

The Prisoner

In the morning of Monday, 22 December 1664 Nicolas was led down to the chapel of the Bastille, where Foucault, the clerk to the Chamber of Justice, sat at a table waiting to announce the prisoner's sentence.[1]

'What is your name?' Foucault asked the prisoner.

'You already know,' answered Nicolas. 'So there's no point in telling you.'

'It's not a question of what we already know,' answered the clerk, 'it's a question of correct protocol.' Once again he asked for the prisoner's name.

'I refused to give the Chamber of Justice my name or to take their oath when they asked me, and I continue to refuse to do anything that might undermine my right to be judged by a court of my peers.'

'What is your name?' asked Foucault for a third time. And once again Nicolas refused to answer.

Having paid due respect to protocol, Foucault proceeded to read out the prisoner's sentence anyway. Nicolas was then led not back to his own rooms but into a chamber near the chapel. When they saw this, Pecquet and La Vallée, who had been watching the prison courtyard from their window, assumed that the verdict must have been death. 'The cries and weeping of those poor men were enough to pierce the heart of any whose heart is not made of stone,' wrote Madame de Sévigné. 'They made such a piteous noise that Monsieur d'Artagnan was constrained to go and reassure them.'[2]

A little later, d'Ormesson dropped by to collect together all the papers in Nicolas's rooms relating to the trial and to pack them away into four sealed chests. A sombre d'Artagnan, who had just received orders to escort Nicolas on the long journey to Pignerol, hugged d'Ormesson warmly and whispered a few discreet words of congratulation. He didn't know what to make of the whole affair, he confided, but would get in touch with d'Ormesson when he returned from Pignerol. As d'Ormesson made his way across the courtyard, he looked up to see Nicolas waving to him from the window of d'Artagnan's room.

'I am your humble servant,' he called.

D'Ormesson waved back.[3]

At midday d'Artagnan put Nicolas into the carriage that would convey him to Pignerol. He himself was going to ride on horseback with an escort of a hundred musketeers. Neither Nicolas's wife nor mother was able to come to say farewell because the King had exiled them both to the Auvergne. But just before the party set off, Nicolas's old servant La Forêt arrived and d'Artagnan, with his usual kindness, allowed him to have a few words with his master.

'Tell our women that they must not worry,' said Nicolas, 'that I am well and have courage to spare.'[4]

A crowd had gathered outside the Bastille to see Nicolas off. As his carriage crossed the square and passed through the Porte Saint-Antoine, he returned their cheers with that 'smiling expression' Madame de Sévigné had remarked upon. Soon after Nicolas's departure, rumours reached Paris that he had fallen ill on the road. 'Everyone's saying, "What? Already?"' wrote Madame de Sévigné.[5]

The general feeling was that the King wanted to finish off the job that the Chamber of Justice had been unable to do for him, and that was why Nicolas had been separated from his doctor and valet, who had previously shared his confinement in five different prisons. When d'Artagnan sent for instructions about what to do with his sick prisoner, the reply came that he should not break the journey. Maybe the King hoped that the passage across the Alps in the middle of winter would kill Nicolas. If so, he would have done better to have appointed a less conscientious minder. For d'Artagnan, with his usual thoughtfulness, had bought extra furs to protect his prisoner against the cold.

Remote and forbidding, the fortress town of Pignerol was a strategic outpost on the furthest edge of France. Apart from the garrison of soldiers, the population consisted of several orders of monks and nuns, who had been drawn to a place so far removed from the temptations of the world. The tower of the citadel vied with the spire of Saint-Maurice church for the title of the town's highest point. Both, perched side by side on their separate knolls, were locked away behind a formidable array of ditches, bastions and ramparts, which in turn were hemmed in by the precipitous peaks of the surrounding mountains.

It would have been hard to imagine a more impregnable fortress, but to make it even more secure the King's architect, François Levé, had been sent ahead to prepare Nicolas's rooms on the second floor of the tower. In a letter to Colbert dated 30 January,[6] Levé complained of the bitter cold that was still impeding his work two weeks after Nicolas's arrival. He was also alarmed to find that the garrison had been using the tower as a powder magazine. It was a death trap, he complained: one spark from a workman's chisel could set the whole place off. He insisted that a separate, purpose-built magazine be built; meanwhile it was 'essential' to house the gunpowder somewhere else at once.

For Nicolas's living quarters, Levé had prepared a bedroom

twenty-six feet long by twelve wide, with a smaller room next door, which served as both dressing-room and bathroom. d'Artagnan, in one final gesture of kindness, insisted that Levé should provide Nicolas with an extra room to use as day quarters, a request that occasioned huge difficulties, since Levé had to make major structural modifications to the tower. But nothing could be done to stop the *bise*, the bitter north wind that howled through the chimney shaft.

D'Artagnan spent a few days in the town attending to the various details of the transfer, but the time finally came for him to say goodbye. Nicolas was to be of good cheer, he said. He was sure that all would turn out for the best. No account exists of their parting, but it must have been the saddest of farewells. Over the more than three years since Nicolas's arrest, guard and prisoner had become devoted friends.

D'Artagnan entrusted Nicolas to the care of his old sergeant, Bénigne Dauvergne Saint-Mars, who – now a captain – had been appointed to be the Governor of Nicolas's new prison. 'Saint-Mars' was actually a *nom de guerre* adopted by the gaoler's father, Louis Dauvergne, a captain in the infantry. Nicolas was pleased with the appointment of 'an honest man', but over the years Saint-Mars would prove pitiless in the execution of his superiors' orders.

In truth, Saint-Mars had little leeway. The minister responsible for communicating the King's wishes concerning the prisoner was François Louvois, the twenty-three-year-old son of Michel Le Tellier. In a letter to Saint-Mars, dated 29 January 1665, Louvois wrote, 'You will please keep me up to date with weekly reports and, even when you have nothing to report, write to me anyway.'[7] He wanted to know exactly what was going on and expected any orders from the King regarding Nicolas's captivity to be followed to the letter.

These orders were designed to ensure Nicolas's total isolation. As a minister to the Crown, Nicolas had been party to some of France's most sensitive secrets, which the King was determined should remain locked up with him. Soon after his arrival Nicolas asked Saint-Mars if he could write to his wife. When the request was passed on to Louvois, he replied, 'I don't doubt that Monsieur Foucquet would like to receive letters from his wife and to reply to them; but before that can happen, it's necessary that the King should agree, and I don't think that's likely just yet.'[8] Nor could he exchange correspondence with anyone else. Nicolas was given a valet, but any solace he might have found in the company was tempered by the fact that the man had obviously been instructed by Saint-Mars to spy on him. Confined to his living quarters, he was unable to take exercise outside. Nor was he allowed to have pen or ink. Every measure was taken to prevent any possible contact with the outside world – not to say worlds. A request for a telescope was turned down.

More leniency was shown when it came to his religious needs. A chaplain was permitted to come and say Mass each day. Nicolas was also given access to a confessor, although he quickly found that it was foolish in the King's custody to rely too much on the privacy of the confessional. When he asked the priest for news, the priest reported the request back to Saint-Mars, warning the gaoler that Nicolas planned to use the books he was given to smuggle out messages. Henceforward, Nicolas was to be permitted to take confession only on the five solemn feast days of the year – Christmas, Easter, the Ascension, the Assumption and All Saints'. His books were now checked both before and after he had read them.

Rigorously guarded and completely cut off, Nicolas began to complain of the harsh conditions of his captivity. But soon an extraordinary event occurred to suggest that at least God was on his side. On the morning of 23 June 1665 a fierce storm raged over the town of Pignerol. A bolt of lightning struck the prison tower, igniting the powder magazine – still there in spite of the specific instructions of the King's architect, François Levé, six months earlier that it should be removed. In a series of spectacular explosions that must have outdone even the fireworks of Vaux, the tower and the surrounding citadel were reduced to ruins. One of the first people on the scene was an officer from the garrison quartered in the town below the citadel, Lieutenant Nicolas Séverat. He reached the entrance to the lower fort to find the bridge destroyed and scattered with the bodies of soldiers. As he hurried on up the hill, he passed heavy cannons that had been turned upside-down by the force of the blast. At the gate to the upper fort there were more dead soldiers. 'It scared me to have come so far without finding anyone alive. I entered the tower, where I found five soldiers who were too stunned by what had happened to say a word; but all the others were dead. Looking up, I saw Monsieur Foucquet standing in the window embrasure.'[9] With Nicolas was his valet. Séverat found a ladder and helped the two men down. Altogether, only fourteen men survived the explosion, with 400 corpses scattered among the ruins.

Back in Paris, Nicolas's supporters argued that the King should take note of this sign from heaven and allow him to go free. The poet Ménage wrote a special petition to Louis in Latin,* ending with the plea: 'O, Louis, likeness of God, you in your turn imitate God supreme and pardon this poor man.'[10] Rather than pardon Nicolas, the King punished Ménage, striking his name off the list of artists who received royal pensions.

François Levé at least had the satisfaction of being able to say

*. . . *Fulmine (causa latet) custodies et ferit arcem / Juppiter: hic moriens, mortuus ille iacet. / Res est sacra miser. Misero vaga fulmina parcunt: / Salvus et illaesus stat, Lodoïce, tibi / Tu quoque, tu misero, Lodoïce, simillime Divum / Exemplo magni parcere disce Iovis.*

'I told you so' when he was sent back to inspect the ruins. His task now was to rebuild Pignerol and to prepare a temporary prison for Nicolas at the fort of Pérouse. Situated high up in the Alps, some sixty miles to the west, it was an even more inaccessible place than Pignerol, which Levé considered to be 'poorly constructed, one might even say a ruin'.[11] In the absence there of any convenient building materials, Levé did the required carpentry and ironwork at Pignerol, then transferred the finished pieces to Pérouse by mule. When the porters realised that for security reasons the job had to be completed quickly, they decided to hold out for extra money. Bandits and an unfriendly local population – in Levé's words 'the nastiest people in the world' – made the work even more difficult, dangerous and unpleasant.[12] A few months later Levé, who was longing to get back to his beloved Paris, fell mortally ill as he hurried to finish the rebuilt prison at Pignerol. As he lay on his death bed in a fever, Saint-Mars quietly retrieved from him a set of locks and keys for the new prison doors.[13]

One effect of the explosion was to expose some of the tricks Nicolas had used to make life a little easier for himself. Amid the wreckage, some handwritten notes were discovered in the broken back of a chair. Nicolas had ingeniously fashioned a pen out of a chicken bone and ink by mixing his sweat with wine. The flames even revealed a kind of invisible ink that Nicolas had used to make notes in his books. 'You must try to find out from Monsieur Foucquet's valet how he wrote the four lines that appeared when that book was heated, and what he used to compose this ink,' Louvois instructed Saint-Mars.[14] But the servant had become so steadfastly loyal to Nicolas that he refused to say a word. A few months later he fell seriously ill and was replaced by a new valet who Saint-Mars had vainly hoped would prove more faithful.

Henceforward, Nicolas would be even more closely guarded and searched every day. And although it wasn't really feasible to stop him eating chicken, any papers on which he could conceivably use his chicken bones to write with were removed. It was the beginning of a battle of wits that involved endless measures and counter-measures. Denied paper, Nicolas began to write on handkerchiefs. Denied handkerchiefs, he began to write on his clothes . . . His guards were rigorous but philosophical. 'People who are in the condition he finds himself,' wrote Louvois, 'try all sorts of tricks to achieve their ends; and the people who guard them must take all sorts of precautions to prevent themselves from being tricked.'[15]

Louis XIV may have wished to give the outward appearance of regarding Nicolas's fate as a trifling matter of little interest to Europe's most powerful monarch, but nonetheless the spectacle of Nicolas's downfall fascinated him. He was curious to know how Nicolas would handle his ordeal. In a note to Saint-Mars, dated 11 April 1666, Louvois wrote, 'Although His Majesty is entirely satisfied with the assurances you have given in your letters that Monsieur Foucquet is securely guarded, it would nonetheless be a good idea to give a few more details for his particular satisfaction; he'd be very pleased if from time to time you'd describe the way in which the prisoner lives – whether he bears his captivity well or badly, what he says, and the things that happen in the course of his imprisonment.'[16]

After a year at Pérouse, Nicolas was transferred, on 14 August 1666, back to a rebuilt Pignerol, where the routine struggle against his distant controllers continued. There were endless petty restrictions: he could have a warmer set of clothes for the winter, but he had to make do with his summer collars; he could read the works of Clavius and Saint Bonaventure, but not Saint Augustin. Most irksome of all were the ever more draconian measures to stop him writing. When his scrawls were discovered on the ribbons with which he fastened his clothes, these were dyed black. A special cleaning regime was established.

Immediately after his laundry had been retrieved from his room – whether clothes, bedlinen or napkins – it would be plunged into a tub of water.[17] A laundress would then take the laundry down to the river and wash the various items in the usual way, but afterwards dry them over a fire in front of a guard, who would inspect them closely for any remaining traces of writing.

When Nicolas's second valet fell seriously ill towards the end of 1666, it was decided to replace him with two valets who would have separate instructions to spy on both Nicolas and on each other. But Nicolas easily won them over, enlisting their help in a new enterprise – which the latest measures of his guards had forced on him – of making paper out of table linen. 'Make sure you take away the paper Monsieur Foucquet has made,' Louvois wrote to Saint-Mars in a letter dated 21 November 1667.[18] 'At the same time you can tell him that if he continues to use his tablecloths to make paper, he mustn't be surprised if you stop giving him any.'

The strict prison regime could be demoralising, but at the same time the constant need to think up new tricks to outwit his guards kept Nicolas as mentally alert as the poems, riddles and commentaries he wrote when these tricks were successful. The writings themselves suggest an inner strength and resilience, but also a surviving sense of irony that helped Nicolas to find a real, if somewhat pained, amusement in his own predicament. For all the privations, he was still capable of the 'smiling expression'.

Even his nemesis Colbert offered an occasion for humour. In December 1666 one of the few items of news to get past the Pignerol information blackout – presumably because of its religious nature – was that Colbert had forbidden the celebration of seventeen feast days, including Saint Nicolas's Day. Nicolas wrote a protest poem to express his solidarity with the saint: 'He has been found guilty, unworthy of exoneration, / Deserving neither respect nor admiration. / Do you wish to know what is his crime? / It has been found that he is a patron of mine.'[19]* It may have been an inconsequential little piece, but the readiness to laugh was a sign of the prisoner's continued will to resist.

But then one day, as unexpectedly as the lightning that had struck the tower, the joking ended. It was the winter of 1669. Idly gazing out of his window one morning, Nicolas was astonished to see the familiar face of his servant La Forêt. With him was someone else Nicolas recognised – a young family friend from Provence called André de Marmet de Valcroissant. The pair had managed to bribe some of the guards to let them approach Nicolas's tower. Hurriedly, he scrawled a note and threw it to them. Although the alarm was soon raised, the two men managed to slip out of Pignerol and across the border into the duchy of Savoy. But the Duke – who was anxious to keep on good terms with his cousin the King of France – refused asylum and had them returned to Pignerol.

The King insisted that an example should be made. La Forêt and four guards were hung. Valcroissant was sentenced to serve five years in a galley ship at Marseilles. To prevent a repetition of what had happened, Saint-Mars had special shutters fitted to Nicolas's windows to prevent him from being able to throw anything out or to make any kind of a sign. Henceforward, all he was able to see was the sky.[20]

*On l'a trouvé coupable, indigne de pardon, / Qu'il ne méritoit plus ni d'honneur ni d'estime. / Voulez-vous en secret savoir quel est son crime? / C'est qu'on a découvert qu'il étoit mon patron.

20

The True King

The price that his friends had had to pay for their loyalty appalled Nicolas. It sapped his will to put up further resistance. Turning his back on this world, he set his eyes firmly on the next, occupying himself in continuous religious devotion. In his reports back to Louvois, Saint-Mars commented on the serenity and calmness of a man who had suddenly become a model prisoner. His only real concern was for Nicolas's health, which was poor. At the end of December 1671, for example, he reported that Nicolas had been suffering from a fever. 'But as he knows how to control himself admirably well and takes his precautions, I'm not bothered by this illness. He hasn't taken to his bed and has a good appetite, so I'm confident he'll get over this sickness and regain his strength as before.'[1]

Health bulletins became a regular feature of Saint-Mars's letters to Louvois. The 'precautions' that Saint-Mars mentioned Nicolas taking were a number of his mother's herbal remedies that he concocted in his room with the help of his valet Champagne, such as water of bitter chicory, peach flower syrup and cherry wine. He was also permitted to receive instructions for a special medicine from his doctor Pecquet, who had been released from the Bastille two months after Nicolas's transfer to Pignerol.

Perhaps as a reward for his more compliant attitude, the King permitted Nicolas in October 1672 to receive and to answer a letter from his wife concerning certain domestic affairs. However, afraid that some secret message might be passed one way or the other, Louvois instructed Saint-Mars to impose some stiff restrictions: 'After you have had the letter read out to him in your presence, you will give him a copy, written in your own hand, and a sheet of paper with ink and a pen. He is to have some hours to think and then, in your presence, to write down his answer.'[2]

Everyone knew that the supposed business matter was a pretext – a thin veil to cover up a huge concession. A second exchange of letters soon followed. The newly relaxed atmosphere led to a revival of hopes, which – absurd as it may have seemed in this place of stone walls and high mountains – even manifested itself in a brief return of past ambition. This was especially so when, through some lapse in security, Nicolas discovered that a huge French army had invaded the Dutch Republic earlier in the year and, after the rejection of an early peace settlement, had now got bogged down in Holland's flooded fields, the Dutch having opened up the dykes.

For a few days it was not a reconciled penitent who inhabited the prison tower, but the ghost of the old Superintendent of Finances. It occurred to Nicolas that France had a need once more for someone of his financial wizardry. Maybe here at last was an opportunity to negotiate his way back into the King's favour. So he asked his gaoler for an interview.

'The conversation turned to the tricks resourceful people use to get hold of money,' wrote Saint-Mars in the inevitable report to Louvois. 'He told me that he wasn't bad at that sort of thing and had managed to find ways of getting hold of funds where others had failed. After one thing or another, he said to me: "As I'm completely washed up, I'm putting my trust in your loyalty to the King that you will tell the marquis de Louvois that I have been considering some ideas that could render His Majesty the greatest of services.""[3]

When Saint-Mars asked Nicolas to be specific about what he had in mind, Nicolas said that it was a matter of such secrecy that he could confide it only to Louvois or the King himself. Over the days that followed he continued to raise the issue at every opportunity, with an insistence that put Saint-Mars into a quandary. He didn't want anyone to think that he had become susceptible to Nicolas's powers of persuasion; but nor did he want to be responsible for thwarting some genuine royal service he was able to provide. So with some hesitation he finally put forward Nicolas's proposal.

Sceptical, Louvois sent back the following instructions: 'You can give him five or six sheets of paper and tell him that he can return them to you written on or blank. Allow him four days, then take back the sheets and send them to me, sealing them in an envelope before him if he so wishes.'[4]

Nicolas complied and Saint-Mars despatched the sealed letter to Louvois by a special courier. Weeks went by while he waited to receive a response. Most days he would ask Saint-Mars if he had heard anything, repeatedly stressing that at stake was not only a very important service to the King but also a chance for Louvois to achieve great glory. Saint-Mars greeted his enquiries with an implacable mask of disinterest.

At last in late March 1673 Louvois gave his reply: 'Having read the documents written by Monsieur Foucquet very carefully, I have come to the conclusion that they do not offer the important service to the King that he promised, or any relief in his troubles. I have therefore judged it inappropriate to present these reports to His Majesty. Inform Monsieur Foucquet of this, let him see his sheets, and then burn them in his presence.'[5]

It amounted to a vindictive slap in the face. But Nicolas did not flinch. He strove to remain as outwardly composed as ever –

'always very calm,' remarked Saint-Mars – as if to say it was their lost opportunity, not his.

Nicolas was like one of those desert creatures that can rest immobile beneath the sands during years of drought, then spring forth again, renewed, when the rains arrive. After his hopes of a possible rehabilitation had been dashed, he resumed the economy of thought and emotion that he knew was the key to his survival. Clinging to his daily routine of prayer, he pulled himself forward through time by observing the feasts and saints' days. But somewhere the quiet hope remained that the rains might return. If he had learned anything at all from his time at Pignerol, it was that no matter how bleak your prospects may seem to be, the most extraordinary things can happen at any moment.

It was perhaps too much to expect lightning to strike twice, but there had been some strange signs. Once, in the depths of winter, when the cold north wind was fighting with the fire in the hearth, a beam in the floor began to smoulder and then catch fire. Nicolas usually tried to give rational explanations for such things, but still he couldn't help viewing what had happened as yet another omen. With the passing of many more saints' days he dismissed the incident from his mind, but then he began to hear some persistent scraping sounds from the chimney.

If such distractions made it hard to concentrate on his prayers, what happened next could easily have caused him to doubt his sanity. One day the marquis de Puyguilhem, Antonin Nompar de Caumont, bedraggled and covered in dust, stepped out of the fireplace and introduced himself. He was staying in the rooms underneath, he said. Since the last time the two had met, well over ten years earlier, Puyguilhem had inherited his father's title and was now known as the comte de Lauzun.

Nicolas remembered a young, hot-headed courtier of little importance, who – in spite of his small stature and unprepossessing appearance – had won a considerable reputation as an accomplished philanderer. But he was not someone it was possible to take seriously in any other walk of life. So Nicolas was astonished when Lauzun told him how he had become a favourite of the King and, in a series of rapid promotions, had been made Captain of the King's Bodyguard, Colonel of the Dragoons and a general in the army.

Nicolas may have longed to catch up on all the news of the last ten years, but hesitated to place any reliance in Lauzun because he told such far-fetched tales. Louise de la Vallière, for example. According to Lauzun, she had borne the King four children and then fled to a convent. From there she had been dragged back by Colbert and forced to share the same apartments as the King's new mistress Madame de Montespan, who had achieved her conquest of the King through the aid of black masses and love potions. When the two mistresses travelled, they had to do so in the same carriage as Louis's wife Maria Theresa, so that onlookers would ask one another whether they had seen 'the Three Queens'.

Lauzun's account of how he came to be at Pignerol was almost as extraordinary. He had been on the verge of marrying Mademoiselle de Montpensier, the King's cousin and the richest woman in France. A date had even been announced for the wedding, but Madame de Montespan had persuaded Louis to veto the engagement. In the bitter feud that followed he took to insulting the King's mistress so openly that Louis decided to send him to the most remote prison in the kingdom to teach him silence.

Nicolas suspected that the real reason why Lauzun had been sent to Pignerol was because he had gone mad. Saint-Mars, who had to look after the new prisoner, would certainly have agreed. Since his arrival in the gaol, Lauzun had refused to eat, allowed his hair to grow long and threatened suicide several times. He had even set fire to his cell. 'Before I got to know Monsieur de

Lauzun,' wrote Saint-Mars in a letter to Louvois, 'I used to think that Monsieur Foucquet was the worst prisoner one could imagine having to look after, but now I think he's a little lamb compared to this one.'[6]

In spite of his fears concerning his new companion's mental balance, Nicolas kept quiet about the passage that Lauzun had managed to make into his chamber and the two men continued to meet in secret. Even the company of a madman was better than no company at all. And in a strange way, Lauzun's clearly unbalanced ravings about the Court – to which he longed to return with all the obsession of an addict – helped Nicolas in his struggle to achieve a spiritual self-sufficiency. For nothing could have better illustrated the folly of his former life.

It was at about the time of Lauzun's arrival that Nicolas, who was no longer considered a danger, was allowed free access at last to ink and paper. He made the most of the opportunity, but the previous levity had been replaced by a consistent strain of repentance: 'Deceitful vanities . . . who enslave the Court, in which the courtiers fritter away their years and their possessions, you no longer own me. Your false bounty, your false charms are now the cause of my tears: I deplore the time I wasted on you.'[7] More sombre and introspective, and increasingly prone to illness, Nicolas now placed his hopes entirely in heavenly redemption. The theme that he returned to again and again was the idea of having won freedom for his soul through his imprisonment. It had taught him the insignificance of earthly authorities. Once he had put his entire faith in the King, but now he thought of the King as an impostor. 'God alone, the God of Gods and the King alone of kings / Deserves our care, devotion and labour: / To him alone do we owe our duty. / Anything given elsewhere is a theft and a crime. / So it is to this king, Christians, that we must give our hearts, / Adoring him and serving him night and day.'

The only earthly kings that he showed any regard for were

those who had paid the proper due to God in heaven. So it was that at last he turned to the Psalms of David. He attempted a translation from the Latin of Psalm 118. At the top of the first page he wrote, 'This psalm has considerable relevance to my present condition and to the eventual release that I hope for, God willing.'

It is easy to imagine which verses would have struck a particular chord:

> The Lord is on my side;
> I will not fear:
> What can man do unto me?

This was the necessary attitude for any prisoner hoping to remain sane in Pignerol.

> It is better to trust in the Lord
> than to put confidence in man.
> It is better to trust in the Lord
> than to put confidence in princes.

To put confidence in princes had been perhaps the greatest mistake in Nicolas's life. The King had punished him for treachery. But really his crime had been faith – faith in a king rather than the faith he ought to have put in God alone.

> I shall not die, but live,
> and declare the works of the Lord.
> The Lord hath chastened me sore:
> but he hath not given me over unto death.

It did not matter how harsh his circumstances had become. So long as there was life there was purpose, which justified a continued existence. Nicolas's purpose now was to declare the works of the Lord. *'J'AIME DE PUR AMOUR; DIEU POUR MA VIE,'* Marie de Maupeou had written many years ago at Saint-Mandé. As Nicolas recalled the spartan little cell his mother had preferred to all the opulence that he had then been able to offer her, as he recalled her poring over the words of Saint Juve's Treatise and the Holy Bible, it must have seemed a strange prefigurement of the life he now led in Pignerol. Then he had been too full of ambition and pride to pay her any attention, but now at last he was ready to follow her example.

> Thou art my God, and I will praise thee:
> Thou art my God, I will exalt thee.
> O give thanks unto the Lord; for he is good:
> For his mercy endureth for ever.

As Nicolas laboured over these verses, putting to use the excellent command of Latin that he owed to the Collège de Clermont, he must surely have thought of the little book that Pierre Deschampsneufs had once dedicated to him. He had been too busy to read the Psalms of David then and it was hopeless to expect his gaolers to allow him to see a copy now. But the act of translation itself was surely a kind of tribute – a belated gesture of gratitude, as well as a reassurance that he had heeded his old teacher's warning.

In that paradoxical way of things, it was just as Nicolas had come truly to put the divine before the temporal, perhaps for the very first time in his life, that the earthly King began to show some clemency. In 1671 Simon Arnauld de Pomponne, who had been a close friend of Nicolas, was appointed Minister for Foreign Affairs. At about the same time Madame de Maintenon, the widow of Paul Scarron, one of the writers Nicolas had supported, became a governess to the children of the King's mistress and, soon after that, the King's new mistress herself. Their influence helped to instil some spirit of compassion within the King, who – having allowed an initial one-off exchange of letters a year and a half earlier – in April 1674 granted Marie-Madeleine Foucquet permission to write to her husband twice a year and to receive his replies.[8] The second of these replies, dated 5 February 1675, has been preserved; it provides a direct portrait of Nicolas after over ten years of captivity:[9]

For three months I have been waiting impatiently to receive your letter. Now it has finally arrived and afforded me as much solace as I can feel in a place of such bitterness and pain. Nothing moves me so much as the cares you have taken over our chapel and the devotions you make there. For a long time now I have felt both the need and the wish to do the same. I have often begged Saint-Mars and the priest who comes here to take my confession to allow me to prepare for my death – which I sense is not far off now – by allowing me free access to a good cleric who is above suspicion, to whom I can open up my conscience without reserve concerning the bad life I have led . . . but I've had no luck so far: I am allowed to attend confession and communion only at Christmas, Easter, Pentecost, on the Assumption and All Saints' Day. The result is that sometimes, as in this year, during four whole months between Christmas and Easter I have to go without the assistance that one might imagine less important than elsewhere, but which is in fact much more necessary because such forced inactivity is the mother of perpetual despair, temptation and restlessness . . . Sometimes I feel as though I have been abandoned or forgotten by those I feel most close to, despised by others, and just a useless burden to everybody. At these moments, the only cure is patience and calm, which usually comes with good use of the Sacraments and the daily intercession of a charitable and religious person who has devoted himself completely to God . . .

Going on to describe his state of health, Nicolas wrote,

> There is always some ill air in our fortress and I'm too unwell and
> not smart enough to know what is best for me . . . My stomach
> fights with my liver, which aches from one night to the next, and
> on top of this I have swollen legs, as well as sciatica, colic attacks
> and, if you don't mind me mentioning this, some really painful
> haemorrhoids . . . But these are just a small part of my ailments.
> I could mention the colds, the fluxions, the headaches, the
> ringing in the ears . . . Finally, my eyes are so weak that I have to
> use glasses, and my teeth are falling out. The best solution is to
> forget about the body completely and to think only of the soul.
> That's what one should do, yet it is the body that makes itself the
> most felt. If only you could come here, that would be the way to
> make both body and soul feel better.

The letter is all the more touching for the snapshot it offers of
Nicolas poised between two worlds – the one he was heading
towards and the one he had left behind. His emotional discipline
told him that it was best not to think of the one he had left behind,
but it was impossible entirely to resist the indulgence. Of his
children, he wrote, 'Please do not try to provide me with their
portraits, as that can only break my heart and there is nothing I
can do to help them; but may your goodness bring it about that I
may one day see the originals.'

Attached to Marie-Madeleine's letter there had been a note
from Nicolas's mother, who was now well into her eighties. 'Her
hand is more sure than mine,' commented Nicolas, 'and the
kindness she shows to a son who has caused her so much pain is
extraordinary . . .'

The King's new mood of clemency manifested itself in
carefully graded increments. After receiving Nicolas's reply,
Marie-Madeleine made several requests to be able to visit to her

husband and also asked that he should be able to see a confessor regularly, not just five times a year. The King turned down both these requests, but in March 1675 did agree that Nicolas should henceforward be able to take Communion every month.

A year later Marie-Madeleine, who was still living in exile away from Paris, met Madame de Maintenon in Bourbon, where the King's mistress had travelled to take the waters. Madame de Sévigné, who witnessed the encounter, was impressed by the skill with which she managed to convey Nicolas's suffering, yet without making any tactless request for Madame de Maintenon to intervene. 'Her words appeared to me perfectly calculated to touch the heart.'[10]

Maybe Madame de Maintenon was moved enough to put in a word on Nicolas's behalf, but the simple passage of time was probably just as significant a factor in improving the conditions of Nicolas's captivity. Nearly forty years old, the King was now a mature and experienced ruler, whose confidence in his authority made it much easier to be magnanimous.

A big thaw occurred in late 1677 when the King gave permission for both Nicolas and the comte de Lauzun to be allowed to take the air on the ramparts that surrounded the prison tower. The King would have preferred Saint-Mars to supervise the promenades of each of the prisoners separately, but appreciating the demands this would make on his gaoler's time, he made it clear that he would not object to Saint-Mars allowing the two prisoners to go out on the terrace together, as long as he monitored their conversations closely. Since this was the first time the two prisoners had been officially permitted to talk to each other in six years, Nicolas must presumably have had to make some comic attempts to feign surprise at all the news he was supposed to be hearing for the first time.

In the flurry of concessions, the pair were also permitted – as always under Saint-Mars's supervision – to play 'honest games' with the officers of the garrison.[11] And Nicolas was allowed to have news of the world outside and began to receive *Le Mercure galant*, a magazine that contained the political and cultural news of the day. Saint-Mars was of course expected to stress the King's extraordinary bounty. 'You can explain to them the great kindness that His Majesty has granted,' Louvois instructed, 'and warn them that the first time you notice any attempt either to give or to receive notes or to make any sign to anyone, they must expect to be confined in their quarters for ever.'[12] But the King did not intend to go on making further concessions without some favour from Nicolas in return.

21

The Predestinate

Pignerol was the place where the King consigned his darkest secrets. One of the most mysterious concerned a servant called Eustache d'Auger, who was incarcerated in Pignerol in the summer of 1669. In a letter to warn Saint-Mars of the prisoner's impending arrival, Louvois wrote, 'It is of vital importance to the King that he be kept in the highest security and that he should not be able to communicate in any way. I give you this advance warning so that you can prepare a dungeon where you can keep him securely.'[1]

This dungeon was to be arranged in such a way that it would be impossible for the prisoner to be overheard by anyone in a neighbouring chamber, and also to be provided with a whole series of security doors that would prevent his guards from hearing anything. 'You yourself must once every day bring this wretch his food and, no matter what the reason, refuse to listen to him, each time threatening to kill him if he dares to speak to you concerning anything other than his daily necessities.'

For five years the prisoner meekly endured his captivity, seeing only Saint-Mars once a day and burying himself in Christian writings. 'He says nothing and lives in contentment, as a man who has given himself up entirely to the will of God and the King,'[2] wrote Saint-Mars. But at the beginning of 1675 Nicolas's valet Champagne died, and as his second valet, La

Rivière, was constantly ill, Saint-Mars suggested that d'Auger should be allowed to become Nicolas's new servant.

Given the original conditions of d'Auger's captivity, it seems surprising that the King agreed, but his stipulation that d'Auger should in no circumstances be confined with anyone other than Nicolas suggests that perhaps Nicolas already knew d'Auger's secret. It's possible, too, that the King hoped that Nicolas might also do some gentle probing on his behalf.

In December 1678 Louvois took the unusual step of writing this note direct to him: 'His Majesty would shortly like to make some considerable improvements to the conditions of your imprisonment; but, as he wishes first to know if the prisoner Eustache d'Auger has said anything in the presence of your other valet about his past life before he arrived in Pignerol, he has ordered me to tell you that he expects you to give him a true answer so that he can take appropriate measures.'[3]

Nicolas was to write down the information in a sealed letter and keep its contents secret even from Saint-Mars. Nicolas's reply was far too confidential to expect a copy of it to exist today, but we do have the letter that Louvois wrote to him in response on 20 January 1679: 'You'll learn from Saint-Mars of precautions that the King wishes to take in order to prevent d'Auger communicating with anyone other than you; His Majesty expects you to help in this regard as best you can, since you know how important it is that no one should be aware of what he knows.'[4]

On the same day, Louvois wrote a long letter to Saint-Mars, headed 'Memorandum on the manner in which the King wishes Monsieur Saint-Mars forthwith to guard the prisoners in his care'.[5] The extraordinary liberalisation of the prison regime that the document set out suggests that the King must have been satisfied with whatever information Nicolas had been able to provide. Henceforward Nicolas, and Lauzun, too, were free to correspond as often as they liked with their friends and relations, as long as that correspondence was communicated via Louvois. They were also free to receive whatever books or journals they wished, and to take a stroll at any time they chose, not just within the precincts of the tower but anywhere in the citadel. The only qualification concerned the comte de Lauzun: 'His Majesty stipulates that he should only be allowed to leave the tower in the company of Saint-Mars, along with two officers and six armed soldiers: His Majesty believes that he is more likely to think of attempting to escape than Monsieur Foucquet.'

The memorandum was notable for a tolerance and an almost thoughtful generosity that was as benign in its spirit as most previous instructions over the length of Nicolas's captivity had been harsh. 'His Majesty is happy for Monsieur Foucquet and Monsieur de Lauzun to see each other in complete freedom, as often and whenever they like. They are free to spend their days together, to dine together and, if it pleases them, Monsieur Saint-Mars may dine with them. His Majesty is also happy for Saint-Mars's officers to converse and to play games with them at any time.'

The King was going out of his way to be kind. There were many possible reasons why. The anger and jealousy of the insecure young man of 1661 had subsided. He was more confident and had long ago ceased to regard Nicolas as a threat. And maybe he even felt a little guilty for having acted with such needless cruelty over the last twenty years – that was something he would have to answer for before God.

The King's kindness did not, however, extend to the lower orders and certainly not to d'Auger, still harbouring his dangerous secret. 'Each time Monsieur Foucquet goes down to Monsieur de Lauzun's room or Monsieur de Lauzun goes up to Monsieur Foucquet's,' the King's memorandum instructed, 'Monsieur Saint-Mars is to take Eustache d'Auger aside, and not allow him to be in Monsieur Foucquet's room when there is anyone else in there besides Monsieur Foucquet and the other valet. Similar precautions must be taken when Monsieur Foucquet goes for a stroll in the citadel. D'Auger must be made to stay in Monsieur Foucquet's chamber, and may only be allowed to accompany him when Monsieur Foucquet is alone with the other valet and limits his walk to the precincts of the tower.'

The King's sudden compassion meant exhausting work for Saint-Mars, who found it much easier to keep his prisoners locked up permanently in their rooms. After the gaoler respectfully drew attention to some of the practical difficulties of implementing all the new concessions, Louis amended his instructions to confine the prisoners to their cells for one day in every week.[6]

But the drift towards increasing tolerance was clear. In the months that followed, the screens were removed from Nicolas's window, new carpets were provided and covers put on his chairs. In his newly refurbished chamber, he was even allowed to entertain the town dignitaries of Pignerol.

The consistent pattern encouraged Nicolas to give rein to some extravagant hopes. In a letter to his mother,[7] he wrote, 'I cannot make better use of the freedom that the King's kindness has granted me than to send you a part of the respects I owe you in this letter, hoping that the same royal clemency – which, after the example of God, shows itself sometimes a little at a time and proceeds by degrees – will allow me to perform the remainder of my duty kneeling before you.' The general expectation, in Paris as much as in Pignerol, was that the King's extraordinary bounteousness was a prelude to an eventual release.

Nicolas went on to express the contrition of a prodigal son, imagining his repentant return home. 'Kneeling before you, my heart, my mouth and perhaps my eyes, through their tears, will explain in depth what you now read in these few words, namely my intense sorrow for the pain that my wrong conduct has caused, disturbing the repose of your honest retirement, and taxing your goodness. Kneeling before you, I shall humbly beg your forgiveness for having made such poor use of your good counsels and taken a path entirely contrary to your good example.'

In June 1679 Nicolas's wife and children made the journey to Pignerol. Marie-Madeleine was allowed to see her husband without restriction and even to sleep in his room. The last time Nicolas had seen his family was fifteen years earlier during the court hearings at the Arsenal. Marie-Madeleine was now nearly fifty and the children had grown up. The youngest, Louis, who had been born during that long-ago summer at Fontainebleau, was meeting his father as if for the first time – a pale, grey-haired and gap-toothed old man.

According to Saint-Simon, one of the first things Nicolas asked his family about was his prison companion Lauzun. To his astonishment, they told him that everything Lauzun had said about his past was true. 'He refused to accept what they told him and was tempted to believe that they had also gone mad. It required a lot of time to convince him.'[8]

Not only was Lauzun telling the truth, but he was probably the reason why Nicolas was now on the threshold of freedom. Mademoiselle de Montpensier was still in love with Lauzun. She wanted him to be released and to be allowed to marry her. Meanwhile the King's mistress, Madame de Montespan, wanted her illegitimate children by Louis to receive the kind of generous settlements that, realistically, only the vast fortune of the King's cousin could make possible. A little horse-trading was required because the lovelorn Duchess had already made over part of her estate to Lauzun. But he would surely be prepared to reconsider in return for his freedom. While the two cousins hammered out the details of a possible deal, Louis decided it would be wise to ease the conditions of Lauzun's imprisonment. But he wanted to do this without singling him out, which would only inflate his already exaggerated sense of his own importance. Nicolas was the chance beneficiary of this scheme. It seemed the King did not work in quite such mysterious ways after all.

Lauzun, however, showed little gratitude for the efforts his intended was making to win him a more comfortable existence. His roving eye, which had had nothing more promising to feast on for the last eight eight years than Saint-Mars's soldiers, settled on Nicolas's extremely attractive twenty-two-year-old daughter – like her mother called Marie-Madeleine. When Nicolas's wife left Pignerol in August to attend to some family business, Lauzun took advantage of her absence to seduce the young Marie-Madeleine, who stayed behind to keep her father company. Driven on by the *démon de midi*, the veteran courtier secured silver buttons for his jerkin and four young horses to parade along the ramparts of the citadel, bringing a touch of Fontainebleau to the grim mountain fortress. Brought up in exile, Marie-Madeleine knew nothing of the Court circles her father had once inhabited and was too flattered to resist the display.

To the extent that Nicolas had genuinely regretted his previous life, perhaps he saw Lauzun's seduction of his daughter as a cruel but poetic justice to add to the long punishment he had already suffered, but it did not prevent him from falling out with Lauzun just the same. Their bickering was so acrimonious that it reached the attention of Saint-Mars, who, however, at Louvois's bidding,[9] allowed the feud to continue in the hope that they would reveal to him each other's secrets.

Nicolas had shown himself at his very best in Pignerol. It was a place which, in its pristine isolation, allowed him to come close to achieving the kind of purity his mother had counselled. But Lauzun's escapades awoke him to the shabby, ignoble nature of the world to which he expected soon to return.

*

As a new year began in Pignerol, the winter winds whistled around Nicolas's alpine tower with the usual ferocity, but although they awoke all his old ailments, he could take some comfort from the thought that in all likelihood this would be the last harsh season he would have to endure.

When on 27 January 1680 he celebrated his sixty-fifth birthday with his daughter Marie-Madeleine, they would have been able to drink a toast to his imminent release. Everyone was expecting the announcement any day. The only thing that seemed to put it off was the inclement weather, which made the roads up to the fortress impassable.

But one last cruel turn of fortune spoiled the reunion that the Foucquet family had over many months been preparing. On 23 March Nicolas passed away after a series of convulsions. The records of the time, which attributed cause of death to that often used but vague term 'apoplexy', do not make clear exactly how he died, but those of his family who had been able to see him during those last months in his cold, austere rooms could understand all too well the attrition of a place that had now, on the threshold of his release, fatally undermined his resilience.

Official circles in Paris greeted his death with near silence, doing little more than to register the bare fact. It was left to his friends to attempt to give some meaning to what had happened. 'Poor Monsieur Foucquet is dead,' Madame de Sévigné wrote to her daughter on 3 April when she first heard the news. 'I am very moved.'[10] She was too upset to write much more than that, but two days later she added a further comment: 'If I were advising Monsieur Foucquet's family, I would tell them not to bring back his body, as apparently they intend to do; for after nineteen years, that is not the way he should leave his prison.'[11]

The death of Nicolas was embarrassing for Saint-Mars, since it led to the discovery of the hole through which Lauzun had been making his way into Nicolas's chamber ever since his arrival ten years before. In response Louvois stipulated some security measures the sense of which it's hard to fathom over 300 years later. Saint-Mars was to tell Lauzun and anyone else who asked that Nicolas's valets La Rivière and Eustache d'Auger had been set free, but in fact he was to shut the pair up in a dungeon, where they were to see and to speak to no one. By degrees, the prisoners were relieved of any vestiges of humanity. Louvois and Saint-Mars ceased in their correspondence even to mention them by name, referring to them instead as the 'Gentlemen at the bottom of the tower'.[12] While La Rivière died in 1687, d'Auger was dragged along to the various gaols that Saint-Mars would subsequently command. When he died in the Bastille in 1703, after over thirty years of imprisonment, he was buried under the name of a prisoner called Matthioli. He never uttered a word that was recorded, but these extreme measures to steal his identity assured him a lasting if anonymous celebrity as the inspiration for the Man in the Iron Mask, more famous even than the man who outshone the Sun King.

Nicolas's body was removed from the tower and kept temporarily in a vault in the church of Saint Claire in Pignerol. A year later it was brought back to Paris, where it was placed in the family vault in the church of Saint Mary of the Visitation. Nicolas's mother, who lived long enough to see his return, died the following month at the age of ninety-one. Perhaps it was she who helped to inspire the appraisal of his life that the nuns of the Visitation recorded in their register of deaths:

On 28 March 1681, Monsieur Nicolas Foucquet was buried in our church, in the chapel of Saint François de Sales . . . In the great offices he held, he demonstrated so extraordinary a talent, so noble a manner and such just and generous feeling, that the past centuries can offer almost no one to rival his accomplishments.

But God, who wanted to make a Predestinate, overturned all these great earthly achievements. He was disgraced, in spite of his important services, put on trial and imprisoned for more than eighteen years. It was during this exile that, stripped of all his honours, he rediscovered virtue and experienced the enlightenment of faith. He began to open his eyes and to recognise the emptiness of worldly splendours . . . So it was that by his disgrace he changed his ways, achieved sanctity and died, full of good deeds and righteousness before God.[13]

Postscript

Vaux-le-Vicomte is still a charmed place 300 years later. To visit it today is to step into a marvellous dream. Nestling in the countryside some three miles outside the town of Melun, it is spared the horde of tourists that afflicts its vulgar offspring at Versailles. There, sightseeing is conducted on an industrial scale, the tour buses dumping before the palace gates visitors from all over the world. The sheer numbers offer obvious testimony to the Sun King's lasting *gloire*.

But although the colossal scale of the enterprise offers an unrivalled standard of majesty, its disregard for measure, its very concern to impress, implies the hidden tale of envy that began at Vaux-le-Vicomte. The serenity, grace and elegance of Nicolas's house were an affront to the young King. It had to be diminished somehow, for no subject should be allowed to display more style than the monarch he was supposed to serve.

Louis's youthful accomplishments were more sporty and practical than reflective. He was a first-class marksman and hunter, he was an excellent dancer, there was nothing he didn't know about riding a horse, but his appreciation of the arts was limited. The young monarch thought reading was dull. But not even a poorly read, previously philistine king could resist the magic of Vaux. Louis already possessed a precocious understanding of all the other kinds of power, but it was Vaux-le-

Vicomte that first introduced him to the power of art and, as a connoisseur of powers, he had to add this one to his collection.

Determined to achieve a swift conquest of this new field – after the manner of generations of impresarios and moguls since – he decided to buy up the best available talent. Nicolas's team became Louis's team. Le Nôtre, Le Vau and Le Brun were put under royal harness, expected at Versailles to outdo what they had achieved at Vaux. We should not blame them too much for the bloated result. Louis's thirst for *gloire* misused their talent every bit as much as Nicolas's good taste had released it. What they had made with perfect measure at Vaux, they were compelled to repeat with vulgar excess at Versailles.

Few of the world's tourists who file through Versailles's magnificent state rooms will have heard of the house that inspired it. As they gaze out at the Grand Canal, on which Louis used to stage mock sea battles, many will have an impression of a domain beyond compare. Louis's descendants may have run into the buffers of the French Revolution, but the palace they once inhabited has been assured a kind of official immortality. While Vaux-le-Vicomte remains little known outside France, Versailles has been designated a World Heritage site of 'outstanding universal value', whose 'sober and colossal architecture' is 'inseparable, even now, from the memory of the Sun King'.

But if only those visitors to Versailles could make the comparison, they would see that Louis's palace is an imitation that causes one to marvel all the more at the original. The Grand Canal, for example, which announces its scale so insistently, seems a very crude display to those who have witnessed the hidden charm of Le Nôtre's earlier effort at Vaux.

From the highest point of Nicolas's house – the belvedere that sits on top of the dome – you can gaze over the entire extent of his domain, but see no stretch of water other than the formal ponds and fountains that line the parterres. It is only when you are in the garden itself and have walked to the end of those parterres that suddenly you come upon the expanse. In the shelter of a great, previously invisible gorge far beneath your feet the canal glistens in the sunlight as it passes serenely between an avenue of chestnuts.

There's something miraculous about this sudden contrast of two domains – one all geometrical precision and order, the other water, grass and trees – the two existing so closely side by side yet each imperceptible to the other. Strolling along the banks of Nicolas's canal, it would be easy for you to imagine that there was no house at all, that you had stumbled through some invisible portal into Arcadia.

But on the far side, you can regain the heights again and from a stone terrace look back the way you have come. In the distance the blue-grey dome projects benevolent authority and purpose – a slaty charisma that every summer attracts a devoted escort of swifts and swallows. Swooping about its brow in a spectacular flying display, they form an airy victory wreath. If you are lucky enough to stand in their midst with the hot summer breeze on your cheeks, you can share in their jubilation, convinced that this must be the closest place to heaven on earth. If I were Nicolas, this is where I would climb.

A pleasing coincidence brings this story to a close. The head gardener of Versailles is talking on the radio about André Le Nôtre. He explains how Vaux-le-Vicomte was an important turning point in his predecessor's career, because before then Le Nôtre had long hesitated over whether he should devote his life to painting or gardening. Nicolas Foucquet provided the faith and support that helped him make up his mind. The gardener goes on to describe the King's jealousy. He tells the story of Nicolas's arrest and punishment, but also how many years later – Le Nôtre – who was on his way to visit the Pope in Rome – made a difficult detour to visit Nicolas in Pignerol, determined before it was too late to express his gratitude to the man who had decided his vocation. But most of all, the gardener recommended that listeners should visit Vaux for themselves:

> It is a magical place that really takes you back through time. And once you are there, you can appreciate the scale of the injustice that occurred. Frankly, Louis wanted to show his authority by destroying the most powerful man in France. But when you are there, when you can see the beauty of the place, when you can experience for yourself the atmosphere that Foucquet created, then you understand how he could not have been the criminal his accusers made him out to be.

Appendix

Ode to a Parrot

Nicolas Foucquet
Attorney-General and Superintendent of
Finances to Louis XIV (1615–1680)

Plutôt le procureur maudira la chicane,
Le joueur de piquet voudra se voir capot,
Le buveur altéré s'éloignera du pot
Et tout le parlement jugera sans soutane

On verra Saint-Amant devenir diaphane,
Le goutteux tout perclus hantera le tripot,
Madame de Rohan quittera son Chabot
Et d'ouïr le sermon sera chose profane,

Un barbier pour raser ira sans coquemar,
Le clocher de Saint-Paul sera sans Jacquemar,
L'évêque Grenoblois fera couper sa barbe,

Que d'oublier jamais ton funeste débris,
Aimable perroquet: j'en jure Sainte-Barbe!
Ton portrait à jamais ornera mon lambris.

References

Prologue: 1644

1 Archives Nationales, E190A, fol. 270.
2 Letter from Nicolas Foucquet to Pierre Séguier, 28 June 1644. Quoted in Boris Porchnev, *Les Soulèvements populaires en France au XVIIe siècle* (Flammarion, Paris, 1972), p. 128.
3 Article, Hôtel-Dieu, in the *Encyclopédie*, 1765, vol. 8, pp. 319–20.
4 Arthur de Boislisle (ed.), *Mémoires de Saint-Simon* (Hachette, Paris, 1924), vol. 36, pp. 68–9.
5 Jacques de Maupeou, *Histoire des Maupeou* (Fontenay-le-Comte, 1959), p. 139.
6 Monsieur de Lauzières to Pierre Sèguier, 28 August 1644, in Hector de la Ferrière, *Deux années de mission à Saint-Pétersbourg* (Imprimerie Impériale, Paris, 1867), p. 144.
7 Justin Lasnier (ed.), *Missions de Cayenne* (Paris, 1857).
8 Pierre Grillon (ed.), *Les Papiers de Richelieu* (Pedone, Paris, 1982), vol. 5, p. 95.
9 Jules Lair, *Nicolas Foucquet: Procureur-Général, Surintendant des finances, ministre d'état de Louis XIV* (Librarie Plon, Paris, 1890), vol. 1, p. 23.
10 For the details of Chalais's trial and execution, see Lair, *Nicolas Foucquet*, vol. 1, pp. 23–47. Especially vivid are his quotations from the *Mercure français*, which provided contemporary accounts of the trial.
11 Lair, *Nicolas Foucquet*, vol. 1, p. 45.

12 Goulas, *Mémoires* (Société de l'Histoire de France, Paris, 1879), vol. 1, p. 127.

Chapter 1: The Second Son

1 Gustave Dupont-Ferrier, *Du Collège de Clermont au Lycée Louis-le-Grand* (E. de Boccard, Paris, 1921), vol. 1, p. 17.
2 François Vavasseur, *Excellentes praeter modum pueros non esse vitales*, quoted in Urbain-Victor Chatelain, *Le Surintendant Nicolas Foucquet, protecteur des lettres des arts et des sciences* (Perrin, Paris, 1905), pp. 18–19.
3 Common Rules for the Teachers of the Lower Classes, rule 31, *Ratio studiorum*, 1599.
4 Rules for the Teacher of the Highest Grammar Class, rule 5, *Ratio studiorum*, 1599.
5 Christophe Balthazar, *Ch. Balthaʒarii Panegyricus. D. Nic. Fulceto*, 1655, quoted in Chatelain, p. 22.
6 Chatelain, *Le Surintendant Nicolas Foucquet*, p. 81.
7 Quoted in Lair, *Nicolas Foucquet*, vol. 1, pp. 75–6.

Chapter 2: The Road to the Top

1 Adolphe Chéruel (ed.), *Journal d'Olivier Lefèvre d'Ormesson* (Imprimerie Impériale, Paris, 1860), vol. 2, p. 51. See also, Michel Pernot, *La Fronde* (Editions de Fallois, Paris, 1994), p. 14.
2 Quoted in Georges Dethan, *The Young Maʒarin* (Thames & Hudson, London, 1977), p. 43.
3 Quoted in Geoffrey Treasure, *Maʒarin: The Crisis of Absolutism in France* (Routledge, London, 1995), p. 14.
4 Quoted in Dethan, *The Young Maʒarin*, p. 89.
5 Claude-Bernard Petitot (ed.), *Mémoires de Richelieu*, vol. 6 (Foucault, Paris, 1823), p. 336.
6 Quoted in Dethan, *The Young Maʒarin*, p. 92.
7 Ibid.

8   Ibid., p. 96.

9   Ibid., p. 94.

10 Ibid., p. 109.

11 Ibid., p. 108.

12 Ibid., p. 112.

13 Ibid., p. 120.

14 *Introduction aux mémoires relatifs à la Fronde*, in A. Petitot (ed.), *Collecion des mémoires relatifs à l'histoire de France* (Foucault, Paris, 1824), 2nd series, vol. 35, pp. 56–7.

15 *Mémoires de Madame de Motteville*, in A. Petitot (ed.), *Collection des mémoires relatifs à l'histoire de France*, 2nd series, vol. 37, p. 317.

16 Quoted in Chéruel (ed.), *Journal d'Olivier Lefèvre d'Ormesson*, vol. 1, p. 417.

17 Ibid., p. 417.

18 Ibid., p. 419.

19 *Mémoires d'Omer Talon*, in A. Petitot (ed.), *Collection des mémoires relatifs à l'histoire de France*, 2nd series, vol. 61, p. 156.

20 Lair, *Nicolas Foucquet*, pp. 111–13.

Chapter 3: Slings

1   Quoted in Marie-Noële Grand-Mesnil, *Mazarin, la Fronde et la presse, 1647–1649* (Armand Colin, Paris, 1967), p. 137.

2   Ibid., p. 142.

3   Cardinal de Retz, *Mémoires*, ed. Michel Pernot (Gallimard, Paris, 2003), p. 405.

4   Quoted in Philippe Erlanger, *Louis XIV* (Weidenfeld, London, 1970), p. 43.

Chapter 4: Fighting for the Cardinal

1   Quoted in Georges Bordonove, *Foucquet: coupable ou victime?* (Editions Pygmalion, Paris, 1979), p. 44.

2   Quoted in Lair, *Nicolas Foucquet*, vol. 1, p. 147.

3   Ibid., p. 152.

4   *Mémoires d'Omer Talon*, Petitot, 2nd series, vol. 62, p. 152.

5   Ibid., p. 156.

6   *Mémoires de Madame de Motteville*, Petitot, 2nd series, vol. 39, p. 156.

7   Ibid., pp. 157–8.

8   Duc d'Aumale, *Histoire des Princes de Condé* (Calmann-Levy, n.d.), vol. 6, p. 57.

9   Quoted in Erlanger, *Louis XIV*, p. 48.

10 Adolphe Chéruel (ed.), *Lettres du Maʒarin pendant son ministère* (Imprimerie Nationale, Paris, 1887), vol. 4, p. 56.

11 Ibid., p. 184.

12 Ibid., p. 47.

13 Pierre Clément (ed.), *Lettres, instructions et mémoires de Colbert* (Imprimerie Impériale, Paris, 1861), vol. 1, p. 73.

14 Quoted in Lair, *Nicolas Foucquet*, vol. 1, p. 161.

15 Ibid., p. 162.

16 Ibid., p. 185.

17 Ibid., p. 164.

18 Ibid., p. 262.

19 Ibid., p. 167.

20 Ibid., p. 167.

21 Accounts of this important day are provided in Dubuisson-Aubenay, *Journal des Guerres civiles* (Champion, Paris, 1883), vol. 2, p. 114; *Journal de Jean Villier, maître d'hôtel du roi* (Renouard, Paris, 1916), vol. 3, p. 6; and Chéruel (ed.), *Journal d'Olivier d'Ormesson*, vol. 2, p. 650.

22 Quoted in Henri Courteault (ed.), *Journal de Jean Vallier, maître d'hôtel du roi* (Renouard, Paris, 1916), vol. 3, p. 7.

23 Lair, *Nicolas Foucquet*, vol. 1, pp. 168–9.

24 Chéruel (ed.), *Lettres du Maʒarin*, vol. 5, p. 22.

25 Lair, *Nicolas Foucquet*, vol. 1, p. 179.

26 Clément (ed.), *Lettres, instructions et mémoires de Colbert*, vol. 1, p. 166.

Chapter 5: The Scoundrel's Return

1 D'Aumale, *Histoire des Princes de Condé*, vol. 6, p. 147.
2 Quoted in Chéruel, *Mémoires sur la vie publique et privée de Fouquet*, vol. 1, p. 66.
3 Ibid., p. 67.
4 Chéruel (ed.), *Lettres du Cardinal Mazarin*, vol. 5, p. 107.
5 Ibid., p. 132.
6 Quoted in Chéruel, *Mémoires sur la vie publique et privée de Fouquet*, vol. 1, p. 114.
7 *Mémoires de Mademoiselle de Montpensier*, in A. Petitot (ed.), *Collection des mémoires relatifs à l'histoire de France* (Foucault, Paris, 1825), 2nd series, vol. 41, p. 262.
8 Chéruel, *Mémoires sur la vie publique et privée de Fouquet*, vol. 1, p. 131.
9 Ibid., p. 145.
10 Ibid., p. 146.
11 Ibid., pp. 147–8.
12 Dubuisson-Aubenay, *Journal des Guerres civiles*, ed. Gustave Saige, vol. 2, p. 277.
13 Ibid., p. 293.
14 Chéruel (ed.), *Lettres du Cardinal Mazarin*, vol. 5, p. 372.
15 *Mémoires de Madame de Motteville*, Petitot, 2nd series, vol. 39, p. 353.
16 *Journal de Jean Vallier, maître d'hôtel du roi*, ed. Henri Courteault, vol. 4, pp. 171–2.

Chapter 6: A Promotion

1 Quoted in Michel Pernot, *La Fronde* (Editions de Fallois, Paris, 1994), pp. 321–2.
2 *Journal de Jean Vallier, maître d'hôtel du roi*, ed. Henri Courteault, vol. 4, p. 106.
3 Quoted in Lair, *Nicolas Foucquet*, vol. 1, p. 253.

4   Chéruel, *Mémoires sur la vie publique et privée de Fouquet*, vol. 1, p. 226.
5   Cardinal de Retz, *Mémoires*, p. 361.
6   Chéruel, *Mémoires sur la vie publique et privée de Fouquet*, vol. 1, pp. 257–8.
7   Ibid., p. 258.
8   Ibid., p. 242.
9   Ibid., p. 248.
10   Ibid., p. 249.
11   Ibid., p. 340.
12   Madame de Sévigné, *Correspondance*, ed. Roger Duchêne (Gallimard, Paris, 1972), vol. 1, p. 36.
13   *Mémoires de Mademoiselle de Montpensier*, Petitot, 2nd series, vol. 42, pp. 296–7.
14   Ibid., pp. 226–7.
15   Ibid., p. 298.
16   Quoted in Bordonove, *Fouquet: coupable ou victime?*, p. 75.
17   Chéruel, *Mémoires sur la vie publique et privée de Fouquet*, vol. 1, p. 277.
18   Ibid., pp. 277–8.
19   Ibid., p. 281.
20   Ibid., p. 282.
21   Ibid., p. 269.
22   *Aegidii Menagii poemata*, 3rd edn (Augustin Courbé, Paris, 1658).
23   Chéruel, *Mémoires sur la vie publique et privée de Fouquet*, vol. 1, p. 270.
24   Ibid., pp. 270–71.
25   *Mémoires de Gourville*, in A. Petitot and Monmerqué (eds.), *Collection des mémoires relatifs à l'histoire de France* (Foucault, Paris, 1826), 2nd series, vol. 52, p. 298.
26   Ibid., p. 319.
27   Ibid., p. 314.
28   Chéruel, *Mémoires sur la vie publique et privée de Fouquet*, vol. 1, p. 324.
29   Ibid., pp. 324–5.
30   Ibid., p. 325.

31   Ibid., pp. 327–8.
32   Ibid., pp. 328.
33   Ibid., pp. 328–9.

Chapter 7: Saint Mandé

1   Madeleine de Scudéry, *The Story of Sappho*, edited and translated by Karen Newman (University of Chicago Press, Chicago, 2003), pp. 15-16.
2   Quoted in Chatelain, *Nicolas Foucquet*, p. 74.
3   Ibid., p. 320.
4   *Archives de l'art français*, ed. Anatole de Montaiglon, 2nd series, vol. 2 (1862), p. 288.
5   Ibid., p. 290.
6   Ibid., p. 291.
7   Ibid., p. 304.

Chapter 8: Vaux-le-Vicomte

1   Paul Pellisson, *Histoire de l'Académie française* (Didier, Paris, 1858), p. 9.
2   Charles Augustin Saint-Beuve, *Tableau Historique de la poésie française* (Charpentier, Paris, 1869), p. 151.
3   Quoted in Joseph Delort (ed.), *Histoire de la détention des philosophes* (Firmin Didot, Paris, 1829), vol. 1, p. 7.
4   Ibid.
5   Quoted in F. L. Marcou, *Pellisson: Etude sur la vie et les oeuvres de Pellisson* (Didier, Paris, 1859), pp. 164–5.
6   Michel Gareau, *Charles le Brun, premier peintre du Roi Louis XIV* (Hazan, Paris, 1992), p. 7.
7   Quoted in Erik Porsenna, *Portrait d'un homme heureux: André le Nôtre* (Fayard, Paris, 2000), p. 101.
8   Quoted in Clément, *Histoire de Colbert*, p. 30.
9   Quoted in Jean-Marie Pérouse de Montclos, *Vaux-le-Vicomte*

(Editions Scala, Paris, 1997), p. 38.

10 Quoted in Jean-Christian Petitfils, *Fouquet* (Perrin, Paris, 1998), p. 268.

11 Chéruel and d'Avenel (eds), *Lettres du Cardinal Mazarin pendant son ministère* (Imprimerie Nationale, Paris, 1894), vol. 8, p. 454.

12 Ibid., p. 505.

Chapter 9: Behind the Façade

1 Foreword to 'Le Songe de Vaux', Jean de la Fontaine, *Oeuvres complètes* (Gallimard, Paris, 1958), vol. 2, p. 79.

2 Ibid., p. 104.

3 In Greek mythology Helicon is the home of the muses.

4 La Fontaine, *Oeuvres complètes*, vol. 2, p. 104.

5 Ibid., p. 81.

6 Lair, *Nicolas Foucquet*, vol. 1, p. 393.

7 Ibid.

8 Chéruel, *Mémoires sur la vie publique et privée de Fouquet*, vol. 1, p. 366.

9 Reproduced in Daniel Dessert, *Fouquet* (Fayard, Paris, 1987), pp. 354–62.

10 Quoted in Lair, *Nicolas Foucquet*, vol. 1, p. 423.

11 Chéruel, *Mémoires sur la vie publique et privée de Fouquet*, vol. 1, pp. 410.

12 Ibid., p. 412.

13 Ibid., p. 413.

14 Ibid., p. 418.

15 Ibid., p. 420.

Chapter 10: Pax Mazarina

1 Chéruel, *Mémoires sur la vie publique et privée de Fouquet*, vol. 2, pp. 2–3.

2 Quoted in Petifils, *Fouquet*, p. 242.

3   Chéruel, *Mémoires sur la vie publique et privée de Fouquet*, vol. 2, pp. 7–8.

4   Clément (ed.), *Lettres de Colbert*, vol. 7, pp. 164–83.

5   *Mémoires de Gourville*, Petitot, 2nd series, vol. 52, p. 323.

6   Chéruel, *Mémoires sur la vie publique et privée de Fouquet*, vol. 2, p. 12.

7   Chéruel and d'Avenel (eds.), *Lettres du Cardinal Mazarin pendant son ministère*, vol. 9, p. 405.

8   Quoted in Bordonove, *Foucquet: coupable ou victime?*, pp. 136–7.

9   Chéruel, *Mémoires sur la vie publique et privée de Fouquet*, vol. 2, p. 19.

10 Bordonove, *Foucquet: coupable ou victime?*, pp. 136–7.

11 Ibid., p. 138.

12 Ibid., p. 139.

13 Ibid., p. 140.

14 Lair, *Nicolas Foucquet*, vol. 1, pp. 548–9.

15 Ibid., p. 550.

Chapter 11: You Can't Take It With You

1   Paul Bonnefon (ed.), *Mémoires de Louis-Henri de Loménie, Comte de Brienne* (Société de l'Histoire de France, Paris, 1917), vol. 2, p. 23.

2   Ibid., p. 24.

3   Jean Loret, *La Muse historique*, ed. Charles-Louis Livet (Daffis, Paris, 1878), vol. 3, p. 231.

4   J.-H., Reveillé-Parise (ed.), *Lettres de Gui Patin* (Paris, 1846), vol. 3, p. 250.

5   Ibid., pp. 296–7.

6   Ibid., p. 314.

7   Abbé de Choisy, *Mémoires pour servir à l'histoire de Louis XIV*, ed. Georges Mongrédien (Mercure de France, Paris, 1966), p. 78.

8   *Mémoires de Louis-Henri de Loménie, comte de Brienne*, vol. 2, pp. 27–8.

9   Ibid., vol. 2, p. 30.

10 Brienne's encounter with the Cardinal in the gallery is related at ibid., vol. 3, pp. 88–90.

11 Ibid., vol. 3, pp. 86–7.

12 Chéruel, *Mémoires sur la vie publique et privée de Foucquet*, vol. 2, p. 85.

13 Ibid., p. 86.

14 Ibid., p. 86.

15 Choisy, *Mémoires*, pp. 70–71.

16 Ibid., p. 57.

17 Bonnefon (ed.), *Mémoires de Louis-Henri de Loménie, comte de Brienne*, vol. 3, p. 92.

18 Ibid., p. 31.

19 Ibid., p. 33.

20 Ibid., p. 36.

21 Ibid.

22 Conrad Van Beuningen, *Lettres et négociations entre M. Jean de Witt, conseiller pensionnaire de Hollande, et M. Conrad Van Beuningen, ministre extraordinaire à la cour de France depuis le 16 mars 1660 jusqu'en 1664* (Amsterdam, 1724), vol. 2, p. 82.

23 *Lettres de Gui Patin*, vol. 3, p. 344.

24 *Lettres Choisies de feu Mr Guy Patin* (Jean Petit, 1692), vol. 2, p. 383.

Chapter 12: Summer at Fontainebleau

1 Quoted in John B. Wolf, *Louis XIV* (Gollancz, London, 1968), p. 69.

2 *Lettres choisies de feu Mr Guy Patin*, vol. 2, p. 385.

3 Elizabeth-Charlotte of Bavaria, duchesse d'Orléans, *Secret Memoirs of the Court of Louis XIV and of the Regency* (Whittaker, London, 1824), p. 148.

4 Madame de Lafayette, *Vie de la Princesse d'Angleterre*, ed. Marie-Thérèse Hipp (Minard, Paris, 1967), p. 32.

5 Quoted in Chéruel, *Mémoires sur la vie publique et privée de Fouquet*, vol. 2, p. 208.

6   Ibid., p. 115.
7   Ibid., p. 174.

Chapter 13: A Thing Apart

1   Chéruel, *Mémoires sur la vie publique et privée de Fouquet*, vol. 2, p. 215.
2   Madame de Sévigné, *Correspondance*, vol. 1, p. 26.
3   See *Lettres de Gui Patin*, vol. 3, p. 289.
4   La Fontaine, *Oeuvres complètes*, vol. 2, p. 506.
5   Mazarin to Louis XIV, 28 June 1659, in Chéruel and Avenel (eds), *Lettres du Cardinal Maҁarin*, vol. 9, p. 155.

Chapter 14: The Party

1   Quoted in Lair, *Nicolas Foucquet*, vol. 2, p. 31.
2   Chéruel, *Mémoires sur la vie publique et privée de Fouquet*, vol. 2, pp. 171–2.
3   Ibid., p. 219.
4   Quoted in Anatole France and Jean Cordey, *Vaux-le-Vicomte* (Calmann-Levy, Paris; 1933), p. 174.
5   Ibid., p. 175.
6   La Fontaine, *Oeuvres complètes*, vol. 2, p. 526.
7   Ibid., p. 527.
8   Ibid.

Chapter 15: The Birthday Present

1   Chéruel, *Mémoires sur la vie publique et privée de Fouquet*, vol. 2, p. 228.
2   Choisy, *Mémoires*, p. 95.
3   *Mémoires de Louis-Henri de Loménie, Comte de Brienne*, vol. 3, p. 54.

4   Ibid., p. 55.
5   Ibid., p. 56.
6   Chéruel, *Mémoires sur la vie publique et privée de Fouquet*, vol. 2, p. 215.
7   *Mémoires de Louis-Henri de Loménie, Comte de Brienne*, vol. 3, pp. 68–9.
8   The account of this second visit can be found in Choisy, *Mémoires*, pp. 97–8.
9   The account of Nicolas's arrest comes from ibid., p. 99.
10   Chéruel, *Mémoires sur la vie publique et privée de Fouquet*, vol. 2, p. 243.
11   Ibid., pp. 247–51.

Chapter 16: 'Lightning Strikes the Highest Mountains'

1   Chéruel, *Mémoires sur la vie publique et privée de Fouquet*, vol. 2, p. 260.
2   Le Tellier to d'Artagnan, 10 October 1661, in François Ravaisson (ed.), *Archives de la Bastille, d'après des documents inédits* (Durand, Paris, 1867), vol. 1, p. 382.
3   Quoted in Chéruel, *Mémoires sur la vie publique et privée de Fouquet*, vol.2, pp. 262–70.
4   La Fontaine, *Oeuvres complètes*, vol. 2, p. 528.
5   Abbé de Choisy, *Mémoires*, p. 101.
6   Chéruel, *Mémoires sur la vie publique et privée de Fouquet*, vol. 2, pp. 282–3.
7   Ibid., p. 283.
8   La Fontaine, *Oeuvres complètes*, vol. 2, p. 505.
9   Chéruel, *Mémoires sur la vie publique et privée de Fouquet*, vol. 2, p. 286.
10   Ibid., p. 289.
11   Madame de Sévigné, *Correspondance*, vol. 1, p. 50.
12   Chéruel, *Mémoires sur la vie publique et privée de Fouquet*, vol. 2, p. 319.
13   Ibid.

14 Chéruel (ed.), *Journal d'Olivier Lefèvre d'Ormesson et extraits des mémoires d'André Lefèvre d'Ormesson*, vol. 2, p. 99.
15 La Fontaine, *Oeuvres complètes*, vol. 2, p. 547.
16 Ibid., p. 548.
17 Louis XIV to d'Artagnan, 3 January 1662, in *Archives de la Bastille*, vol. 1, p. 413.

Chapter 17: Justice

1 Lair, *Nicolas Foucquet*, vol. 2, p. 69.
2 Pellisson's pamphlet, 'Discours au Roi par un de ses fidèles sujets, sur le procès de M. Foucquet', was reprinted in Paul Pellisson-Fontanier, *Oeuvres diverses*, (Didot, Paris, 1735), vol. 2, pp. 25–59.
3 La Fontaine, *Oeuvres complètes*, vol. 2, p. 529.
4 Madame Foucquet to Louis XIV, 30 July 1662, in Ravaisson (ed.), *Archives de la Bastille*, vol. 1, p. 58.
5 Ibid., p. 59.
6 Ibid., pp. 60–61.
7 Lair, *Nicolas Foucquet*, vol. 2, p. 175.
8 Ibid.
9 Chéruel (ed.), *Journal d'Olivier Lefèvre d'Ormesson et extraits des mémoires d'André Lefèvre d'Ormesson*, vol. 2, p. 20.
10 Ibid., p. 81.
11 Ibid., p. 74.
12 Ibid., p. 82.
13 For the conversation between Nicolas and Chamillart, see ibid., p. 86.
14 Ibid., p. 89.
15 Ibid., p. 100.
16 Ibid., p. 101.
17 Ibid., p. 100.
18 Ibid., pp. 136–8.
19 Ibid., pp. 174–5.
20 Ibid., p. 195.

Chapter 18: The Trial

1 For d'Ormesson's account of the first day, see Chéruel (ed.), *Journal d'Olivier Lefèvre d'Ormesson*, vol. 2, pp. 239–46.
2 Ibid., pp. 246–7.
3 Ibid., p. 250.
4 Ibid., p. 251.
5 Madame de Sévigné, *Correspondance*, vol. 1, p. 59.
6 Ibid., p. 64.
7 Ibid., p. 69.
8 Ibid., pp. 71–2.
9 Quoted in Lair, *Nicolas Foucquet*, vol. 2, p. 363.
10 Ibid., p. 366.
11 Madame de Sévigné, *Correspondance*, vol. 1, p. 72.
12 Ibid.
13 Ibid., p. 74.
14 Ibid., p. 76.
15 Chéruel (ed.), *Journal d'Olivier Lefèvre d'Ormesson*, vol. 2, p. 283.
16 Quoted in Petitfils, *Fouquet*, p. 453.

Chapter 19: The Prisoner

1 For descriptions of Nicolas's encounter with Foucault, see Madame de Sévigné, *Correspondance*, vol. 1, p. 79; and Chéruel (ed.), *Journal d'Olivier Lefèvre d'Ormesson*, vol. 2, p. 286.
2 Madame de Sévigné, *Correspondance*, vol. 1, p. 79.
3 Chéruel (ed.), *Journal d'Olivier Lefèvre d'Ormesson*, vol. 2, p. 287.
4 Madame de Sévigné, *Correspondance*, vol. 1, p. 81.
5 Ibid., p. 81.
6 Ravaisson (ed.), *Archives de la Bastille*, vol. 2, pp. 396–7.
7 Joseph Delort (ed.), *Histoire de la détention des philosophes et des gens de lettres à la Bastille et à Vincennes, précédée de celles de Foucquet, de Pellisson et de Lauzun* (Firmin Didot, Paris, 1829), vol. 1, p. 85.

8   Ibid., p. 85.
9   Nicolas Séverat, *Mémoire historique de la vie d'un fantassin de vingt-cinq ans de service* (Lyon, 1711).
10 Quoted in Petitfils, *Fouquet*, p. 466.
11 Levé to Colbert, 25 July 1665. Ravaisson (ed.), *Archives de la Bastille*, vol. 2, p. 435.
12 Levé to Colbert, 1 August 1665. Ravaisson (ed.), *Archives de la Bastille*, vol. 2, p. 439.
13 Saint-Mars to Colbert, 12 June 1666. Ravaisson (ed.), *Archives de la Bastille*, vol.3. p. 24.
14 Louvois to Saint-Mars, 26 July 1665. Delort (ed.), *Histoire de la détention des philosophes*, vol. 1, pp. 103–104.
15 Ravaisson (ed.), *Archives de la Bastille*, vol. 3, p. 119.
16 Delort (ed.), *Histoire de la détention des philosophes*, vol. 1, pp. 120–1.
17 Ravaisson (ed.), *Archives de la Bastille*, vol. 3, pp. 118.
18 Delort (ed.), *Histoire de la détention des philosophes*, vol. 1, pp. 144–5.
19 Quoted in Chatelain, *Le Surintendant Nicolas Foucquet*, p. 541.
20 Delort (ed.), *Histoire de la détention des philosophes*, vol. 1, p. 161.

Chapter 20: The True King

1   Ravaisson (ed.), *Archives de la Bastille*, vol. 3, p. 139.
2   Ibid.
3   Ibid., p. 142.
4   Delort, *Histoire de la détention des philosophes*, vol. 1, p. 213.
5   Ibid., p. 218.
6   Quoted in *Archives de la Bastille*, vol. 3, p. 134 (Saint-Mars to Louvois, 30 July 1672).
7   Quoted in Chatelain, *Nicolas Foucquet*, p. 545.
8   Delort (ed.), *Histoire de la détention des philosophes*, vol. 1, p. 229.
9   Chéruel (ed.), *Mémoires sur la vie publique et privée de Fouquet*, vol. 2, pp. 452–60.
10 Madame de Sévigné, *Correspondance*, vol. 2, p. 294.

11 Delort (ed.), *Histoire de la détention des philosophes*, vol. 1, p. 267.

12 Ibid.

Chapter 21: The Predestinate

1 Delort, *Histoire de la détention des philosophes*, vol. 1, pp. 155–6.

2 Ravaisson (ed.), *Archives de la Bastille*, vol. 3, p. 175.

3 Louvois to Foucquet, 23 December 1678. Ravaisson (ed.), *Archives de la Bastille*, vol. 3, p. 208.

4 Service historique de l'armée, A1 617, folio 513, quoted in Petifils, *Fouquet*, p. 489.

5 Delort (ed.), *Histoire de la détention des philosophes*, vol. 1, pp. 280–5.

6 Louvois to Saint-Mars, 15 February 1679. Delort (ed.), *Histoire de la deténtion des philosophes*, vol. 1, p. 286.

7 Dated 20 February 1679. Ravaisson (ed.), *Archives de la Bastille*, vol. 3, p. 210.

8 Arthur de Boislisle (ed.), *Mémoires de Saint Simon*, vol. 41, p. 261.

9 Delort (ed.), *Histoire de la détention des philosophes*, vol. 1, p. 314.

10 Madame de Sévigné, *Correspondance*, vol 2, p. 889.

11 Ibid., p. 894.

12 Petitfils, *Fouquet*, p. 510.

13 Quoted in Ravaisson (ed.), *Archives de la Bastille*, vol. 3, p. 213.

Sources

Aumale, duc d', *Histoire des Princes de Condé* (Calmann-Levy, Paris, 7 vols, 1885–96)

Boislisle, Arthur-Michel de (ed.), *Mémoires de Saint Simon* (Hachette, Paris, 1929)

Boissi, M. A. L. de (ed.), *Mémoires de Mademoiselle de Montpensier* (4 vols, Paris, 1806)

Bonnefon, Paul (ed.), *Mémoires de Louis-Henri de Loménie, comte de Brienne* (Société de l'Histoire de France, Paris, 3 vols, 1916–19)

Bordaz, Odile, *D'Artagnan, mousquetaire du roi* (Balzac, Paris, 2001)

Bordonove, Georges, *Foucquet: coupable ou victime?* (Editions Pygmalion, Paris, 1979)

Bussière, Mademoiselle de (ed.), *Mémoires de Monsieur de Gourville* (2 vols, Maestricht, 1782)

Chatelain, Urbain-Victor, *Le Surintendant Nicolas Foucquet, protecteur des lettres des arts et des sciences* (Perrin, Paris, 1905)

Chéruel, Adolphe (ed.), *Journal d'Olivier Lefèvre d'Ormesson* (Imprimerie Impériale, Paris, 1860–1)

Chéruel, Adolphe, *Mémoires sur la vie publique et privée de Fouquet, Surintendant des Finances* (Charpentier, Paris, 2 vols, 1862)

Chéruel, Adolphe and Georges d'Avenel (eds.), *Lettres du Cardinal Mazarin pendant son ministère* (Imprimerie Nationale, Paris, 9 vols, 1876–1906)

Choisy, Abbé de, *Mémoires pour servir à l'histoire de Louis XIV*, ed. Georges Mongrédien (Mercure de France, Paris, 1966)

Clément, Pierre, *Histoire de Colbert et son administration* (Didier, Paris, 1874)

Clément, Pierre (ed.), *Lettres, instructions et mémoires de Colbert* (Imprimerie Impériale, Paris, 9 vols, 1861–82)

Courteault, Henri (ed.), *Journal de Jean Vallier, maître d'hôtel du roi 1648–1657* (Renouard, Paris, 4 vols, 1902–18)

Delort, Joseph, *Histoire de la détention des philosophes* (Firmin Didot, Paris, 3 vols, 1829)

Dessert, Daniel, *Fouquet* (Fayard, Paris, 1987)

Dethan, Georges, *The Young Mazarin* (Thames & Hudson, London, 1977)

Dumas, Alexandre, *Louise de la Vallière*, ed. David Coward (Oxford University Press, Oxford, 1995)

Dumas, Alexandre, *The Man in the Iron Mask*, ed. David Coward (Oxford University Press, Oxford, 1991)

Dumas, Alexandre, *The Three Musketeers*, ed. David Coward (Oxford University Press, Oxford, 1991)

Dumas, Alexandre, *Twenty Years After*, ed. David Coward (Oxford University Press, Oxford, 1993)

Dumas, Alexandre, *The Vicomte de Bragelonne*, ed. David Coward (Oxford University Press, 1995)

Erlanger, Philippe, *Louis XIV* (Weidenfeld, London, 1970)

France, Anatole and Jean Cordey, *Vaux-le-Vicomte* (Calmann-Lévy, Paris, 1933)

Gareau, Michel, *Charles le Brun, premier peintre du Roi Louis XIV* (Hazan, Paris, 1992)

Grand-Mesnil, Marie-Noële, *Mazarin, la fronde et la presse* (Armand Colin, Paris, 1967)

Lafayette, Madame de, *Vie de la Princesse d'Angleterre*, ed. Marie-Thérèse Hipp (Droz, Geneva, 1967)

La Fontaine, Jean de, *Oeuvres complètes*, ed. Pierre Clarac (Gallimard, Paris, 2 vols, 1958)

Lair, Jules, *Nicolas Foucquet: Procureur-Général, Surintendant des finances, ministre d'état de Louis XIV* (Librarie Plon, Paris, 1890)

Marcou, François Léopold, *Etude sur la vie et les oeuvres de Pellisson* (Didier, Paris, 1859)

Mitford, Nancy, *The Sun King* (Hamish Hamilton, London, 1966)

Morand, Paul, *Fouquet ou le Soleil offusqué* (Gallimard, Paris, 1961)

Motteville, Françoise Langlois de, *Mémoires pour servir à l'histoire d'Anne d'Autriche*, ed. Blaisot Desbordes (Amsterdam, 1723)

Pellisson-Fontanier, Paul, *Histoire de l'Académie française*, ed. Charles-Louis Livet (Didier, Paris, 2 vols, 1858)

Pernod, Michel, *La Fronde* (Editions de Fallois, Paris, 1994)

Pérouse de Montclos, Jean-Marie, *Vaux-le-Vicomte* (Editions Scala, Paris, 1997)

Petitfils, Jean-Christian, *Fouquet* (Perrin, Paris, 1998)

Petitot and Monmerqué (eds.), *Collection des mémoires relatifs à l'histoire de France* (Foucault, Paris, 78 vols, 1820–29)

Porsenna, Erik, *Portrait d'un homme heureux: André le Nôtre* (Fayard, Paris, 2000)

Ravaisson, François (ed.), *Archives de la Bastille, d'après des documents inédits* (Durand, Paris, 1867)

Retz, Cardinal de, *Mémoires*, ed. Michel Pernot (Gallimard, Paris, 2003)

Saige, Gustave (ed.), *Journal des Guerres Civiles de Dubuisson-Aubenay* (Champion, Paris, 2 vols, 1883–5)

Sévigné, Madame de, *Correspondance*, ed. Roger Duchêne (Gallimard, Paris, 2 vols, 1972)

Tapié, Victor-Lucien, *France in the Age of Louis XIII and Richelieu* (Macmillan, London, 1974)

Treasure, Geoffrey, *Mazarin: The Crisis of Absolutism in France* (Routledge, London, 1995)

Voltaire, *The Age of Louis XIV*, trans. Martyn Pollack (Dent, London, 1926)

Wolf, John B., *Louis XIV* (Gollancz, London, 1968)

List of Illustrations

12 Paul Fontanier-Pellisson by unknown artist, Châteaux de Versailles et de Trianon, Versailles. Photo © RMN/ © Droits réservés.

13 Louise de la Vallière as the goddess Diana, by Claude Lefebvre (1632–1675), Châteaux de Versailles et de Trianon, Versailles. Photo © RMN/ © Gérard Blot.

14 Louis XIV before Maestricht, 1673 by Pierre Mignard (1612–1695), Châteaux de Versailles et de Trianon, Versailles. Photo © RMN/ © Daniel Arnaudet.

15 The Trial of Nicolas Foucquet at the Arsenal.

16 Pignerol: frontispiece to *Histoire de la détention des philosophes* by Joseph Delort (Firmin Didot, 1829).

17 Saint Mary of the Visitation, 17 rue Saint-Antoine, Paris.

Glossary

Ecu a silver coin which during the seventeenth century fluctuated in value between about three and five *livres*. See *livre*.

Lettres de cachet letters signed by the King and bearing the royal seal (the *cachet*), which communicated the sovereign's direct will. During the *ancien régime* their use often led to the arbitrary exercise and abuse of power.

Lit de justice a formal session of the Parlement of Paris that took place in the presence of the King to implement the compulsory registration of royal edicts. During the hearing, the King would take his place on a *lit* of five cushions in a corner of the Great Chamber of the Parlement.

Livre a unit of currency established by Charlemagne to equal one pound of silver. It was subdivided into twenty *sous*. At the end of the seventeenth century – according to a report by the British mint whose authors included Sir Isaac Newton – there were approximately fifteen *livres* to the British pound. Using the retail price index, a pound from this period would be worth about £120 today.

Masters of Requests (maîtres des requêtes) officers in the Parlement, who served as deputies to the Chancellor and provided scrutiny over legal procedure.

Ordonnance de comptant an order for cash that the king made to the Treasury without issuing any official receipt or indicating the purpose for which the money was needed.

Pistole a gold coin worth about 10 livres. See *livre*.

Présidents à mortier chief magistrates in the appeal courts, who distinguished themselves from the presidents of the lower chambers by wearing a black velvet hat with two gold braid ribbons – the *mortier*.

Index*

Page numbers followed by 'n' refer to footnotes.